Research, Records and Responsibility

Ten Years of PARADISEC

Edited by Amanda Harris, Nick Thieberger and Linda Barwick

SYDNEY UNIVERSITY PRESS

First published in 2015 by Sydney University Press

Sydney University Press
Fisher Library F03
University of Sydney NSW 2006 AUSTRALIA
Email: sup.info@sydney.edu.au
sydney.edu.au/sup

National Library of Australia Cataloguing-in-Publication Data

Title:	Research, records and responsibility : ten years of PARADISEC / edited by Amanda Harris, Nick Thieberger and Linda Barwick.
ISBN:	9781743324431 (paperback)
ISBN:	9781743324448 (ebook : epub)
Notes:	Includes bibliographical references and index.
Subjects:	Pacific and Regional Archive for Digital Sources in Endangered Cultures (PARADISEC).
	Cultural property--Protection--Digitization.
	Archival materials--Digitization.
	Digital preservation.
Other Creators/	Harris, Amanda, editor.
Contributors:	Thieberger, Nicholas, editor.
	Barwick, Linda, editor.
Dewey Number:	306.0285

Cover photo by Nick Thieberger (September 2012). NABU is the name of the PARADISEC
catalogue, taken from the word for path or road in Nafsan, the language of South Efate,
Vanuatu. The image is of a panel in Heidelberg bearing the word NABU. Serendipitously
NABU is a German organisation that works to protect biodiversity.

Cover design by Miguel Yamin

Contents

PARADISEC: its history and future

Nick Thieberger, Amanda Harris and Linda Barwick

In 2002, linguists and musicologists at the Universities of Sydney and Melbourne and the Australian National University formulated a grant application with a view to establishing a digital archive.[1] Most of the researchers had accumulated field recordings of language and culture from the Pacific region and South-East Asia, near neighbours of Australia. While the Australian Institute for Aboriginal and Torres Strait Islander Studies (AIATSIS) caters for recordings and materials originating in Australia, there was no local repository for the research materials of Australian researchers who collected materials beyond Australia's borders. The group set about learning what were the best ways to digi-

Thieberger, Nick, Amanda Harris and Linda Barwick (2015). 'PARADISEC: its history and future.' In *Research, Records and Responsibility: Ten Years of PARADISEC*, edited by Amanda Harris, Nick Thieberger and Linda Barwick. Sydney: Sydney University Press.

1   Chief investigators on the first application (Australian Research Council (ARC) Linkage Infrastructure, Equipment and Facilities (LIEF) program grant LE0346848) included Allan Marett, William Foley, Jane Simpson, Linda Barwick, David Nathan (all University of Sydney), Peter Austin, Nicholas Evans, Janet Fletcher, John Hajek, Catherine Falk, Steven Bird, Alexander Adelaar (University of Melbourne) and Andrew Pawley and John Bowden (ANU). Subsequent LIEF applications funded were LE0453247, LE0560711 and LE110100142.

tise the audio and what metadata should be used to describe it, and undertook a stocktake of known relevant collections and a digitisation trial at the University of Sydney in 2002. We sought advice from relevant agencies (in particular from the National Library of Australia and the National Film and Sound Archive). This advice was particularly valuable in allowing us to determine appropriate metadata standards (we use Dublin Core and Open Archives Initiative metadata terms as a subset of our catalogue's metadata) and for the more hands-on requirements of cleaning and repairing mouldy or damaged analogue tapes.

Having designed the system, we applied for Australian Research Council (ARC) funding to buy a Quadriga workstation and associated equipment (playback machines, a vacuum oven for treating tapes) and to fund staff to begin digitising the several hundred tapes that had been part of our first survey of such material. The newly funded Pacific and Regional Archive for Digital Sources in Endangered Cultures (PARADISEC) began in 2003 by digitising collections of audio recordings made since the early 1960s by Australian National University (ANU) researchers, and also took in recordings from the Universities of Sydney and Melbourne digitised as part of the 2002 trial. We designed a metadata system and built a metadata catalogue, initially written in File-MakerPro, then, after a couple of years, moved to an online SQL/PHP system. With a further round of Linkage Infrastructure, Equipment and Facilities (LIEF) funding in 2011, we built our own online system (called Nabu) that manages the ingestion, description and curation of our repository.

The design of PARADISEC from its inception was for a long-term, secure storage facility for the precious materials gathered by fieldworkers, and one which would not only keep the materials safe, but would make them ultimately accessible to the communities from which they came, as well as to future researchers. In this chapter, we explore the evolution of PARADISEC as a digital archive aspiring to long-term sustainability in a funding environment based around short-term project funding models. We also describe the changing face of PARADISEC, and document attempts to make the materials within the archive more widely accessible, while still safeguarding the privacy of those whose words and ideas have been recorded.

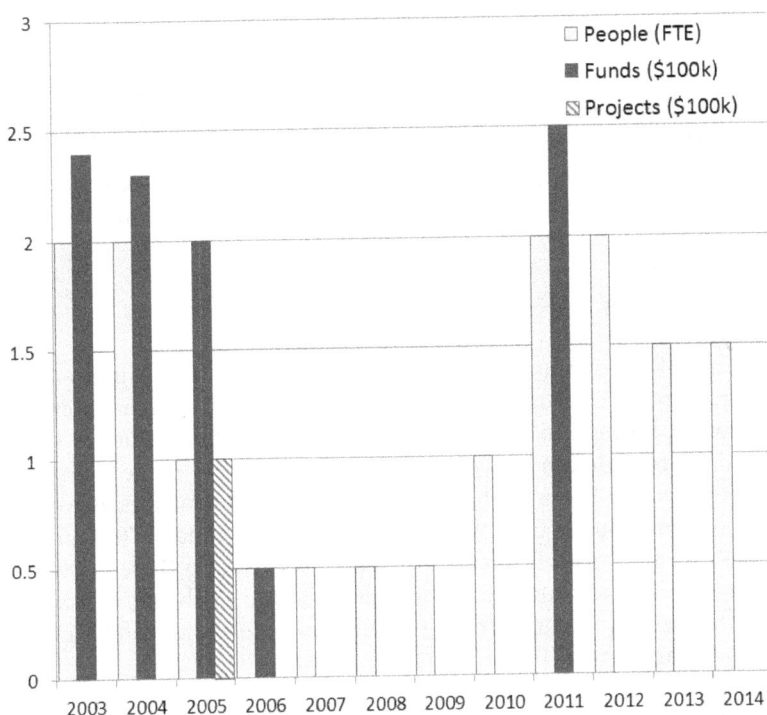

Figure 1 Funding and staffing history of the PARADISEC repository.

As can be seen in Figure 1, funding over the past decade has been sporadic. In only four years (2003, 2004, 2005 and 2011) were we successful in obtaining infrastructure funding, despite several additional applications to the ARC's LIEF program. To keep staff employed between grants, we have been supported by our host institutions and have also been able to attract paid work digitising audio collections for other parts of our universities and for relevant external bodies.

Over the ten years of PARADISEC's operation, the repository has grown to represent over 860 languages from across the world (see Table 1). While initially the archive was confined to cultural materials from the Pacific region and South-East Asia, demand for a suitable

3

repository for research materials led to an expansion of scope. A smaller number of materials from North America, Africa and Europe now form part of the archive. As of September 2015 the repository holds 94,500 files, of which 14,200 are WAV audio files, amounting to over 5100 hours of audio. In 2011 we initiated an online survey[2] to locate further endangered analogue collections and to work with their custodians to find funds to digitise and curate them before they are lost.

What is in the PARADISEC repository?

PARADISEC collections range in size and scope from hundreds of recordings on a particular language made in the course of extensive fieldwork, through to small opportunistic compilations of a few short examples recorded in a given language. Record types range from narratives through to sung, chanted and spoken performances as well as instrumental music. The collections from the 1960s and 1970s typically represent the work of deceased or retired scholars so there is usually limited contextual information to include in the catalogue. Occasionally there are handwritten transcripts of these recordings which we have included as scanned TIF or PDF files.

PARADISEC makes information available in an ethically appropriate way and we have established working relationships with agencies in our region such as the Vanuatu Cultural Centre, Institute of Papua New Guinea Studies, University of French Polynesia, and the University of New Caledonia, among others (Thieberger and Barwick 2012). In 2014 we received funding to digitise some hundreds of tapes held by the Solomon Islands Museum in Honiara. We have started a crowdfunding campaign to try to raise the funds necessary to do this work and to locate more endangered collections of analogue recordings.[3]

The value and potential for ongoing enrichment of the archive by making it as discoverable as possible was made clear when we had a request from Diana Looser, then a PhD candidate in Theatre at Cornell University in the USA, who was writing a dissertation on Oceanic

---

2 http://www.paradisec.org.au/PDSCSurvey.html.
3 http://paradisec.org.au/sponsorship.htm.

Name	Value
Number of resources	9266
Number of resources online	9189
Distinct languages	839
Distinct linguistic subfields	4
Distinct linguistic types	3
Distinct DCMI types	3
Average elements per record	26.8
Average encoding schemes per record	12.3
Average metadata quality score	9
Record views per month	489
Click-throughs per month	139
Last updated	2014-11-19
Known integrity problems	0
Overall rating	★★★★★

Table 1 Open Language Archives Community statistics on the PARADISEC collection. Note: record views and click-throughs are for the month of September 2014.

theatre and drama. She needed access to a play that was listed in our catalogue but existed nowhere else that she could find. In his collection TD1, the linguist Tom Dutton had included a tape of playwright Albert Toro's *Sugarcane Days* recorded from Australian Broadcasting Corporation (ABC) Radio Port Moresby.[4] Looser transcribed the tapes and prepared the only extant version of the script, which she then redeposited in the collection. This re-use of research material in new ways can only be achieved if that material is stored in accessible locations with licences for use in place and with a catalogue that provides sufficient information to allow it to be located.

Technicalities

We began by installing a Quadriga analogue-to-digital workstation and developing a system architecture that included data storage and backup, naming conventions, a metadata schema, a workflow for identifying eligible recordings (by assessing their physical state and contents), deposit and access conditions and a catalogue. This catalogue presents a set of metadata elements to the user with dropdown menus to enforce standard forms, in particular for terms that are exposed to external harvesting tools to allow remote searching of the catalogue. These terms include country names (ISO 3166-1), language names (ISO 639-3), and datatypes, among other elements.

The online catalogue (Nabu[5]) has been redeveloped over time in response to users' comments. It currently exports a feed that is harvested by the Open Archives Initiative, the Open Language Archives Community, and the Australian National Data Service, all of which helps make items in the archive more discoverable. Each item in the archive has its own deposit conditions and over half (some 5500 items out of 9800) can be seen or listened to online by registered users – that is, those who have agreed to the conditions of use and registered their email addresses. The remaining items require some kind of permission from the depositor, but we are working with depositors to reduce the number of items in that category.

The structured metadata requirements of our catalogue oblige the depositor to provide rather basic information that they may not previously have compiled, including, for each item, a title, date of creation,

---

4   Registered users can hear the first of the audio files of this performance here: http://catalog.paradisec.org.au/collections/TD1/items/P02179/essences/1019890.
5   http://catalog.paradisec.org.au – the open source code of the catalogue software is available at https://github.com/nabu-catalog/nabu.

language spoken, and country in which the item was recorded. Further information can include: the role of participants; the language name as it is known locally (which may vary from the standard form); the type of information (lexicon, song, narrative and so on); geographic location (given by a bounding box on a map); and a free text description of the item which can be as rich as the depositor wants. All of this can be improved on by subsequent researchers who may re-use the data in their own projects (as we saw above with the item from Tom Dutton's collection).

Research uses of PARADISEC

An example of the research use that a citable archival repository like PARADISEC offers is the work done by Åshild Næss (2006) on the nature of the languages of the Reefs-Santa Cruz (RSC) (Solomon Islands). The late Professor Stephen Wurm (of the ANU) had a considerable number of recordings from these languages in his house and office when he died. Næss was based in Norway and unable to get copies of the recordings, most of which were uncatalogued and known to her only by oblique references in Wurm's work. As she notes, 'Although Wurm published a number of papers on RSC, the actual data cited in these publications is limited to word lists and a few handfuls of frequently repeated example sentences. This makes it difficult to determine to what extent the structural claims, in particular, are actually supported by the data. Being able to evaluate and analyse Wurm's primary data will be of invaluable help in the effort to resolve the question of the origins of the RSC languages' (Næss 2006, 159).

Such recordings are important for researchers, and we present them as playable objects in our online repository for users to access. An important additional functionality we have developed to make it easier to present interlinked text and media corpora is the Ethnographic E-Research Online Presentation System (EOPAS),[6] which takes the media outputs of linguistic fieldwork together with texts[7] that are time-aligned to the source media and presents them online. EOPAS provides infor-

---

6 http://www.eopas.org.

mation about a text that satisfies several different needs at the same time. It gives the casual web user information about a text, showing grammatical and morphological complexity, but also allowing that complexity to be hidden via a toggle switch if desired. It allows a corpus of any number of texts in a language to be presented and searched, with a keyword-in-context view of any given word or morpheme (parts smaller than a word), all resolving via a mouse click to the context of the morpheme.

Community access to PARADISEC

A key aspect of the creation of digital repositories like PARADISEC is that they can provide access to primary material for any authorised user. This is essential in the current archiving environment where cultural heritage communities have become increasingly active users of digitised archival material originating in their communities (Barwick 2004). Digitised collections of primary data are now easily findable, but people also expect to be able to access them (Landau and Fargion 2012, 128). In Australia, the increasing involvement of Indigenous people in decision-making for archives and their collections means that objects are no longer removed from their creators and preserved in distant locations. The return of historical and archival materials in digital forms has become central to discussions of technology in Indigenous Australia, as evidenced by the outcomes of recent conferences: the AIATSIS National Indigenous Studies Conference (2009) and the Information Technologies and Indigenous Communities Symposium (2010). In Ormond-Parker et al.'s summary of these discussions, the group calls for 'increased support for programs which support the return to community-based archives of digitised heritage objects, including photographs, audiovisual recordings and manuscripts from national repositories' (2013, xii).

The accessibility of archival collections is essential to their long-term sustainability, and the solutions offered by digital distribution

---

7   Actually *interlinear text*, that is, text with translations at the word or smaller level.

make it possible for a digitised recording to be held in a central location and yet be accessible from any other location in the world. This means that digital recording archives are able to circumvent some of the problems faced by museums and archives of physical objects. Several Indigenous scholars have noted that careful decisions about making materials accessible are essential for Indigenous people to consent to the ongoing curation of their cultural materials (O'Sullivan 2013; Aird 2002). PARADISEC's access conditions allow for restrictions to be placed on access so that online digital objects are both easily accessible to individuals with the correct permissions, but also able to be hidden from others. Cultural restrictions notwithstanding, in the long-term, the aim is to make the repository as openly accessible as possible.

Authorisation for access to most material is obtained by supplying a valid email address. Delivery of media allows for web or mobile phone access, and, in cases where there is not yet easy internet or mobile coverage, we have also trialled simpler solutions, like making CDs or creating iTunes installations for school computer systems, as author Nick Thieberger did in Erakor village in central Vanuatu. Each time he visited his fieldsite, he was asked for copies of photos or recordings, and he realised the need for these to be available when he was not present. When he first visited Erakor village there was intermittent electricity available, usually, in the house he lived in, only in the evenings. CD players were common enough, so he was able to make audio CDs with tracks made up of various villagers telling stories or singing songs, or the choir singing hymns. These and the liner notes came out fairly readily from his text/media corpus; creating the template CD took about two hours and burning multiple copies was then a simple matter. Over the years the electricity supply has become more reliable, and the school was given a set of ten computers by their sister school in Australia. Having heard about Linda Barwick's experience (Barwick and Thieberger 2006) in establishing an iTunes installation at Wadeye,[8] he decided to do the same thing at Erakor school. With time-aligned transcripts, it is not a large task to locate the parts needed to create a set of stories

---

8   See also http://paradisec.org.au/blog/2006/08/ indexing-and-managing-song-recordings-for-e-publication.

told by elders, which become tracks in iTunes. Users can then establish favourites and burn their selection to a CD for their use at home.

The change in access to archives has also had a significant impact on archiving practice itself. While PARADISEC was originally designed to house digitised but born-analogue recordings, now it is being inundated with born-digital material. These collections are created from the outset in formats that can be deposited in the archive directly from the field or soon after researchers' return from fieldwork. In this way researchers have a safe copy of their primary records, and are able to cite those records with the persistent identification provided by an archive. Archiving *before* the analysis makes the research grounded and replicable and turns on its head the more traditional approach of archiving primary recordings at the end of one's research career (Barwick 2004). Through publications and numerous training workshops, over the years PARADISEC has also provided information to assist researchers and cultural heritage community members to plan their fieldwork so as to create recordings that are archivable from the outset.

Transcription

While many cultural heritage communities find access to the original recordings made by fieldworkers far more valuable than what has been written about those recordings by foreign researchers (Seeger and Chaudhuri 2004), a media recording with a transcript is more useful than a recording on its own. A transcript that is time-aligned to the media it transcribes is more useful again, providing the possibility for linking the text (utterances or words) directly to the position that they occur in the media. Current field methods include the use of tools like ELAN[9] for creating such transcripts, but emerging methods for automated alignment of a transcript and media (e.g., WebMAUS[10]) promise to speed up this otherwise time-consuming process and can, as a first step, identify segments in the recording according to acoustic characteristics. Many legacy items in the PARADISEC repository have little

---

9 http://tla.mpi.nl/tools/tla-tools/elan.
10 http://phonetik.uni-muenchen.de/BASWebServices.

metadata and no transcripts and would benefit from having a simple description of their content as a first step towards creating more
detailed descriptions. In this way it may be possible to automatically
identify different speakers, varying performance types, and spoken tape
identification at the beginning of the recording, all in order to improve
the description of their contents.

Some PARADISEC collections, on the other hand, are heavily annotated and will allow re-use and re-analysis in future research projects,
and can also be presented in online services representing languages of
the world. Over 860 languages are represented in PARADISEC with a
variety of styles, including songs, narratives and elicitation. Given this
rich reserve of material, there are great possibilities for re-use of these
collections (subject of course to deposit conditions). It may be possible,
for example, to establish crowd-sourced annotation of legacy material,
either at the level of simply identifying parts of a recording or – where
suitably skilled transcribers are available – to provide transcripts. We
are also developing methods for delivery of the catalogue and files via
mobile devices.

Citing primary research records

As mentioned above, we are particularly interested in providing advice
and training for researchers so that their records (be they recordings,
photographs, transcripts or more analytical work like corpora, dic-
tionaries or grammars) will be archivable and re-usable by others in
future, emphasising the importance of linguistic data management
(Thieberger and Berez 2012) and based on the principles established
by Bird and Simons (2003) for the portability of research material. It is
obvious from this training that the more a researcher knows and imple-
ments methods for creating good archival forms of their data, the easier
it is for an archive to accession that material. The researcher's own research materials will also be easier for them to access in the future.

PARADISEC has a blog[11] that often provides examples of new
methods or summaries of projects using innovative approaches. We

---

11   http://paradisec.org.au/blog.

also helped to establish the Resource Network for Linguistic Diversity[12] which has a mailing list and FAQ page on relevant topics aimed at supporting many aspects of language documentation and language revitalisation.

Recognition

We have created nine terabytes of curated records that, without our work, would otherwise be only uncatalogued analogue material. As a result, PARADISEC was cited as an exemplary system for audiovisual archiving using digital mass storage systems by the International Association of Sound and Audiovisual Archives[13] and was also included as an exemplary case study in the Australian government's *Strategic Roadmap for Australian Research Infrastructure*.[14] In 2008 we won the Victorian eResearch Strategic Initiative (VeRSI) eResearch Prize (Humnities, Arts and Social Sciences category). In the words of the judges: 'PARADISEC is an outstanding application of ICT tools in the humanities and social sciences domain that harnesses the work of scholars to store and preserve endangered language and music materials from the Asia-Pacific region and creates an online resource to make these available.'

We are rated at five stars (the maximum rating) in the Open Language Archives Community[15] for the quality of our metadata. In 2012 PARADISEC was awarded a European Data Seal of Approval[16] and, in 2013, PARADISEC's collections were inscribed in the UNESCO Australian Memory of the World program.

12 http://rnld.org.
13 International Association of Sound and Audiovisual Archives (2004). *Guidelines on the Production and Preservation of Digital Audio Objects (IASA-TC04)*. Aarhus: International Association of Sound and Audiovisual Archives (IASA), p. 51.
14 http://www.nectar.org.au/sites/default/files/ Strategic_Roadmap_Aug_2008.pdf, p.42 (viewed 26 March 2014)
15 http://www.language-archives.org/metrics/paradisec.org.au.
16 https://assessment.datasealofapproval.org/assessment_75/seal/html.

About this volume

This publication commemorates the first ten years of PARADISEC with a selection of papers that originated in a conference held in December 2013.[17] As a reflection on the ways that the archive has developed over the last decade, the chapters included here come not only from the archive itself but from collaborations between archivists, users and researchers depositing materials in the archive.

The volume is divided into three parts, each of which deals with a different aspect of PARADISEC's archiving legacy. The first part considers how archiving practices feed into broader methods of research practice. Daniela Kaleva applies models of performativity to questions of research quality and impact in assessing the contribution of archival collections in research outputs. Andrea Berez shows how approaches to teaching can be informed by a long-term view, which compels students to practice archiving even at the beginning of their collection of field data. David Nathan seeks to define the reach of digital archives in the current context, exploring how audiences discover, access and interact with modern archives.

In the second part of the volume, the focus is on how archives themselves can be enriched. Peter Withers demonstrates KinOath, a program enabling the documentation and preservation of kinship data across diverse cultural contexts. Catherine Bow, Michael Christie and Brian Devlin then take the archive back to communities, demonstrating how archival materials can be mobilised by creating interactive materials for the use of current community members. Jennifer Post considers how archives can enrich musical instrument data so that it is contextualised by practices, recordings, images and experiences of music.

The focus of the third part is on communities and the way the products of the archive feed back into community practice. Andrea Emberly considers some of the ethical dilemmas inherent in dealing with archival materials that depict children. Sally Treloyn and Rona Googninda Charles show how community interactions with ethnomusicological archival collections can lead to innovative contemporary practices in endangered dance-song traditions.

---

17   http://paradisec.org.au/2013Conf.html.

As a postscript to the issues of reach, community and access for ethnographic archives explored in the main body of the volume, we end with Lisa MacKinney, Cat Hope, Lelia Green and Tos Mahoney's introduction of the Western Australian New Music Archive and its objective to create a lasting repository of new music performance.

Conclusion

Archiving of research outputs is central to language documentation and to the preservation of recorded oral tradition. Researchers have to ensure that speakers are able to locate records made with them or with their ancestors; properly constructed repositories can provide that function. From a research perspective, the provision of carefully curated scholarly material provides the basis for further research, and for validation of the research that motivated the collection of the material in the first place. PARADISEC aims to be as responsive as possible (given our shoestring budget) to the individual needs of researchers, in particular those located in isolated and remote communities who will be the main beneficiaries of the digitised set of materials we have produced over the past decade.

Works cited

Aird, Michael (2002). 'Developments in the repatriation of human remains and other cultural items in Queensland, Australia.' In *The Dead and Their Possessions: Repatriation in Principle, Policy and Practice*, edited by Cressida Fforde, Jane Hubert and Paul Turnbull, 302–11. London: Routledge.

Barwick, Linda (2004). 'Turning it all upside down … Imagining a distributed digital audiovisual archive.' *Literary and Linguistic Computing* 19(3): 253–63.

Barwick, Linda, and Nicholas Thieberger (2006). 'Cybraries in paradise: New technologies and ethnographic repositories.' *Libr@ries: Changing Information Space and Practice*, edited by Cushla Kapitzke and Bertram C. Bruce, 133–49. Mahwah: Lawrence Erlbaum. http://repository.unimelb.edu.au/10187/1672.

Bird, Steven, and Gary Simons (2003). 'Seven dimensions of portability for language documentation and description.' *Language* 79: 557–82. http://tiny.cc/2003-7dim-birdsimons.

Landau, Carolyn, and Janet Topp Fargion (2012). 'We're all archivists now: Towards a more equitable ethnomusicology.' *Ethnomusicology Forum* 21(20): 125–40.

Næss, Aashild (2006). 'Past, present and future in Reefs-Santa Cruz research.' In *Sustainable Data from Digital Fieldwork: From Creation to Archive and Back*, edited by Linda Barwick and Nicholas Thieberger, 157–62. Sydney: Sydney University Press. http://hdl.handle.net/2123/1299.

Ormond-Parker, Lyndon, Aaron Corn, Cressida Fforde, Kazuko Obata, and Sandy O'Sullivan, eds (2013). *Information Technology and Indigenous Communities*. Canberra: AIATSIS Research Publications.

O'Sullivan, Sandy (2013). 'Reversing the gaze: Considering Indigenous perspectives on museums, cultural representation and the equivocal digital remnant.' In *Information Technology and Indigenous Communities*, edited by Lyndon Ormond-Parker et al., 139–49. Canberra: AIATSIS Research Publications.

Seeger, Anthony, and Shubha Chaudhuri, eds (2004). *Archives for the Future: Global Perspectives on Audiovisual Archives in the 21st Century*. Calcutta: Seagull Books.

Thieberger, Nicholas and Andrea Berez (2012). 'Linguistic data management.' In *The Oxford Handbook of Linguistic Fieldwork*, edited by Nicholas Thieberger, 90–118. Oxford: Oxford University Press.

Thieberger, Nicholas and Linda Barwick (2012). 'Keeping records of language diversity in Melanesia, the Pacific and Regional Archive for Digital Sources in Endangered Cultures (PARADISEC).' In *Melanesian Languages on the Edge of Asia: Challenges for the 21st Century*, LD&C Special Publication No. 5, edited by Nicholas Evans and Marian Klamer, 239–53. Honolulu: University of Hawai'i Press. http://hdl.handle.net/10125/4567.

Part 1
Archiving as research

1
Through the lens of performance and performativity: reframing the research quality and impact of ethnographic digital research archives

Daniela Kaleva

Digital research archives such as PARADISEC were established as part of research projects temporarily funded by government research grants. On the tenth anniversary of PARADISEC, its founders, contributors and users are celebrating, among other achievements, a wealth of knowledge encompassing more than 9 terabytes of data, over 5000 hours of audio recordings of language and music from the Pacific, Asia and worldwide, and prestigious international recognition as a member of the UNESCO Memory of World Register (see Thieberger et al., this volume; Clement et al. 2013). While PARADISEC has received several government grants in the past, the archive's sustainability is threatened by diminishing government funding and increasingly demanding mechanisms of institutional and government research quality and impact reporting. PARADISEC must balance these challenges with its obligation and responsibility to preserve cultural heritage materials in order to continue to pursue its vision. Many ethnographic digital research archives are facing the same challenge.

Kaleva, Daniela (2015). 'Through the lens of performance and performativity: reframing the research quality and impact of ethnographic digital research archives.' In *Research, Records and Responsibility: Ten Years of PARADISEC*, edited by Amanda Harris, Nick Thieberger and Linda Barwick. Sydney: Sydney University Press.

This raises questions about how research quality and the impact of ethnographic digital research archives can be articulated more effectively as research outputs for the purposes of reporting and grant writing in order to safeguard the archives' economic sustainability and further development. Analogue and digital ethnographic research materials that are preserved and accessed through digital archives impact communities in different and more far-reaching ways than initially anticipated. Perhaps this social significance can be used as an entry point for reframing the research quality and impact of ethnographic digital research archives. The lens of performance and performativity can provide a new theoretical perspective or even create a new stage in the development of ethnographic research databases. In an article on the vocabulary of performance, Sruti Bala (2013, 19) states that the concept of performance 'reveals the attempts of various disciplines of the Humanities to self-critique their working terms by reassessing their mutual relationship'. The lenses of performance, both as a goal and as a process, and performativity, as a way of identifying linguistic traits as actions within a sociocultural context, where identity manifests through iterability and citationality, afford a fresh look into the content and identity of ethnographic digital research archives.

Performance and performativity

The etymology of the word performance references the execution of action. In business terminology, it means 'the way a job or task is done by an individual, a group or an organisation' (Statt 2004, 113). There are particular aspects of the operation that can be measured; for example, technical and business performance can be gauged according to how particular technical mechanisms or business processes perform against technological standards and planned output. The technical performance of the structure of digital research archives is constantly assessed against international standards, but is there more room for developing ways to measure the performance of these archives against government and institutional reporting mechanisms? Further, how can this be reflected back into infrastructure? What are the indicators and standards there, and how can the content, services and operations perform better in this context? Assessing the research quality and impact of digital research archives and their collections could be considered in the context of performance as a goal.

At the same time, performance is a process. Performance studies scholar Richard Schechner differentiates between 'is performance' and 'as performance'. Dance and music performances, drama spectacles and rituals entail particular traditional, expressive forms and embodied practices within specific cultural contexts. While there are limitations as to what constitutes artistic or cultural performance, Schechner (2006, 38) suggests that 'just about anything can be studied "as" performance'. This so-called cultural turn indicates a shift towards explorations of process over product and practices that are not perceived as encapsulated in text objects but as living, embodied practices. This has prompted scholars to question the modes of scholarly research and their roles within this research (Bala 2013, 17). The lens of performativity demands realignment from text-based or captured objects to considering their performative nature in the context of the social and cultural processes within which artefacts are born and exist, and where meaning is shaped and interpreted. Besides making its mark on disciplines such as linguistics, philosophy, anthropology, gender studies, literary studies, social sciences, theatre studies and performance studies, performativity has been a potent theoretical grounding for research in information technology (IT) and management. For instance, tracing the linguistic characteristics of communications related to IT in organisations indicates how such discourses *perform* IT differently depending on the industry and the culture of the organisation (De Vaujany et al. 2012, 19).

The concept of performativity was introduced in the discipline of linguistics during the William James Lectures delivered at Harvard University in 1955, when linguist J. L. Austin used the term 'performative utterances' to describe words that constitute action. A typical example of such performatives is the 'I do' uttered by the groom and bride during a wedding ceremony. Austin posits that speech is a performative act, and an important correlation exists between language and action (Bala 2013, 18–19). Furthermore, Austin proposes a multilateral analysis of such performative utterances that includes the specific words in locution, the purpose of the utterance and the effect of the locutions

(Austin 1962, 4–6). These linguistic subtleties can be useful when considering how language and its performative dimension change in the realm of information management. 'The performative refers to the way things assume shape and are constituted by way of naming, of being called and interpellated' (Bala 2013, 19). For instance, to ensure that digital collections are semantically accessible, their curators must negotiate the tension between the language used to describe the stored objects and the language familiar to the users, which affects both the discoverability and the interpretation of these objects (Tahmasebi and Risse 2013). Similarly, we can consider the evolution of language when we articulate the purpose, function and value of ethnographic digital research archives and their collections in the context of higher education and society at large. This raises the issue of identity, which has been a major focus of performativity theory, especially in the work of Judith Butler. Butler calls attention to gender identity not as inborn behaviour but as enacted and dependent on social constructs, embodied practice that is 'tenuously constituted in time – an identity instituted through a stylized repetition of acts' (Butler 1988, 520). This perspective can inform how we perceive and articulate the identity of digital research archives and the roles of the people involved in their operation and use.

Various types of performance processes, including cultural, linguistic and gender performance processes (Bala 2013, 15–16), co-exist in the operation, use and evaluation of digital research archives. These processes include both the collected content of intangible digital artefacts representing particular, established cultural practices and the performance of the archives as research spaces. The latter plays out within the dynamic realm of the virtual world of digital archives, which is driven by human actors through the technological system processes of locating, storing and providing access to cultural and linguistic artefacts (Reitz 2004, 216).

In science and technology studies, performativity has allowed for deeper scrutiny of the material elements of cultural artefacts in various knowledge cultures and their roles therein (Waterton 2010, 650–52). Waterton suggests that through 'performativity, we can see the archive as a technology that constitutes not only a record of our representations of the world, but as an active and iterative making of the world and of entities and selves within it'. The digital research archive is a locus of the performative interplay between the technological components of the system and humans occupying various roles, the involved organisations and specific sociocultural contexts. One of them is the higher education context, upon which the existence and sustainability of such research systems depends.

Digital collections of cultural artefacts in digital research archives could be considered not only as objects of knowledge but as 'a way of knowing' (Taylor 2003). Their curation, conversion into digital objects and use create a lens of knowing, where the information object and user, researched and researcher, are intertwined in virtual and embodied material performance processes of cultural practices, information management, cultural preservation, cultural brokerage and the act of research. Performance and performativity provide a different ontological and epistemological perspective that can uncover new strategies for digital research archives and indicate how they can be evaluated in terms of what they do and what role they play in knowledge discovery and production.

Reframing content: cultural performative findings

Digital research archives, such as PARADISEC, hold audio, text and visual (photographic and video) archival material in the form of downloadable files. Despite the fact that they are captured for the purposes of linguistic research, these materials contain considerable by-products in the form of oral history, music and dance narratives that are essential in Indigenous cultures' knowledge transfer (Christie 2005). Ethnographic fieldwork materials are carriers of performative aspects of speech through paralinguistic signs that include gestures, movements and facial expressions. A good example of such by-products is the new knowledge generated by Rutkowski et al. (2013) of Polish Sign Language (PJM) under the umbrella of the PJM Corpus Project. They created an array of tools for transcribing, systematising and coding video material capturing PJM and, in the process, made a serendipitous discovery of specific cultural intricacies. These videos are an important component of knowledge transfer in the context of the community of practice to which they belong – in this case, both the scholarly and deaf communities.

In the discipline of linguistics, archives aim to preserve and provide access to data sets as evidence for new research publications in the form of verifiable primary data. Therefore, media-rich archival material is reduced to quantified searchable metadata for the purposes of preservation, access and discoverability. Linguistics scholars aspire to see increasingly direct citations of data in the electronic publishing of linguistic research and a move towards the recognition of curated data as a format of scholarly publication (Musgrave and Hajek 2013). These needs for linguistic scholarly practice and knowledge dissemination are challenging both current publishing practices and research performance indicators. However, the danger is in perceiving media-rich archival materials of linguistic research as only research data (Christie 2005), thus ignoring the depth of the cultural knowledge encrypted in their content by means of performative material signs. This performative nature of archival material that is rendered as data, but is actually made of performative material signs, allows for reframing of how we evaluate the content of archival databases.

Creative practice research has opened a new epistemology that takes into account the practice-led nature of knowledge production and the dissemination that takes place in creative arts disciplines. In response to the specifics of artistic practice research, a third paradigm of scholarly enquiry was identified along with the quantitative and qualitative research paradigms (Haseman 2006, 2010). Performative research, proposes Haseman (2010, 151), is led by practice and is 'expressed in non-numeric data, but in symbolic forms of data other than words in discursive text. These include material forms of practice, of still and moving images, of music and sound, of live action and digital code.' Media-rich archival materials could be viewed as collections of cultural performative findings. When accompanied by exegetical writing and peer reviewed in scholarly and professional journals, such curated collections could meet the requirements of existing quality reporting systems and could present stronger research output arguments in grant writing.

The quality assessment of traditional scholarly outputs within the publication categories counted in the Higher Education Research Data

Collection (HERDC), such as books, book chapters, articles in peer-reviewed journals and refereed conference papers (Department of Education 2014, 26–34), pertains largely to traditional processes and formats of scholarly publishing. The content of digital research archives, on the other hand, could be considered in the context of the Excellence in Research for Australia (ERA) initiative, and more precisely in light of non-traditional categories of scholarly outputs.

The ARC's definition of research is 'the creation of new knowledge and/or the use of existing knowledge in a new and creative way so as to generate new concepts, methodologies and understandings' (ARC 2012a, 3). This could include synthesis and analysis of previous research to the extent that it is new and creative. Experimental and creative knowledge discoveries are reiterated here in reference to an earlier document elaborating that it is 'creative work undertaken on a systematic basis in order to increase the stock of knowledge, including knowledge of humanity, culture and society, and the use of this stock of knowledge to devise applications' (OECD 2002, 30). ERA's non-traditional categories of scholarly outputs, introduced for trial in 2009, constitute a major milestone in the process of recognising performative material signs within artistic practice research as valid evidence of knowledge discovery.

ERA's submission guidelines specify four categories of non-traditional outputs: original creative works, live performance of creative works, recorded/rendered creative works, and curated or produced substantial public exhibitions and events. There are two categories that can be exploited for the purpose of reporting ethnographic digital research archives as curated research outputs. Computer programs that are often written for ethnographic digital research archives can be categorised as recorded/rendered creative works, while entire websites or curated collections could be considered under curated or produced substantial public exhibitions and events, where the curatorial role of the researcher is at the forefront of the major output (ARC 2012b, 47–48).

Research statements can argue the research background, contribution and significance of such non-traditional outputs. The research contribution of curated databases must relate to both scholarly knowledge and practice and the community of practice regarding open access transmission. Innovation can be linked to the availability of research outcomes to researchers, specific communities and the public, and it is advantageous if the work is interdisciplinary and funded by multiple organisations. The research significance can be supported by evidence of dissemination at conferences and in the media. Quality or excellence can be argued by means of the peer review of such websites, supported by published critical reviews of these resources and the scholarly essays that reference them, through citations in scholarly writing and in the media, and evidence of a high degree of cultural significance, complexity of structure and innovative techniques of digitally searchable archival content. The standard output in this category implies the curatorial leadership of the scholars involved.

The above mechanism brings to the forefront the decisive role of the peer review process in the humanities as a quality indicator for non-traditional outputs. Since peer review is performed by well-established scholars in the discipline and is predominantly subjective, new ideas that push current boundaries can be promoted from the bottom up by engaging in discipline and higher education research debates, by exemplifying new modes of knowledge discovery and transmission, and by creating new technological pathways. For instance, performance-specific information can be included in the metadata of the databases. This has been demonstrated in the field of the creative arts and specifically in the curation of artistic works with technological components, such as computer-generated musical scores. Boutard et al. address issues of appropriation in the digital creation of music, suggesting that preservation models need to consider the life cycles of archival and creative processes. This includes performance information containing tacit knowledge that is vital for future interpretations of the work and records of knowledge interactions between different stakeholders (Boutard et al. 2013, 19). Another example from creative practice research is the combination between creative artefacts and exegetical writing (Haseman 2010, 156). Exegetical notes often include reflective analysis, reflexive questioning and citations from the researcher's diary that complement or deliberate the philosophical and practical aspects of the research. Exegetical information could add value to media-rich files within digital archival research collections.

The reiteration of the performative paradigm and media-rich archival content of digital research archives as performative evidence of captured cultural performances will be necessary until it becomes fully recognised in higher education mechanisms of reporting and funding. In addition, performative archival content and systems that hold significant cultural knowledge fit several currently prioritised research themes: Indigenous research, understanding our region and the world, promoting an innovation culture and economy, smart information use, and strengthening Australia's social and economic fabric (ARC 2012b, 74).

Reframing identity

Judith Butler's perspective on performativity in gender studies illuminates the formation of identity not as a given and inherited phenomenon but as a series of repeated acts within a social context. This can be transferred to the process of identity building in relation to digital research archives and the individuals and groups of actors involved in their management, operation and use. The current ERA categories of non-traditional research outputs in academic reporting and quality evaluations necessitate that the cultural performative findings housed in ethnographic digital research archives are identified using the notions of 'exhibition' and 'curation/curator'. The questions to be asked are what are digital research archives, and how do they perform in the context of academia, the Indigenous cultures with which they engage and society at large?

By definition, digital research archives or repositories are systems 'designed for locating, storing, and providing access to digital materials over the long term' (Reitz 2004, 216). The purpose of digital research archives is to preserve and disseminate research data and information. They hold components of new knowledge discoveries in data and information formats. The processes associated with digital research archives are locating, storing and providing access to data and information, digital preservation, standardised description of content, information access and discovery of primary data and research publications, as well as the direct citation of primary data in research publications. Research data or captured media-rich research materials can sit within research archives as separate collections. The above language describes the information content of such research resources using IT terminology to refer to the intrinsic specialised characteristics and processes that are crucial for the maintenance and development of these information systems.

Just as the semantic language of digital library collections needs to develop according to the usability demands driven by users' language (Tahmasebi and Risse 2013), we in Australia need to consider whether operational IT language does justice to the performance of digital research archives in the current evolved state of their operation and in a climate where impact has become another research quality measurement in academic reporting. IT vocabulary, such as digital archives, archival databases and digital repositories, presupposes a technical interpretation focusing on product and structure, where collections are reduced to the sum of the information objects rather than seen as carriers of performative signs of cultural knowledge and wisdom. This linguistic articulation is derived from information management terminology and predetermines a semantic interpretation that affects how government auditing and funding bodies and administrators perceive and evaluate ethnographic digital research archives. Using IT language to refer to ethnographic digital collections falls short of describing and measuring the significance of this social interaction, the impact these online resources have on Indigenous communities and their cultural sustainability, and the crucial role of scholars as cultural brokers.

Derrida (1996, 29) posits that the archive is 'only a notion, an impression with a word and for which, together with Freud, we do not have a concept', as well as 'an irreducible experience of the future' (Derrida 1996, 68). The identity of the archive is dynamic and dependent on knowledge actors and social contexts. How identity is articulated and reiterated, therefore, affects how the archival research databases are marketed and reported within the academic context. The scholars involved in the curation of digital research archives need to negotiate the semantic tensions pertaining to language referring to information content and develop a more holistic citation that encompasses the wider impact of digital archival databases on research and sociocultural environments. The ontological aspects of this shift in thinking indicate a 'move from an archival universe dominated by one cultural paradigm to an archival multiverse; from a world constructed in terms of "the one" and "the other" to a world of multiple ways of knowing and practising, of multiple narratives co-existing in one space' (Shepherd 2011, 5).

Collections of cultural performative findings are vital cultural documents. They constitute cultural capital which, when in action – or when being accessed and used by scholars, community members or government bodies – impacts new research and community sustainability, and has economic implications. A classic example is the generation of Aboriginal music recordings used in land claims archived by the Native Title Research Unit of the Australian Institute of Aboriginal and Torres Strait Islander Studies (AIATSIS) (Koch 2008). Grace Koch (2008) discusses how, owing to the *Native Title Act 1993*, more ritual songs were recorded as part of the native title claim process, raising issues of responsibility and illuminating the challenges of archival practices. The impact of the repatriation of such collections is gaining importance and contributes to the development of a stronger sense of identity among the younger generations of cultural heritage communities. An intriguing case is the repatriation of Junba dance-songs in Western Australia that has enabled new generations to cherish their musical heritage and engage in the community (Treloyn and Charles, this volume). These examples demonstrate that cultural performative archival content is not composed of frozen data or information but of dynamic cultural artefacts that represent cultural capital with the potential to affect health and wellbeing while also generating knowledge discoveries.

Archival databases have been criticised for not being suited to cultural work with Indigenous communities and for being incapable of finding 'an active place in knowledge work' due to their reliance on Western taxonomy and hierarchy with categories and classes that are insufficient when working with Indigenous knowledge (Christie and Verran 2013, 307). Furthermore, Kimberly Christen (2012, 2882) expresses concern that some digital databases come to an end as expensive projects that have addressed only specific needs at a particular point in time without mechanisms for a sustainable future due to lack of ownership by users that would continue to engage with the content and update the infrastructure. Instead of being spaces of 'large collections for people who do not know what they might find' (Christie and Verran 2013, 307), Indigenous archival material is specific and requires culturally sensitive tools that do not resonate with the notions of open access that dominate information management and scholarly dissemination policies (Christen 2012, 2874–81). Christen considers issues of privacy and sociality, and traces how Indigenous people contribute their local understanding and histories to the notions of 'social relations back to place-based mapping practices' (2012, 2881).

Michael Christie, however, warns against perceiving archives as repositories of knowledge and suggests seeing them instead as 'a memory source containing assemblages of traces of previous truth-claim episodes' (Christie 2005, 64). A new step in this direction is the Mukurtu CMS – a culturally sensitive platform that is flexible to serve and adapt to the cultural needs of any Indigenous community, referred to by its creators as a 'safe keeping place' (Christen 2012, 2881–88). Moreover, Turnbull proposes the radical solution of adopting a 'transmodern' approach with the capacity to dilute the negative sides of the unequal power between custodians of data and those of Indigenous knowledge. This approach avoids integration by maintaining the tension between different traditions and, in this way, opens possibilities for the concurrent creation of knowledge (Turnbull 2012, 25). Turnbull approaches this work with multiple narratives of different knowledge traditions via complexity theory and distributed systems:

> Performativity and practices come together with complex adaptive systems in sharing a coproductive constructivist account of reality in terms of agency, actions, enactments, and processes in interaction without invoking plans, rules, instructions, laws, or external space or time, everything is to be understood as an emergent effect of systematically connected interactions, where the system and the agents coproduce each other. (Turnbull 2012, 11–12)

Turnbull argues that language and narrative are central to the development of networks, and underscores that languages have local, spatial and temporal dimensions that construct locality and time. In this way, they are performative not of a linear and single dominant historical narrative but as 'sites where social and political processes are enacted' (Turnbull 2012, 14). The practical viability of Turnbull's proposed framework, which promotes cultural diversity, is demonstrated in the work of the Emergent Databases, Emergent Diversity project.[1] This project allows users to actively engage with the databases of the Zuni Pueblo in New Mexico and the Cambridge Museum of Archaeology and Anthropology. Such online spaces depart from the notion of 'storage facilities' and approach a new identity that has the potential for significant knowledge discovery and social impact. Digital research archives that contain ethnographic media-rich files that engage with Indigenous cultures can be reframed into platforms marked by complexity, adaptivity and systematicity, where the ways of knowing are considered as social processes (Turnbull 2012, 20). Ethnographic digital research archives are evolving into complex adaptive systems. Their emerging identity as research and knowledge environments that facilitate knowledge transfer and co-creation overrides the perception that their performance is solely constituted of preservation and access to materials about endangered languages and cultural heritage.

Scholars have examined how different disciplines look at archives and archival processes, and have concluded that the future of archives will be embedded in stronger collaborative associations between libraries and scholars (Clement et al. 2013; Manoff 2004). The business model of the Australian Literature Resource (AustLit) demonstrates the successful collaboration between scholars, libraries, the University of Queensland and the National Library. AustLit is a non-profit venture undertaken by scholars and librarians with a mission 'to be the definitive information resource and research environment for Australian literary, print, and narrative cultures'. AustLit is identified as a multifaceted online centre, organised according to information structure: 'a database about Australian literature and storytelling'; according to function: 'a research environment'; as a stakeholder: 'a publisher of scholarly research' and 'a partner and collaborator in scholarly research'; and according to social structure: 'a team of scholars, librarians, researchers, volunteers'.[2] This description addresses identity, the

---

1 For more details about this project, see http://www.digitalinnovations.ucla.edu/2007/ccc/projects/Srinivasan.htm.

research context and process, and is exemplary of a more holistic approach to marketing the performance and value of this multifaceted resource and community.

One of the implications of the dynamic expansion of digital research archives is that it will progressively motivate more and more structural changes to how societal, research and individual impact data are generated. In a presentation given on 28 June 2012, Professor Aidan Byrne, the CEO of the Australian Research Council (ARC), singled out papers and patents as relevant spin-offs of research activities, due to their commercial value, with impact projected onto new government policy development, new research paradigms and the creation of commercial products and enterprises (Byrne 2013). The ARC's definition of impact is 'the demonstrable contribution that research makes to the economy, society, culture, national security, public policy or services, health, the environment, or quality of life, beyond contributions to academia.'[3]

Calculating impact is challenging for the humanities. Nevertheless, new measurements of research impact in the context of virtual environments are opening the door to rich impact data stories and impact cases that can be applied at the individual file, collection and archive levels. The impact of research articles can be traced more comprehensively through altmetrics (non-traditional citations of research products such as downloads) than bibliometrics (traditional citation metrics such as impact factor) by employing categories such as viewed, saved, discussed, recommended and cited. Impact can be measured not only through the citation of data or symbolic data in scholarly articles but by creating impact statements which are based on the altmetrics applied to various materials and stakeholders that track how research collections perform outside of scholarly publishing in communities of practice and society at large. This includes not only full-text citations but views, downloads, references and presence in the media, and, in some cases, such as in the web-based and open source impact story, separating the impact between the scholarly community and the public depending on the altmetrics sources (Lin and Fenner 2013). In addition, altmet-

2 *AustLit.* Accessed 25 June 2015. http://www.austlit.edu.au.
3 http://www.arc.gov.au/general/impact.htm.

rics can be applied to stakeholders: curator, creator, depositor, collector, custodian and so on, while social networks can be highlighted using webometrics (research data showing the World Wide Web's structure and usage), virtual ethnography and web mining.

Some of these tools have been used in the performing arts database AusStage. AusStage has been described as 'an accessible online resource for researching live performance in Australia' that 'enables research on live performance as a wealth-producing creative industry, a generator of social capital and an indicator of the nation's cultural vitality.'[4] It is hosted at Flinders University and is supported by a consortium of universities, government agencies, industry organisations and collecting institutions, and funded mainly by government bodies. Since the database's collections encompass performance events and the artistic personnel involved in those events, networks of artists are a prominent indicator of artistic endeavours, status and collaborations in the field. AusStage has introduced data visualisation technologies to provide visual mapping of geographic displays of live performance data over time, titled the AusStage Mapping Events service, and to illustrate collaborative networks of professionals through the AusStage Navigating Networks service.[5] These tools are capable of creating a detailed picture of the complex networks and knowledge life cycles to reference the sociocultural implications of such knowledge platforms.

Stakeholders and roles become blurred in the process of ethnographic research and the curation of archival collections. Scholar-creators, scholar-curators, scholar-collectors, scholar-librarians, IT experts, research librarians and archivists all work in the digital humanities sphere, relying on interdisciplinary technical and research skills and the ability to perform ethical stewardship while building trust with the custodians of Indigenous communities. These are complex skills which need specialist training and prolonged mentoring as part of the research process. Berez (this volume), for instance, demonstrates the benefits of involving research students in archiving practices at the postgraduate level. Identifying this interdisciplinary capacity is necessary both to source funds and to challenge established roles in acad-

---

4   *AusStage*. Accessed 25 June 2015. http://ausstage.edu.au.
5   Ibid.

emia. Currently, Australian universities divide their human resources into academic and professional staff, with little space for hybrid roles, such as librarian-scholars working in academic faculties or information expert-scholars working on research projects. While information professionals can integrate more thoroughly into the research processes of open access publishing (Clement et al. 2013, 119), bridging roles would allow digital research archives to tap into university operational infrastructures and their budgets. Hybrid roles can be established by reiterating the need to adapt current staffing categories to the changes in scholarly publishing and can be promoted from the bottom up by scholars and information professionals.

Conclusion

Having established vital infrastructure, collection and digitisation processes, ethnographic digital research archives are evolving into dynamic, multifaceted virtual research spaces and subcultures that work across the quantitative, qualitative and performative paradigms. They are a locus of knowledge preservation and access with the capacity to generate new knowledge through the exchange and interaction between various knowledge actors, such as academics, communities and the public. The lens of performance and performativity enables the strategising of reporting avenues within the ERA framework and funding applications, the creation of new metadata to collect impact metrics and the evolution of language to better reference the identity of ethnographic digital research archives and the social significance of their structure and operation. Reframing archived material content into symbolic data of cultural knowledge and an identity that departs from information management language would allow for a better understanding of what archives do within a social context and of the actions and processes in which scholars, information professionals and community members engage. While the launch of ethnographic digital research archives as complex adaptive systems may not be in full sight for most archives, the example of AustLit is intriguing, as it articulates a hybrid business model that uses the resources and expertise of both information professionals and scholars. Furthermore, the structural innovations of creative arts research reporting and creative arts databases, as exemplified by AusStage, may be helpful in understanding the ways in which content is presented and described and social data are visualised as maps and networks.

Works cited

Austin, J. L (1962). *How to Do Things with Words*. Oxford: Clarendon Press.

Australia, Department of Education (2014). *Higher Education Research Data Collection: Specifications for the Collection of 2013 Data*. Canberra: Commonwealth of Australia. http://tiny.cc/2014-2013data-depted.

Australian Research Council (2012a). *ERA 2012 Evaluation Handbook: Excellence in Research for Australia*. Canberra: Commonwealth of Australia. http://tiny.cc/2012-eval-arc.

Australian Research Council (2012b). *ERA Submission Guidelines: Excellence in Research for Australia*. Canberra: Commonwealth of Australia. http://tiny.cc/2012-eraguide-arc.

Australian Research Council (2015). *Research Impact Principles and Framework*. http://arc.gov.au/general/impact.htm.

Bala, Sruti (2013). 'The entangled vocabulary of performance.' *Rupkatha Journal on Interdisciplinary Studies in Humanities* 5: 12–21.

Boutard, Guillaume, Catherine Guastavino and James Turner (2013). 'A digital archives framework for the preservation of cultural artefacts with technological components.' *International Journal of Digital Curation* 8: 42–65.

Butler, Judith (1988). 'Performative acts and gender constitution: An essay in phenomenology and feminist theory.' *Theatre Journal* 40: 519–31.

Byrne, Aidan (2013). *Presentation on the Australian Research Council, Ballarat University, 28 June 2013*. Ballarat: Australian Research Council. http://tiny.cc/2013-arc-byrne.

Christen, Kimberly (2012). 'Does information really want to be free? Indigenous knowledge and the politics of open access.' *International Journal of Communication* 6: 2870–93.

Christie, Michael (2005). 'Aboriginal knowledge traditions in digital environments.' *Australian Journal of Indigenous Education* 34: 61–66.

Christie, Michael and Helen Verran (2013). 'Digital lives in postcolonial Aboriginal Australia.' *Journal of Material Culture* 18: 299–317.

Clement, Tanya, Wendy Hagenmaier and Jennie Levine Knies (2013). 'Toward a notion of the archive of the future: Impressions of practice by librarians, archivists, and digital humanities scholars.' *The Library Quarterly* 83: 112–30.

De Vaujany, François-Xavier, Sabine Carton, Carine Dominguez-Perry and Emmanuelle Vaast (2012). 'Performativity and information technologies: An inter-organizational perspective.' *Cahier de Recherche* 2012(9): E5.

Derrida, Jacques (1996). *Archive Fever: A Freudian Impression*. Chicago: University of Chicago Press.

Haseman, Brad (2006). 'A manifesto for performative research.' *Media International Australia, Incorporating Culture and Policy* 118: 98–106.

Haeman, Brad (2010). 'Rupture and recognition: Identifying the performative research paradigm.' In *Practice as Research: Approaches to Creative Arts Enquiry*, edited by Estelle Barrett and Barbara Bolt, 147–57. London: I. B. Tauris.

Koch, Grace (2008). 'Music and land rights: Archival recordings as documentation for Australian Aboriginal land claims.' *Fontes Artis Musicae* 55: 155–64.

Lin, Jennifer and Martin Fenner (2013). 'Altmetrics in evolution: Defining and redefining the ontology of article-level metrics.' *Information Standards Quarterly* 25: 20–26. doi:10.3789/isqv25no2.2013.

Manoff, Marlene (2004). 'Theories of the archive from across the disciplines.' *Libraries and the Academy* 4: 9–25.

Musgrave, Simon and John Hajek (2013). 'Linguistic scholarship in the data-driven 21st century.' Paper presented at Research, Records and Responsibility (RRR): Ten Years of the Pacific and Regional Archive for Digital Sources in Endangered Cultures (PARADISEC), University of Melbourne, 2–3 December. http://hdl.handle.net/2123/9847.

OECD (2002). *Frascati Manual: Proposed Standard Practice for Surveys on Research and Experimental Development*. Paris: OECD. doi: 10.1787/9789264199040-en.

Reitz, Joan M (2004). 'Digital archive.' In *Dictionary for Library and Information Science*. Westport: Libraries Unlimited.

Rutkowski, Paweł, Joanna Łacheta, Piotr Mostowski, Joanna Filipczak and Sylwia Łozińska (2013). 'The corpus of Polish sign language (PJM): Methodology, procedures and impact.' Paper presented at Research, Records and Responsibility (RRR): Ten Years of the Pacific and Regional Archive for Digital Sources in Endangered Cultures (PARADISEC), the University of Melbourne, 2–3 December. http://hdl.handle.net/2123/9841.

Schechner, Richard (2006). *Performance Studies: An Introduction*. New York: Routledge.

Statt, David A (2004). 'Performance.' In *The Routledge Dictionary of Business Management*. London: Routledge.

Tahmasebi, Nina and Thomas Risse (2013). 'The role of language evolution in digital archives.' In *Proceedings of the 3rd International Workshop on Semantic Digital Archives*, edited by Livia Predoiu et al., 16–27. Aachen: CEUR-WS.

Taylor, Diana (2003). *The Archive and the Repertoire: Performing Cultural Memory in the Americas*. Durham: Duke University Press.

Turnbull, David (2012). 'Performativity and complex adaptive systems: Working with multiple narratives across knowledge traditions.' *Studia Universitatis Babes-Bolyai-Philosophia* 57: 9–32.

Waterton, Claire (2010). 'Experimenting with the archive: STS-ers as analysts and co-constructors of databases and other archival forms.' *Science, Technology and Human Values* 35: 645–76.

2

Reproducible research in descriptive linguistics: integrating archiving and citation into the postgraduate curriculum at the University of Hawaiʻi at Mānoa

Andrea L. Berez

On valuing reproducibility in science and linguistics

The notion of *reproducible research* has received considerable attention in recent years from physical scientists, life scientists, social and behavioural scientists, and computational scientists. Some readers will be familiar with the criterion of *replicability* as a tenet of good execution of the scientific method, in which sound scientific experiments or studies are those that can be recreated elsewhere leading to new data, and in which sound scientific claims are those that are confirmed by the new data in a replicated study. For example, if a researcher conducts a scientific study by surveying 5000 people selected at random, that study and claims arising from it are replicable if another researcher can make the same claim based on new data that come from a random survey of 5000 different people. Likewise, claims can be disproven in a replication, if the new researcher finds different results arising from

Berez, Andrea L. (2015). 'Reproducible research in descriptive linguistics: integrating archiving and citation into the postgraduate curriculum at the University of Hawaiʻi at Mānoa.' In *Research, Records and Responsibility: Ten Years of PARADISEC*, edited by Amanda Harris, Nick Thieberger and Linda Barwick. Sydney: Sydney University Press.

new data. Nonetheless, because the original study was replicable, the research method itself is considered to be sound, even if the original results are later disproven.

Reproducibility is similar to replicability, but reproducible research aims to provide accountability by allowing other researchers to reach the same (or different) conclusions using the same data set as the original publication, rather than from new data arising from the same experimental conditions. The term *reproducible research* was developed mainly in computer science (e.g., Buckheit and Donoho 1995; de Leeuw 2001; Donoho 2010), with the intention that researchers should provide not only the academic paper, but also the data and computer code upon which the paper is based, thus allowing readers to reach the same conclusions about the same data set. Summarised by Dan Gezelter of the Open Science Project:

> If a scientist makes a claim that a sceptic can only reproduce by spending three decades writing and debugging a complex computer program that exactly replicates the workings of a commercial code, the original claim is really only reproducible in principle ... Our view is that it is not healthy for scientific papers to be supported by computations that cannot be reproduced except by a few employees at a commercial software developer ... it may be *research* and it may be *important*, but unless enough details of the experimental methodology are made available so that it can be subjected to true reproducibility tests by sceptics, it isn't Science. (Gezelter 2009, emphasis original)

Reproducibility is potentially useful in other scientific enterprises beyond the physical sciences and computer science. In many fieldwork-based life and social sciences, precise replicability is impossible to achieve. The variables contributing to a particular instance of observation are too hard to control for – for instance, the mechanisms by which frog-eating bats find prey in the wild (Ryan 2011). Even in semi-controlled situations like studying primate tool-use in captivity (Tomasello and Call 2011) it is difficult to reproduce every environmental or non-environmental factor that may contribute to which tool, for example, a chimpanzee will select in a given situation.

Reproducible research in language documentation and description

Linguistics, which can also be considered a social science dealing with observations of complex behaviour, is another field that would seem to lend itself to the kind of scientific rigour that reproducibility provides, but until now there has been little discipline-wide discussion of how we might implement reproducibility, or even a widespread identification of a need to do so. The goal of reproducible research as discussed here is intended to increase accountability in the search for understanding the nature of language, rather than to reproach colleagues. The discussion has not been so benign in other fields, however: compare the recent controversy in social psychology, in which Diederik Staple was found to have fabricated data in 15 to 20 years' worth of publications (Crocker and Cooper 2012). Fang et al. (2013) surveyed more than 2000 biomedical and life sciences journals and found that while 21.3% of article retractions were due to honest investigator error, fully 67.4% of retractions were due to 'misconduct, including fraud or suspected fraud (43.4%), duplicate publication (14.2%) and plagiarism (9.8%)' (Fang et al. 2013, 1). This has led to discussions of solutions including a 'transparency index' (Marcus and Oransky 2012) and a 'retraction index' (Fang and Casadevall 2011) for journals, watchdog websites (e.g., http://retractionwatch.com/) and indices, and blogs (e.g., http://reproducibleresearch.net/blog/).[1]

Within linguistics, investigations into possibilities for reproducible research have mostly been in the context of language documentation and description, in which the documentary fieldwork methodology has been noted for its potential to provide substantiation of scientific claims by promoting attention to the care and structuring of language data (Himmelmann 1998, 2006; Woodbury 2003, 2011; Thieberger 2009; Thieberger and Berez 2012; among others). Digital multimedia and annotations including transcripts and translations ostensibly allow readers to confirm claims about language structure by allowing direct access to the original observational data. This would mean that not only could

---

1 Misconduct in the life sciences has arguably greater consequences than it does in linguistics, and I am not necessarily advocating policing publications in our field.

example sentences in a grammar be confirmed as correctly transcribed, parsed and translated, but a sceptical reader could also determine whether or not she would reach the same conclusions about the phenomenon the example is meant to illustrate by providing access to the utterance in context. As with the example of frog-eating bats above, it is too cumbersome to require that descriptive linguistic claims be fully replicable, but it is not too cumbersome – in fact, it is desirous for the sake of 'good science' – to make them reproducible. A creative rewording of the Gezeltner quote above makes this clear:

> If a linguist makes a claim that a sceptic can only reproduce by spending three decades working in the same language community in the same sociolinguistic and fieldwork conditions, the original claim is really only reproducible in principle ... Our view is that it is not healthy for linguistic descriptions to be supported by examples that cannot be reproduced except by doing one's own fieldwork ... it may be *research* and it may be *important*, but unless enough details of the utterances in context are made available so that it can be subjected to true reproducibility tests by sceptics, it isn't Science. (modified from Gezeltner 2009, underlined words replaced, emphasis original)

Clearly, linguists cannot expect their colleagues to replicate fieldwork conditions (and doing so would not even necessarily lead to replicated utterances), but reproducibility may not be out of the question. Several authors have explored possibilities for providing direct access to the data upon which grammars are written, usually involving some appeal to the extensibility of structure that digital formats provide. Thieberger (2009), representing perhaps the most ardent endorsement of the benefits of reproducible grammar writing, outlines general principles for linking descriptions to corpora and lexica, but notes that generalised tools for doing so are not yet widely available. Thieberger was able to create such a tool for his own (2006) grammar of South Efate, but software development is not often part of the ordinary working linguist's skillset. Maxwell (2012) provides an even more specific menu of data structures and software needs for producing a fully replicable grammar, including data structured as robust XML and a series of parsing engines and tokenisers. Unfortunately, the publishing industry upon which most linguists rely has not yet caught up with these digital visionaries and we are still years away from a discipline-wide endorsement of radically linked grammars and source texts.

A simpler, albeit less robust, apparatus for linking linguistic claims to data may be available through a mechanism that already exists in academic publication: citation. If authors of descriptive linguistic materials can provide resolvable citations to original data in context – that is, a citation via a permanent handle to an archived language resource – it would be at least a step in the right direction. This of course presumes that the linguist has prepared source materials for archiving and has then deposited them in an appropriate digital archive (i.e., not a website, but a digital repository with an institutional commitment to preserving and migrating data in perpetuity) (Thieberger and Berez 2012, 100), a practice that is increasingly becoming the norm. Then the linguist need only provide an identifying handle or URL and a time code for each example in the grammar.

Practices in descriptive linguistics

In theory, providing sufficient citation sounds fairly simple. Provided the linguist archives well-structured digital files that link textual annotations to specific points in a media file (e.g., an ELAN file and an audio file), simple citation should be a straightforward process.[2] Many descriptive linguists have already long been providing at least some form of citation for examples; for instance, the initials of the speaker who uttered the example, or a reference to a field notebook. But linguistics has not fostered a culture of providing full citation or even of making data locatable. Berez et al. (in prep) is a study of data citation practices in descriptive grammars, descriptive PhD theses, and linguistics journals from a ten-year span between 2003 and 2012, beginning five years after Himmelmann's (1998) position paper on language documentation as, among other things, a way to provide accountability in linguistics: '[Language] documentation ... will ensure that the collection

---

2 In practice, linguists will need to decide on discipline-wide formats for citing many kinds of primary data, not just digital media.

and presentation of primary data receive the theoretical and practical attention they deserve' (1998, 164). Berez et al. (in prep) have found that by and large, authors of grammars, theses and articles rarely even indicate *if* or *where* data is stored, let alone provide some indication of from where in a corpus a particular example was retrieved.

In a sample of 45 published grammars, among those authors who stated explicitly where their data were located, the largest number of them (eight) had archived the data in a dedicated repository. Five authors indicated a plan to archive data in the future, and nine made some textual materials available via paper publication, either in the same volume or in a different volume. Two authors clearly stated that their data were unpublished (with no indication of a plan to make data available); one made data available on an accompanying website; one stated that data was backed up at his place of residence; one stated the data had fallen victim to a political uprising. Importantly, fewer than half the authors surveyed even considered it important to mention the location of data: 29 of the 45 surveyed did not make explicit statements about the location of their data. A sceptical reader would not even know where to look.

Berez et al. (in prep) also investigates methods of citation of example sentences. In the same 45 published grammars discussed above, the tendency is to provide less information to readers, rather than more, and 25 grammars used no discernable method for citing example sentences back to the primary data from whence they came. Of those that did, however, the citation form is ad hoc, usually with minimal information like speakers' initials or name (e.g., *JM*), sometimes with a date (e.g., *Tom Smith, 2009-04-07*) or, rarely, with a reference to the linguistic data type (e.g., *narrative*). In some cases, the author makes no reference to the data even being part of a larger corpus, but it some instances there is at least *some* indication that an item is a member of a group of materials conceived as unified along some parameter (e.g., *Notebook 12, p. 16* or *KC, tape 3 of 27*).

Only three of the 45 grammars so far examined in Berez et al. (in prep) include a citation in the format recommended by Thieberger (2009), in which an (ostensibly) resolvable permanent handle links to an item or items stored in a digital archive, with or without time offsets for the utterance. For example, this could be of the form *Peter Wee,*

oai:scholarspace.manoa.hawaii.edu: NL1–042, 00:02:44.4–00:02:46.0.[3]
In this example, the author cites the name of the speaker, the resolvable
URL to a file named NL1–042 that is stored in the ScholarSpace repository at the University of Hawaiʻi at Mānoa (aka, Kaipuleohone, see
below), and the starting and ending timecodes of the utterance in the
recording (here, starting two minutes, 44.4 seconds from the beginning of the recording and ending two minutes, 46 seconds from the
beginning of the recording).

Teaching postgraduate students to be more scientific

Language documentation at UHM

The Department of Linguistics at the University of Hawaiʻi at Mānoa
(UHM) offers advanced degrees (MA, PhD) focusing on language documentation.[4] As such, it seems we have a responsibility to investigate
novel ways to promote the methods and goals of language documentation in our curriculum. Calls for training in language documentation
invariably include training in linguistic data management techniques
(Jukes 2011; see also the curricula of the InField[5] and CoLang workshops,[6] as well as the grantee training of the Endangered Languages
Documentation Programme[7]), and these very techniques are those that
would enable linguists to prepare data in ways that facilitate archiving
and citation. However, given that the publishing world does not require
authors to cite back to archived primary data, how can we expect students to undertake this task? Even in the program at UHM, most of the
PhD theses over the last ten years have not cited examples back to resolvable resources, with the result that most of our students' linguistic
claims are not reproducible.

3 Many thanks to Huiyung Nala Lee for providing this citation example.
4 http://www.ling.hawaii.edu.
5 http://www.linguistics.ucsb.edu/faculty/infield and
http://linguistics.uoregon.edu/infield2010/home.
6 http://idrh.ku.edu/colang2012, http://www.uta.edu/faculty/cmfitz/swnal/
projects/CoLang.
7 http://www.eldp.net.

Fortunately, however, we are well-positioned to instil good habits in our students because of a number of fortuitous features of the program. First, we have several required courses in which proper data management and the creation of structured digital media and annotations can be learned, practised, and then mined for evidence for claims. These include LING 710: Methods in Language Documentation; LING 630: Field Methods; LING 617: Language Revitalization; and LING 640: Methods of Language Conservation. The result is that when students begin their own fieldwork data collection, they have already had enough experience at creating structured data so that they can begin using best digital practices immediately, rather than needing to go back and retrofit a less well-structured corpus of materials later. In addition to targeted coursework, we are also home to the Kaipuleohone University of Hawai'i Digital Language Archive,[8] a digital repository hosted in the University of Hawai'i Library's D-Space repository, ScholarSpace.[9] Kaipuleohone is fully compliant with the Open Language Archive Community's (OLAC[10]) metadata standards, and is a member of the Digital Endangered Languages and Music Archives Network (DELA-MAN[11]) (Berez 2013).

Recent changes to our requirements

As mentioned above, only two of the descriptive PhD theses (i.e., grammars) from the past decade (i) indicate that field data was archived and (ii) provide citations for examples back to the archived data. In response to this low level of archiving and citation, during the 2013–14 academic year the faculty in the department decided that encouraging archiving and citation was insufficient if we are to effectively communicate to our students that we value reproducibility. In the fall semester, the faculty elected to make the first of two major changes to the PhD

---

8   http://www.kaipuleohone.org. Kaipuleohone means 'gourd of sweet words' in Hawaiian. We are grateful to Laiana Wong for suggesting this name for the archive.
9   http://scholarspace.manoa.hawaii.edu.
10   http://www.language-archives.org.
11   http://www.delaman.org.

Handbook. This change added language stating that (i) students whose theses were based on data collected during their own fieldwork, regardless of linguistic subfield, were required to properly archive their data; (ii) students were to develop an archiving plan as a component of the required thesis proposal; and (iii) proof of deposit must be given to the thesis committee before a thesis could be approved. This change ensured that students would plan for archiving early in their graduate careers, and would hopefully train them to continue the practice into their professional lives.

Later, in the spring semester of 2014, the faculty elected to make the second change to the PhD Handbook, this time requiring proper citations to archived materials. Data in theses coming from a student's own archived materials must now be cited via a persistent identifier to the source file. After some discussion, it was determined that because different subfields have different practices for citation, the exact format and level of granularity – for instance, to a timecode in a specific audio file for examples from discourse, or to a collection of scanned field notebooks for historical linguistics, or to a dataset from an experiment – would be developed in consultation with the thesis advisor. The final wording of the new additions to the PhD Handbook are below:

> The Department of Linguistics values proper data management and citation. Students whose dissertations are based on data collected during the course of their own fieldwork are required to properly archive their data in an appropriate language archive in order to ensure the longevity of the data. Students will develop an archiving plan early and will include a description of this plan in the Dissertation Proposal. Data can be archived with Kaipuleohone, the University of Hawai'i Digital Language Archive or with another accepted archive (for example, a member archive of the DELAMAN network). For students archiving their data in Kaipuleohone, the archiving plan should be developed in consultation with the current archive director. All students will be required to submit proof of deposit to the committee before the dissertation can be approved.
>
> In addition, each student is required to cite data in the dissertation coming from his or her own archived materials via a persistent identifier URL to the source file in the archive. The exact format of

the citation and the level of granularity (e.g., timecode in an audio file; collection of files; dataset; etc.) can be developed in consultation with the dissertation advisor, and should reflect the best practices in the student's linguistic subfield.

Frequently asked questions

The new requirements for archiving and citation apply to students entering the program from fall 2014 onwards. Before the changes came into effect, three PhD students voluntarily followed the proposed requirements and provided feedback on workflow integration. We continue to work with these students, but so far their response has been positive, even enthusiastic.[12] Nonetheless, a few (rhetorical and actual) questions arise. Preliminary answers to some of these are below, and no doubt we will continue to refine how we put our new policies into practice.

Q: After the thesis is submitted, the author wants to revise a transcription, gloss, parse, analysis, etc. Is the citation now incorrect?

A: No. The citation is to the primary data itself (i.e., the media file), not the transcription or analysis per se.

Q: The student wants or needs to keep data temporarily private or inaccessible, either because of privacy concerns with the data provider, or to discourage 'scooping'. Is this going to put the student's degree at risk?

A: No. The student will still cite the archived materials. Requests for access to files that are not freely available will be handled like any other such request, by contacting the depositor. We are still able to balance the need for privacy.

---

12 One student writes, 'I have to say that archiving is one of the best things I ever decided to do for this dissertation. After four chapters, I have almost 400 example sentences, all attributed to specific timings in specific files in my archive. Metadata and a mix of software makes everything so easy to find. If it wasn't for the archive, I can't imagine even getting to this stage relatively unscathed. So thanks!' (Email from Nala Lee, 1 April 2014).

Q: The student later archives multiple 'versions' of the same primary data. Is the citation now incorrect?

A: No. Students, like other depositors, are encouraged to reference the original, unedited version of the primary data. Later versions can be associated to the original file in the archive metadata.

Q: Isn't it overwhelming to archive and cite while also writing a thesis?

A: Students are taught early to integrate preparing for archiving and citation early through required coursework. The intention is for this to become part of expected departmental culture, and for students to accept archiving and citation as part of the rigorous steps for thesis research and beyond.

Conclusion

Linguistics departments routinely make values declarations by requiring milestones to a degree. For instance, by requiring students to write qualifying papers, we are stating that we value the ability to write article-length research papers. By requiring comprehensive exams, we are stating that we value being able to talk and write eloquently about linguistics. By requiring PhD theses, we are stating that we value being able to plan and execute independent research. Given that we are ultimately training linguistic scientists, why would we value reproducibility any less than the aforementioned skills? Students, like anyone, are less likely to adopt practices that are seen as unessential, and will not often spend their time on activities they do not get credit for doing, but by teaching students how to archive and cite data properly, and then not only recommending but requiring it, we are making a statement that we value reproducibility.

Works cited

Berez, Andrea L (2013). 'The digital archiving of endangered language oral traditions: *Kaipuleohone* at the University of Hawai'i and *C'ek'aedi Hwnax* in Alaska.' *Oral Tradition* 28(2).

Berez, Andrea L., Lauren Gawne, Tyler Heston and Barbara Kelly (2015). 'Citation and transparency in descriptive linguistics.' (unpublished manuscript)

Buckheit, Jonathan B. and David L. Donoho (1995). 'Wavelab and reproducible research.' In *Wavelets and Statistics*, edited by Anestis Antoniadis and Georges Oppenheim, 55–81. New York: Springer.

Crocker, Jennifer and M. Lynne Cooper (2012). 'Addressing scientific fraud.' *Science* 334: 1182. doi: 10.1126/science.1216775.

Donoho, David L (2010). 'An invitation to reproducible computational research.' *Biostatistics* 11(3): 385–88.

Fang, Ferric C. and Arturo Casadevall (2011). 'Retracted science and the retraction index.' *Infection and Immunity* 79(10): 3855–59.

Fang, Ferric C., R. Grant Steen, and Arturo Casadevall (2013). 'Misconduct accounts for the majority of retracted scientific publications.' *PNAS Early Edition* 334: 1–6.

Gezeltner, Dan (2009). 'Being scientific: Falsifiability, verifiability, empirical tests, and reproducibility.' *The OpenScience Project.* http://openscience.org/blog/?p=312.

Himmelmann, Nikolaus P (1998). 'Documentary and descriptive linguistics.' *Linguistics* 36: 161–95.

Himmelmann, Nikolaus P (2006). 'Language documentation: What is it good for?' In *Essentials of Language Documentation*, edited by Jost Gippert, Nikolaus P. Himmelmann, and Ulrike Mosel, 1–30. Berlin: Mouton de Gruyter.

Jukes, Anthony (2011). 'Researcher training and capacity development in language documentation.' In *The Cambridge Handbook of Endangered Languages*, edited by Peter K. Austin and Julia Sallabank, 423–45. Cambridge: Cambridge University Press.

de Leeuw, Jan (2001). 'Reproducible research: The bottom line.' *UCLA Department of Statistics Papers.* http://escholarship.org/uc/item/9050x4r4.

Marcus, Adam and Ivan Oransky (2012). 'Bring on the transparency index.' *The Scientist.* http://tiny.cc/2012-transp-marcus.

Maxwell, Mike (2012). 'Electronic grammars and reproducible research.' In *Electronic Grammaticography (Language Documentation and Conservation Special Publication No. 4)*, edited by Sebastian Nordhoff, 207–34.

Ryan, Michael J. (2011). 'Replication in field biology: The case of the frog-eating bat.' *Science* 334: 1229–30.

Thieberger, Nicholas (2006). *A Grammar of South Efate: An Oceanic Language of Vanuatu.* Honolulu: University of Hawai'i Press.

Thieberger, Nicholas (2009). 'Steps toward a grammar embedded in data.' In *New Challenges in Typology: Transcending the Borders and Refining the*

Distinctions, edited by Patricia Epps and Alexandre Arkhipov, 389–408. Berlin; New York, NY: Mouton de Gruyter Mouton.

Thieberger, Nicholas and Andrea L. Berez (2012). 'Linguistic data management.' In *The Oxford Handbook of Linguistic Fieldwork*, edited by Nicholas Thieberger, 90–118. Oxford: Oxford University Press.

Tomasello, Michael and Josep Call (2011). 'Methodological challenges in the study of primate cognition.' *Science* 334: 1227–28.

Woodbury, Anthony C. (2003). 'Defining documentary linguistics.' In *Language Documentation and Description, Volume 1*, edited by Peter K. Austin, 35–51. London: The Hans Rausing Endangered Languages Project.

Woodbury, Anthony C. (2011). 'Language documentation.' In *The Cambridge Handbook of Endangered Languages*, edited by Peter K. Austin and Julia Sallabank, 159–86. Cambridge: Cambridge University Press.

3
On the reach of digital language archives

David Nathan

The aim of this chapter is to extend previous work on archival 'access and accessibility' (Nathan 2013) in order to make initial suggestions towards a set of criteria for thinking about archives' 'reach' – their multifaceted capacity to successfully provide language resources to those who can gain value from them. Several of our archives now think of themselves as publishers (Holton 2013; Nathan 2011b), which leads naturally to thinking about intended audiences and the appropriateness and usability of the archives' materials and services.

The origins of this theme can be traced to the Open Archive Information Systems (OAIS) project initiated by the Consultative Committee for Space Data Systems in the 1990s (CCSDS 2012; OAIS 2012; the CCSDS committee currently has 11 members, including NASA, the European Space Agency, and similar agencies from Canada, China, Japan, Russia and several European countries). The committee's context was a need to deal with massively accruing digital data from space programs, at the same time as preservation strategies were diverging, or worse:

Nathan, David (2015). 'On the reach of digital language archives.' In *Research, Records and Responsibility: Ten Years of PARADISEC*, edited by Amanda Harris, Nick Thieberger and Linda Barwick. Sydney: Sydney University Press.

Problems had often stemmed from terms – such as archives/archiving or metadata – that were used so widely and for so many different purposes that it was difficult to determine if they were being used in the same way by different actors. The combination of pressing need, available expertise, and inconsistent language meant the time was ripe for developing a reference model that could codify and support greater consistency in discussions of digital archives.[1] (Lee 2010, 4021)

Recognition of these wider problems, and the goal of establishing a 'common framework of terms and concepts' rather than specific designs or implementations (CCDSD 2012, iii, 1–3) led to their activity and impact reaching far beyond the scope of space data to 'become a fundamental component of digital archive research and development in a variety of disciplines' (Lee 2010, 4020).

The OAIS Reference Model recognises, in addition to long-term preservation, the importance of data dissemination and availability, and archives' accountability to their users and stakeholders. These concepts are expressed in relation to 'data consumers', and in particular *designated communities*:

[a] special class of Consumers is the Designated Community. The Designated Community is the set of Consumers who should be able to understand the preserved information ... [i.e., information expressed] in a form that is understandable using the recipient's Knowledge Base. The Designated Community, and its associated Knowledge Base, for whom the information is being preserved by the Archive is defined by that Archive, and that Knowledge Base will, as described below, change over time. The definition of Designated Community may be subject to agreement with funders and other stakeholders. (CCSDS 2012, 2–3)

---

1   Some readers will recognise some of these problems as still remaining to be solved – or perhaps being recapitulated – for the archiving of language documentation.

Figure 3.1 illustrates two aspects of the OAIS model that I wish to expand on in this paper. Firstly, the term 'designated communities' highlights the importance of archives being explicit about *who* they serve and in turn *how* they do so; but while many archives pay homage to the OAIS model (Nathan 2011a),[2] few actually make identifying, understanding and appropriately serving audiences a significant part of their scientific endeavour (see below criteria *2. Audiences*; *4. Delivery*; *5. Access management*; *6. Information accessibility*; and *9. Feedback channels*). Secondly, notice the essentially linear progression from depositor ('producer') to archive and then to consumers/users – an architecture now superseded by today's potent combination of ethically based community inclusion in research and current social networking technologies that enable wider participation (see below criteria *2. Audiences*; *3. Discovery*; *5. Access management*; *7. Promotion*; *8. Communication ecology*; and *9. Feedback channels*).

I have borrowed the term 'reach' from Chang (2010), who uses it as a subordinate category in her 'Target, Access, Preservation, and Sustainability' (TAPS) grid of evaluative criteria for archives. There are several other evaluative systems that digital archives can use to claim and demonstrate conformance to standards and good practices, including the National Initiative for a Networked Cultural Heritage (NINCH) guide (NINCH 2002), DRAMBORA,[3] and the Data Seal of Approval.[4] While these are largely focused on policies, strategies, resources, and technologies for digital preservation, TAPS also included a criterion addressing access and relevance to the archives' intended audiences, recalling the OAIS architectural principle devoted to identifying, understanding, and serving users. The components of 'reach,'

---

2   See also http://dobes.mpi.nl/meetings/aab-meeting-report-nov-05-v2.pdf and http://www.robertmunro.com/research/munro05elar.ppt. The Data Seal of Approval evaluative scheme (for details, see below), for example, requires approved archives to have 'technical infrastructure [which] explicitly supports the tasks and functions described in internationally accepted archival standards like OAIS' – see guideline #13 of the DSA Guidelines at http://datasealofapproval.org/en/information/guidelines.
3   Digital Repository Audit Method based on Risk Assessment. http://www.repositoryaudit.eu.
4   http://www.datasealofapproval.org/en.

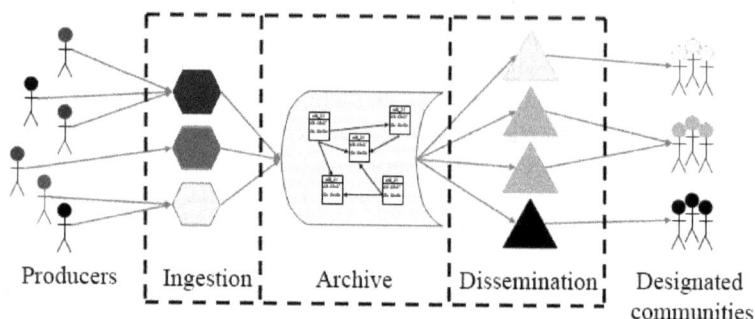

Figure 3.1 The OAIS model proposes three types of packages: ingestion, archival, and dissemination. There can be multiple dissemination packages to serve the archive's 'designated communities'.

described below, should be seen as complementary to these existing evaluative schemes.

The body of this chapter unpacks 'reach' into a set of ten criteria, illustrating them by examples from some of the DELAMAN archives:[5]

1. *Acquisition*, the archive's collection policies and its acquisition processes and resources;

2. Archives' understanding of their key *audiences* in order to provide appropriate services for them; for example identifying a range of relevant audiences, their languages of access, their varied technological and information literacies, interface design and usability;

3. *Discovery*, drawing on the understandings of audiences in order to help them browse, navigate, search, identify and select their items of interest;

---

5 The archives mentioned in this paper are: AILLA (Archive of the Indigenous Languages of Latin America), ANLA (Alaska Native Language Archive), ELAR (Endangered Languages Archive), DoBeS (Dokumentation Bedrohter Sprachen), and PARADISEC (Pacific and Regional Archive for Digital Sources in Endangered Cultures). See http://www.delaman.org/members for details. For DELAMAN, see http://www.delaman.org.

4. *Delivery*, that is, making available selected resources according to users' preferences, whether by download, view-in-browser, through apps or other means;
5. *Access management* such that resource delivery follows depositors' and communities' preferences, and where users have ways of applying for and negotiating access;
6. *Information accessibility*, where the actual desired content is accessible to users, whether in terms of contextualisation or appropriate complexity, language, or modality;
7. *Promotion*, raising the profile of archive deposits and activities, and bringing 'outreach' versions to the intended (or new) audiences;
8. *Communication ecology*, the place of archives' core activities within growing media and informational environments;
9. *Feedback channels*, where users can utilise the archive to provide feedback to depositors or to enhance deposits with user-generated content; and
10. *Temporal reach*, where long-term preservation seems to be at odds with today's 'short-termism' of funders and the (apparent) ephemerality of digital media.

Through considering how archives are providing such services, we can see a transition from being repositories of memory to being facilities for fostering participation and understanding.

The ten components of reach

1. Acquisition

Users are drawn to archives when they expect to find resources relevant to their needs. The clarity of an archive's collection and acquisition policies (Conathan 2011, 240) and the vigour with which it seeks new materials will thus draw users, increase usage, and provide regular update topics for announcements (which can be disseminated through the archive's 'information ecology': see below).

The PARADISEC archive,[6] for example, actively invites and seeks out legacy analogue materials that are vulnerable or valuable,[7] thereby increasing its coverage and relevance to users. Acquisition for the

Endangered Languages Archive (ELAR) and the Documentation of Endangered Languages (DoBeS) archives,[8] by contrast, is largely driven by associated grant-giving – as of early 2014, 90% of ELAR's incoming materials were from Endangered Languages Documentation Programme (ELDP) grantees.

2. Audiences

If the mission of archives is preserving and disseminating resources, then audiences are their *sine qua non*. We can think of audiences as being the sum of all individuals that access collections over their entire lifespan, or as aggregated 'types' based on certain shared criteria (such as 'researchers', 'community members' and the like). We can alternatively think of audiences as being those using archives today, or those in the (possibly distant) future who discover and access materials, if the archives have fulfilled their preservation role (Woodbury 2014, 1; Holton 2013).[9]

Whether thinking of individuals with varied motivations and literacies, or groups who have particular preferences or constraints (e.g., language and other skills, availability of computers etc.), effective reach will take into account whether the archives provide suitable content versions and appropriate ways of searching, browsing, viewing and downloading (see *4. Delivery* and *6. Information accessibility* below for more on different methods of delivery and alternative versions of content, also OAIS 2012, Nathan 2006).

---

6   See http://paradisec.org.au.

7   See, for example, http://www.paradisec.org.au/blog/2014/04/paradisec-stats-for-2014 and Thieberger et al., this volume.

8   ELAR at http://elar-archive.org; DoBeS at http://dobes.mpi.nl.

9   Some might include other stakeholders such as funders and host institutions as audiences as well – and increasingly those who require reports about research; e.g., Australians report on their archive deposits for research evaluation in the ERA system. However, for the purposes of this paper, I do not include these categories; while those stakeholders might be those that we are required to 'play to' to sustain our existence, they are not our *raison d'être*. Funding sources come and go according to fashion or particular funders' strategies, but archives' collections have enduring value.

How well do archives know their audiences? Audiences are fundamental to what archives do, and archives should take a scientific approach to defining, researching, describing, serving and reporting about them. Yet it appears that some language archives take a peremptory approach to audiences, sometimes in contrast to the careful attention they pay to technical issues. Schwiertz (2012, 126), for example, describes DoBeS archive's attempt to address the limitations of its navigational interface:

> When considering the exploitation of language documentation data contained in language archives, three major user groups can be identified: The speaker community, the scientific community, i.e. linguists and scholars of related disciplines, and the general public. Each of these user groups has different interests and different needs, all of which are hardly satisfied by the IMDI-tree representation of the DoBeS archive. For the community users, community portals have been created in some projects ... we have [also] created a general portal to the DoBeS archive.[10]

This looks like an admirable advance, but we might ask whether it is sufficient to simply proclaim the reality of these 'major user groups'? Are there other yet undiscovered user groups? What research took place? What shared properties define these 'groups'? How is the archive collecting and reporting evidence about usage by these groups, what counts as serving them, and how well are they being served? How is the archive improving its methods and services based on its growing understanding of these putative groups?

ELAR requires users to register and create a basic profile. Answers to the profile question asking registrants to describe their connection

---

10   Schwiertz is the latest of several authors to write about user groups in this way. Wittenburg et al. (2002, 36) write: 'Besides the linguists, ethnologists and other researchers we see interests from school and university educators, journalists, and especially from the indigenous people themselves.' Farrar and Langendoen (2003, 97) arbitrarily identify linguists, indigenous communities, and language learners as groups who will gain from web access to linguistic resources. They urge data producers to adopt ontology and the 'semantic web' which would seem to have limited benefit to most of these groups.

with endangered languages inform the archive about the proportion of its users who are community members, researchers, and professionals in particular disciplines, and about their affiliations, motivations, heritages, interests and language activities.

It is easier for archives with more specific areal coverage and targeted collection policies to be transparent about the users they say they serve. For example, the Archive of Indigenous Languages of Latin America[11] offers its interface in Spanish, which is a *lingua franca* for the region it serves. It is not feasible for international archives like ELAR or DoBeS to provide interfaces to serve all their audiences; however, at the level of the individual deposit, depositors can be encouraged to provide metadata and descriptive information in the subject language of each deposit, or a relevant *lingua franca*. For example, the Movima deposit in DoBeS has metadata and descriptive material in Spanish.[12] Shenkai Zhang, ELAR depositor of Pinjiang love songs,[13] edited her deposit's home page to provide contextual information in Chinese to help facilitate access to the Pinjiang community from which these songs come (see Figure 3.2). See also below under 6. *Information accessibility* for Eli Timan's ELAR collection,[14] which forgoes analytical linguistic content to provide what Timan, a community member himself, understands that his community wants: transliteration in Arabic, translation into English, and pictures drawn by the storyteller.[15]

Considering language choice in the context of audiences highlights the fact that by typically presenting services in a given language (usually English), archives are either making a (probably covert) assumption that English is a *lingua franca* for their audiences or else simply imposing English as a condition of using the archive.

Other audience-related factors include what modalities people would like to access materials in, their computer and literacy styles and preferences, and what computer hardware, software and connectivity they have available. Without appropriate research, archives may be in-

---

11 http://www.ailla.utexas.org.
12 http://dobes.mpi.nl/projects/movima.
13 http://elar.soas.ac.uk/deposit/0079.
14 http://elar.soas.ac.uk/deposit/0026.
15 See these materials at http://jewsofiraq.com.

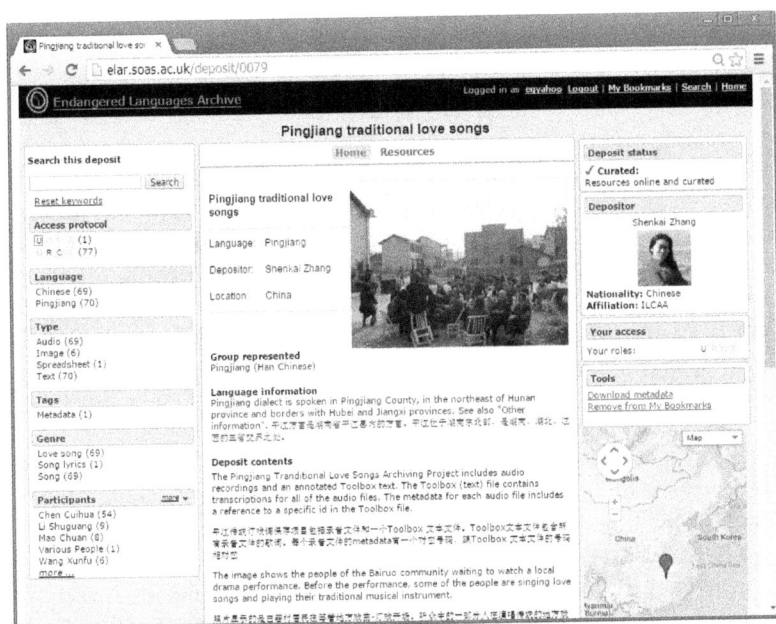

Figure 3.2 Shenkai Zhang has edited her ELAR deposit to add Chinese text to aid access by language community members.

sufficiently aware of these factors, or even whether factors pattern with groups or vary more according to the individual user.[16]

---

16   It might be objected that research of these factors might 'run into the same language and accessibility issues' that this paper identifies as obstacles to 'reach' (I am grateful to an anonymous reviewer for raising this). While it is beyond the scope of the paper to suggest a full research program, I would suggest that much might be learned if a small fraction of the time and intellectual rigour applied to language documentation and analysis were applied to scientific investigation of a community's preferences, skills and receptiveness to various kinds of language materials. Such research could even be recognised as part of documentation methodology (Nathan and Fang 2014, 53).

3. Discovery

Archives have a long-standing tradition of providing methods for helping users to find materials; in archive-speak this is usually called resource discovery (Bird and Simons 2003). There are a variety of methods, from search over cataloguing metadata to additional finding aids produced by curators. Discovery strategies (and users' expectations) are shifted in the digital domain. On the one hand, discovery is facilitated by the ability of computers to support search over large amounts of text material. On the other hand, language archives increasingly contain large amounts of media (audio, images, video) that are generally as opaque to computers as uncatalogued objects were in a traditional archive, so metadata (labelling and description of content) are as crucial as ever for resource discovery.

Debates about the extent to which metadata categories need to be standardised have largely given way to concern for encouraging depositors to provide as broad and deep metadata and metadocumentation as possible (Austin 2013), since these represent the unique, irreplaceable knowledge that only depositors are likely to possess, and are the keys to carrying a profound understanding of the materials into the future, for future users and usages. Rich metadata, when combined with multiple languages and well-designed interfaces to facilitate search and browse, increase an archive's reach to a greater range of users.

Archives need to understand audiences in order to provide a range of ways for them to search, browse, and navigate effectively to materials they are interested in. While we may make generalisations about real or imagined user groups, it would seem a good starting point for online catalogues to take best advantage of known and effective digital genres. ELAR designed its catalogue to use some of the contemporary visual and interactive methods of social networking applications (e.g., Facebook), a decision that has been validated by various fieldworker reports that many language communities have recently and rapidly acquired access to the internet with predominant use of social networking apps on mobile devices.

Providing discovery mechanisms means more than presenting users with search screens allowing them to search 'thin' metadata (Nathan and Austin 2005). This is especially important for endangered languages, where language names can vary widely due to spelling variations or by being expressed in different languages or as exonyms or endonyms, where not all of the 'target audience' are likely to have relevant literacies (but see *2. Audiences* above), where the materials tend to be at the edges of mainstream knowledge rather than the centre, and where certain users are simply fishing about out of interest rather than being focused on finding particular linguistic material. Thus it is important to provide ways to discover what is available in the archive through browsing. Browsing, as illustrated in Figure 3.3, enables users to recognise and select items, even randomly. Many archives now also provide maps to enable discovery by browsing according to location. This has many advantages: it lessens dependence on traditional literacies, it encourages serendipitous discovery, it better supports people who 'think visually', and it conveys additional information such as proximity and clustering of materials and likely landform/environment information.

Archives can also join with others by 'federating' their discovery mechanisms; that is, sharing and pooling some or all of their metadata so that users can search or browse a larger virtual collection without having to know (at least initially) where a given resource is located (Broeder et al. 2008). The best known example in the language documentation field is the Open Language Archives Community (OLAC) catalogue.[17]

Archives' choices – whether explicit or not – about metadata and interfaces control users' ability to discover materials they are looking for, and/or discover materials they were not previously aware of but which prove to be interesting or valuable to them. Constraining discovery strategies to structured search via standard, English, academic-centric categories and pre-defined ontologies can limit the reach of archives.

4. Delivery

This criterion is concerned with how a resource, typically a file, is actually delivered to a user. Whether the resource file is text, audio or video, it may be offered for download, or it may be shown directly in the browser or in some kind of browser-embedded player (e.g., a media-

---

17 http://search.language-archives.org/index.html.

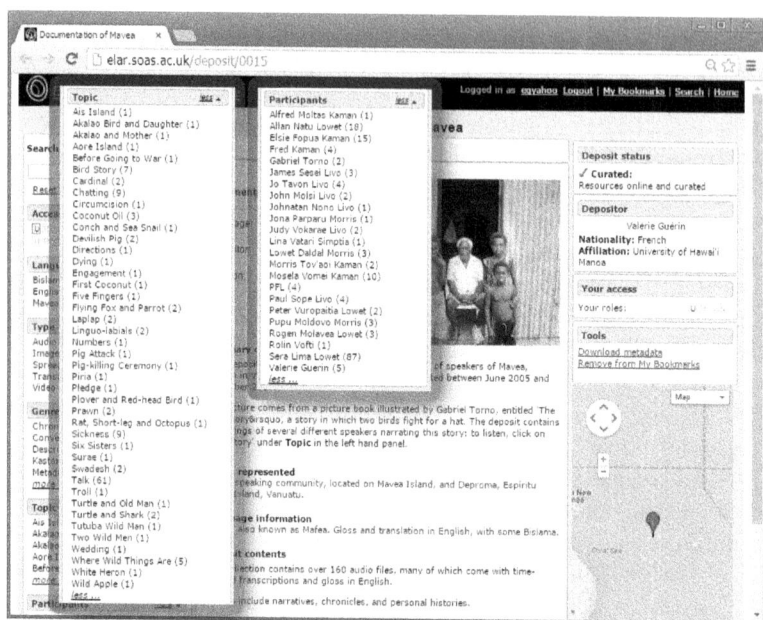

Figure 3.3 Showing the range of terms available in faceted browse of Valerie Guerin's ELAR deposit (the scrolled sections have been superimposed onto this image). See http://elar.soas.ac.uk/deposit/0015.

player plugin). The best option for a user will depend on their purposes, skills, devices, software, and internet connection. Viewing a video sample in the browser may be preferable because downloading the whole file would entail a high data cost, especially on mobile; another user might download a video file but not know how to play it. On the other hand, some users will want to view or work with the video or view it later offline.

Consider the choices available for viewing media annotation files produced using ELAN software.[18] Data files produced by ELAN are encoded as opaque XML structures that can only effectively be viewed

18   http://tla.mpi.nl/tools/tla-tools/elan.

Figure 3.4 Annex runs as a browser plugin, requiring no software installation.

using bespoke software (typically, the ELAN software itself). Those who want to work with the detail of an ELAN file will likely have ELAN installed and will want to download the ELAN file.[19] On the other hand, those who do not have ELAN (or the correct version of it) installed, who are not interested in technical annotations, or who do not have the skills, time or motivation to find and install software, would rather simply view some version of the material in their browser. To serve them, DoBeS (aka The Language Archive, the authors of ELAN) created a browser plugin, 'Annex' (Annotation Explorer; see Figure 3.4).[20] Other software developers have also created ELAN content viewers – see 6. *Information accessibility*.

---

19 In fact, such users will also need certain configuration files to display the ELAN file as its producer intended.
20 http://tla.mpi.nl/tools/tla-tools/annex.

Archives can extend the reach of their resources by providing different ways of delivering them. This is going to become increasingly important as more non-Western communities catch up with, if not overtake, Western modes of using the internet, often in different ways, such as solely through mobile devices.

5. Access management

Today, matters of privacy and control of personal information are of increasing general concern. Such concerns are amplified in the case of recordings of endangered languages. Endangered language communities and their speakers are typically under various pressures and deprivations that are often also contributing causes to the decline of their languages and cultures. These difficulties are amplified by the methodologies of documentary linguistics, which most highly values the recording of spontaneous and conversational speech. As the contexts in which languages are spoken decrease (which is what primarily drives endangerment), people tend to use their languages more and more to speak of private, local, sensitive and secret matters. So the primary data of documentary linguistics maximises the likelihood of it including content that can cause embarrassment or harm to the recorded speakers. As a result, it is broadly agreed among endangered languages documenters and archives that they need to collect, preserve and disseminate materials in accordance with the wishes of the information providers and their communities (Rice 2012; Austin and Grenoble 2007).[21]

The ELAR archive developed an approach to access management that locates it within a larger framework called *access protocol*. This term refers to the sum of processes extending from the beginning of documentation activity (e.g., starting when a documenter seeks informed consent from speakers) and then collects metadata on the rights and sensitivities associated with documentation materials, through to the mechanisms for dynamically providing, restricting, or negotiating about access to archived materials. It involves careful attention to how

---

21   This stance has recently come under pressure from funders campaigning for their variant of 'Open Access'.

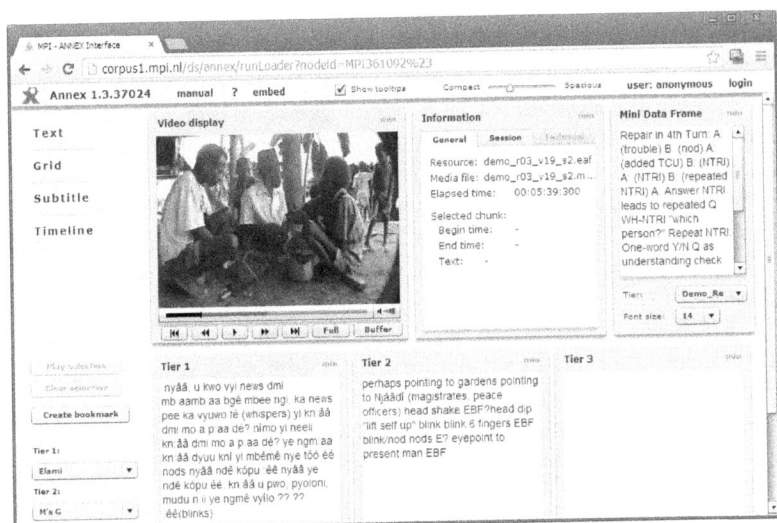

Figure 3.5 Annex displaying a simpler view of an ELAN file.

the interface represents and guides users around both accessible and controlled-access materials,[22] and includes methods for negotiating access, and detailed reporting to depositors and others. It is described in detail in Nathan (2010).

Respect of privacy and control of personal information impose legal as well as ethical obligations. Therefore it is important that an archive's policies and mechanisms for safeguarding access, and its methods for processing and deciding access applications, are transparent, accountable, and ethically and legally sound.

---

22   Prior to 2014, ELAR's catalogue interface provided coloured labels clearly showing any user which resources s/he could and could not access. Helpfully for users, these included navigational controls, which enabled users to restrict a search or browse to only those materials that they could (or could not) access. Following a funder's campaign for 'Open Access', ELAR staff felt pressured to modify this system.

6. Information accessibility

A user might be delivered a resource (see *4. Delivery* above), perhaps after negotiating access to it (see *5. Access management* above), but there remains the question: how accessible is the actual *content* of that resource? Consider again the case of an ELAN file: it might have a wealth of linguistic detail, but for some users that detail can obscure a simpler experience or bit of information they are after. To help, Annex provides alternative views of the data; for example, by showing simpler text versions of the content (see Figure 3.5).

Figures 3.6 and 3.7 show two simpler applications that provide alternative renderings of the information contained in an ELAN file. Figure 3.6 shows an example from Eli Timan, who documented Jewish Iraqi (a dialect of Arabic), and worked with Stuart McGill to develop a Flash app that runs in a browser.[23] The app draws data from an ELAN file but bypasses the more complex ELAN software to show a simple display that synchronises the audio with scrolling Arabic orthography and English translation. According to Timan, himself a member of the Jewish Iraqi community, this makes the relevant information more accessible to his target audience for the materials.[24]

Another more adventurous example, developed by Edward Garrett using HTML5, is a speech bubble player.[25] This player selects and pulls data from an ELAN file and presents it in a familiar comic-book style. A user can 'play' with the speech bubbles, manipulating the interface not only in terms of the linguistic data but in terms of how the display is composed and experienced (a 'thick interface' in the terms of Nathan 2006).

I recount here an interesting audience reaction to demonstration of the speech bubble player during the presentation of the talk on which this chapter is based. When Garrett's speech bubble player was being demonstrated in morpheme-by-morpheme mode (representing speech content as interlinearised/glossed) several audience members burst into

---

23   The app is similar to Christopher Cox's CuPED; see
http://sweet.artsrn.ualberta.ca/cdcox/cuped.
24   See an example at http://jewsofiraq.com/texts/
shlomo_kuwaity1.xml#shlomo_kuwaity1.008.
25   See http://lah.soas.ac.uk/projects/dev/bubble-player/wilbur.html.

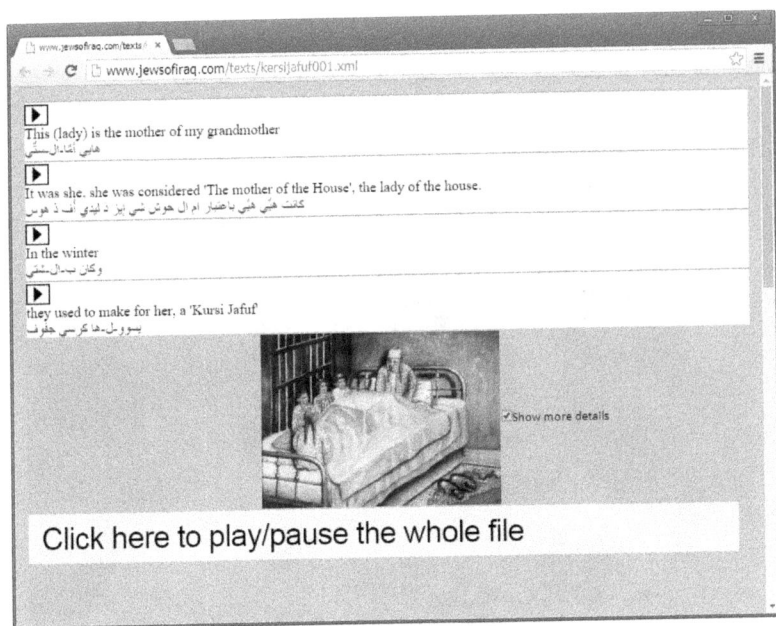

Figure 3.6 Eli Timan and Stuart Gill's simple Flash-based ELAN player.

laughter. It took me a few moments to realise that what was amusing them was the dissonance between on the one hand watching video of people in informal conversation, their speech visualised in speech bubbles, while on the other hand seeing the *content* of their speech rendered as analytical, morpheme-by-morpheme stuff. The friendly video/ speech bubble view clashed with the 'technical' interlinearisations. Oddly, perhaps, I had never before seen anybody respond this way despite many years of viewing materials together with others in purely 'technical' contexts such as ELAN. This audience response suggests a challenge to the way we routinely render language events as de-contextualised and asocial without a second thought as to the transformation that we have imposed.

Although in both cases illustrated above the original data file is an ELAN file, the same principle of multiple content-rendering, as per the OAIS model, applies across many types of files and content. For exam-

Figure 3.7 Edward Garrett's speech bubble player. The speakers, conversing in Pite Saami, are Henning Rankvist (left) and Elsy Rankvist (right). From an ELAR collection deposited by Joshua Wilbur, *Pite Saami: Documenting the Language and Culture*, http://elar.soas.ac.uk/deposit/0053.

ple, a video can be provided with subtitles in a variety of languages (or with varied levels of detail in the transcription or annotation, cf. Jukes 2011); a text file could be presented as a print-ready PDF document or in very large font to aid the vision-impaired or elderly. An audio file could be represented spatially and labelled by keywords or images representing topics being spoken about so that a user can easily navigate to sections of interest. Such considerations raise questions about the resources required to produce multiple dissemination versions, and it is an index of the infancy of our field that it is not at all clear whether the onus lies with the archive itself, with the producers/depositors, or even the eventual consumers. In favour of the onus falling on the archive is the OAIS Reference Model, which assigns to archives decisions about 'designated communities' and thus the materials appropriate to them (in addition, an archive can potentially amortise investment in methods across multiple deposits). On the other hand, producers/depositors are most likely to know best about the nature of the materials and their key user communities, and they may have other motivations for reworking materials. Leaving the burden to the eventual consumers is the default but inexplicitly stated scenario for most present archives.

7. Promotion

Archives can increase their reach by raising awareness of their services and activities among both existing and new audiences. Up until recently, the activities of endangered languages archives have mainly been disseminated within linguistics and related fields through conferences, workshops, articles, and websites. A few endangered-language-related projects have managed to receive significant mainstream press attention, including the Endangered Languages Alliance[26] (whose stories have been picked up by the *New York Times*), the Endangered Languages Project[27] (which made news in several major newspapers), the Living Tongues Institute[28] (funded and promoted by *National Geographic*), and the World Oral Literature Project[29] (whose director, Mark Turin, has appeared in BBC documentaries). However, these are not archives, which raises questions of whether archives are generally too absorbed in their curatorial, preservation or technical services, whether the term 'archive' turns off users, and whether archives should partner with more 'sexy' and outgoing projects like those mentioned, or with institutions experienced in outreach such as the British Library or the Smithsonian Institution.

Nevertheless, archive activities can draw wider interest. For example, 'Endangered Languages Week', an outreach event originally initiated by ELAR and the Endangered Languages Academic Programme at HRELP,[30] drew up to 1000 students, staff and visitors annually to events

---

26   See http://elalliance.org.
27   See http://www.endangeredlanguages.com.
28   See http://www.livingtongues.org.
29   See http://www.oralliterature.org.

targeted at a wide range of disciplines and the wider public. In some years, a parallel event was run at other institutions, and, during its lifetime from 2007 to 2013, HRELP's Endangered Languages Week came to be seen as a fixture in the calendar for those interested in languages more broadly.[31]

There are other opportunities for raising awareness and usage of our archives among students and particular language communities. Recently Adam Schembri, depositor (together with Trevor Johnston) of the Australian Sign Language (AUSLAN) corpus in ELAR,[32] posted a series of Facebook messages about the corpus, and following those posts the staff at ELAR noticed an increase in the rate of archive user registrations and archive accesses. Gary Holton (2014) reports a similar upsurge in community interest as a result of online communications about archive materials.

Joshua Wilbur widened awareness of and access to his Pite Saami materials deposited with ELAR[33] by working with local archives in Sweden to encourage and help them hold language materials so Saami community members can access them (Wilbur 2014).

An archive may decide to promote particular deposits locally in order to attract users. For example, the DoBeS archive entry page prominently features attractive videos, thus literally promoting the featured deposits.[34] ELAR sponsored a short series of blog posts by postgraduate intern Zander Zambas titled 'Meet an Endangered Language', each of which offers thematic discussion and walk-through of the deposit highlights.[35] Archives could also cross-promote their holdings; for example, by listing 'interesting' deposits in partner archives, or by systematic efforts to cross-reference related holdings across archives.

---

30   The Hans Rausing Endangered Languages Project at SOAS, which was originally established with three components: the Academic Programme, the Documentation (funding) Programme, and the Archive Programme.
31   For more details about ELW, see http://www.hrelp.org/events and the annual reports at http://www.hrelp.org/publications/newsletter.
32   http:// elar.soas.ac.uk/deposit/0001.
33   http://elar.soas.ac.uk/deposit/0053.
34   http://dobes.mpi.nl.
35   http://elar-archive.org/blog/category/elar-collections/meet-an-endangered-language.

8. Communication ecology

As expressed so well by the title of the 2008 conference of the International Association of Sound and Audiovisual Archives, 'No Archive Is an Island', archives exist as institutions and services within an interconnected network of communication and interaction types: conferences, workshops, publications, posters, mailing lists, social media (Facebook, Twitter etc.), blogs, podcasts, and other events such as training and outreach events. And of course archives can be linked together, through common portals such as OLAC,[36] or by placing links in deposits to relevant deposits in other archives (Steven Bird, personal communication). These all provide possibilities for disseminating information about archives and their collections, and for interaction and exchange.[37] These channels are complementary and mutually reinforcing: Melissa Terras (2012) has shown through experiments with social media that using the right combination of blogging and Twitter – with the right timing ('timing is everything') – it is possible to increase the number of article downloads by up to 11 times.

9. Feedback channels

Archives can implement additional channels to facilitate communication with and between themselves, depositors and users. ELAR provides depositors with detailed real-time information about who has accessed their materials. Reports from depositors and communities confirm that this enhances their trust in the archive. For example, the Warm Springs community (Oregon, USA) has language materials deposited in ELAR with access restricted to 'Community only'.[38] Community members reported their relief on seeing ELAR's access reports explicitly showing zero downloads. In other cases, depositors worried about rampant downloading are reassured on seeing that access to their deposits seems to be moderate, and can be more willing to relax access restrictions.

---

36 http://www.language-archives.org.
37 As well as to identify new sources of materials for collections.
38 These were produced with linguist Nariyo Kono; see http://elar.soas.ac.uk/deposit/0066e.

ELAR implemented an innovative feedback channel for negotiating access to restricted materials (see also 5. *Access management* above). Called the 'Subscription system', this system caters to depositors who are willing to share access to materials but only under the condition of express permission, so that they can be aware of access and usage of their data. ELAR conducted research (Nathan 2010) and found a very salient preference for this condition, with the proportion of items under Subscriber access ('S') varying between 25 and 50% over time. The system places a link next to all S-labelled items. Users can click on the link to bring up a dialogue box where they can send a request message to the depositor. In turn, the depositor is notified and supplied with the user's request message and the user's profile information; based on these the depositor can grant or deny access, or send a message back to the user (or both). The system has proved to be a very effective solution both for satisfying depositors' preference for 'need to know' and for delegating access management to those in the best position to handle it. Furthermore it has proved to be a fertile channel for exchange of information, as depositors and users discover the value of reciprocal exchange of information around the topic of the language materials. Although a limited implementation, this transformation of the archive from being a static repository to being a living platform for building and conducting relationships *around* language materials could eventually be extended to include communication around all deposits, involving exchange between various constellations of depositors, users, and language speakers.

Many archives work with depositors and provide feedback about their materials during the depositing/curating process; in this way the archive is 'reaching' future users through its contribution to the content, organisation, and properties of the deposit itself.[39]

---

39 This process makes explicit the influence of archives on the records they preserve and hence on the representation of the world they attempt to record, recalling Jacques Derrida's *Archive Fever* (1995) and its proposal – or accusation – that archives manipulate and construct the historical record through their policies and practices (Nathan 2012). Perhaps the main issue for us is whether archives wield this influence in a transparent, collaborative and scientific way.

While ELAR's subscription system (described above) enables users to negotiate directly with depositors about access to materials, a richer feedback channel between them could result in more effective usage of those materials. Users of data – and especially less experienced users such as students – can benefit from ongoing access to documenters so that the latter can provide methodological guidance or warnings about the limitations of the materials (indeed a free exchange may lead to fruitful collaboration between them). While in general scientific data can be utilised in its own terms, language documentation materials often consist of recordings and other material captured in complex situations that are only partially understood, and where the descriptive aspects can be limited, preliminary, and under revision. In addition, such materials are often unique, with little contextualising, corroborating or cross-referencing literature. While general archive principles encourage depositors to provide metadata and metadocumentation (Austin 2013) to ensure that data is understood and used appropriately, there remain many methodological limitations that can be ameliorated by connecting users and depositors.

10. Temporal reach

Reach across time is conventionally assumed to be archives' mission. However, this can no longer be taken for granted as funds become harder to get, host institutions look for short-term returns, and even the concept of 'archive' becomes crowded out by the proliferation of digital services that appear to converge with what archives do, especially as archives also increasingly portray themselves as publishers (cf. Holton 2014, Nathan 2011b) or software engineers (Koenig et al. 2009).

Gary Holton (2013) has pointed out that the value of archives can be realised through serendipitous discovery in the (perhaps distant) future, and is not calculable in terms of inputs and outputs, impact, or other contemporary evaluative measures. In his example, Eyak materials, after lying unused for some 40 years in the Alaska Native Language Archive, were 'discovered' and suddenly received much attention and use by the community; they went rapidly from zero to 100% reach after 40 years of archival dormancy. Holton has pointed out that in the digital domain, and given today's popular engagement with ephemeral digital data, it is all too easy to delete, revise and substitute – all actions which can dilute or distort the historical record.

Conclusion

This paper has listed a provisional set of ten criteria that, taken together, could be used to describe an archive's reach. As a coda, I would like to add that they are not proposed as measuring yardsticks or evaluative criteria. That kind of quantitative or box-ticking approach does not take into account the concept of *value*. As archives struggle to justify their existence to host institutions and funders, they find themselves citing facts and numbers: being a member of this or that body, having X terabytes of data and Y deposits/files/hours (Dobrin et al. 2007). While archives might well be proud of some of their numbers (although cf. Woodbury 2014, 2, who honestly discloses disappointingly low access and usage), they also need to work out ways to detect and describe the value found in archive usages. Such information would not only tell us more about the reach of an archive (for example, if a teacher amplifies the dissemination of archive holdings by creating classroom teaching materials from them) but also about the *significance* and *meaning* of the materials to those who access them. Endangered languages archives have an important responsibility as custodians of the resources contributed by communities, documenters, and funders, and so any efforts they make to increase their reach will amplify the efforts of all.

Acknowledgements

I would like to thank two anonymous reviewers and Peter Austin, Stephen Bird and Birgit Hellwig for valuable comments and corrections to this paper and the presentation on which it is based. However, I am solely responsible for all remaining errors and provocations.

Works cited

Austin, Peter K. (2013) 'Language documentation and metadocumentation.' In *Keeping Languages Alive: Documentation, Pedagogy and Revitalization*, edited by Sarah Ogilvie and Mari Jones, 3–15. Cambridge: Cambridge University Press.

Austin, Peter K., and Lenore Grenoble (2007). 'Current trends in language documentation.' In *Language Documentation and Description, Volume 4*, edited by Peter K. Austin, 12–25. London: SOAS.

Bird, Steven, and Gary Simons (2003). 'Seven dimensions of portability for language documentation and description.' *Language* 79: 557–82. http://tiny.cc/2003-7dim-birdsimons.

Broeder, Daan, David Nathan, Sven Strömqvist, and Remco van Veenendaal (2008). 'Building a federation of language resource repositories: The DAM-LR project and its continuation within CLARIN.' In *Proceedings of the Sixth International Conference on Language Resources and Evaluation (LREC 2008)*, edited by Nicoletta Calzolari et al. Marrakech: European Language Resources Association (ELRA). http://www.lrec-conf.org/proceedings/lrec2008.

Chang, Debbie (2010). 'TAPS: Checklist for responsible archiving of digital language resources.' MA thesis, Graduate Institute of Applied Linguistics, Dallas.

Consultative Committee for Space Data Systems, The (CCSDS) (2012). 'Reference model for an Open Archival Information System (OAIS)' *Recommended Practice Issue 2*. Washington: CCSDS Secretariat. http://public.ccsds.org/publications/archive/650x0m2.pdf.

Conathan, Lisa (2011). 'Archiving and language documentation.' In *The Cambridge Handbook of Endangered Languages*, edited by Peter K. Austin and Julia Sallabank, 235–54. Cambridge: Cambridge University Press.

Derrida, Jacques (1995). *Mal d'archive: une impression freudienne*. Paris: Éditions Galilée.

Dobrin, Lise, Peter K. Austin and David Nathan (2007). 'Dying to be counted: Commodification of endangered languages in documentary linguistics.' In *Proceedings of the Conference on Language Documentation and Linguistic Theory*, edited by Peter Austin, Oliver Bond and David Nathan, 59–68. London: SOAS.

Farrar, Scott and Terry Langendoen (2003). 'A linguistic ontology for the semantic web.' *Glot International* 7(3): 97–100.

Holton, Gary (2013). 'Thanks for not throwing that away: How archival data unexpectedly inform the linguistic and ethnographic record.' Paper presented at Research, Records and Responsibility (RRR): Ten Years of the Pacific and Regional Archive for Digital Sources in Endangered Cultures (PARADISEC), University of Melbourne, 2–3 December. http://hdl.handle.net/2123/9835.

Holton, Gary (2014). 'Mediating language documentation.' In *Language Documentation and Description, Volume 12*, edited by David Nathan and Peter K. Austin, 37–52. London: SOAS. http://elpublishing.org/PID/136.

Humanities Advanced Technology and Information Institute (HATII), University of Glasgow and National Initiative for a Networked Cultural Heritage (NINCH) (2002). *The NINCH Guide to Good Practice in the Digital Representation and Management of Cultural Heritage Materials.* http://www.ninch.org/guide.pdf.

Jukes, Anthony (2011). 'Culture documentation and linguistic stimulus.' In *Sustainable Data from Digital Research*, edited by Nick Thieberger et al., 49–65. Melbourne: University of Melbourne.

Koenig, Alexander, Jacquelijn Ringersma and Paul Trilsbeek (2009). 'The Language Archiving Technology domain.' In *Proceedings of the Fourth Language and Technology Conference: Human Language Technologies as a Challenge for Computer Science and Linguistics*, edited by Zygmunt Vetulani, 295–99. Poznan: Springer. http://tiny.cc/2009-lat-koenig.

Lee, Christopher A. (2010). 'Open Archival Information System (OAIS) reference model.' In *Encyclopedia of Library and Information Sciences, Third Edition*, edited by Marcia J. Bates and Mary Niles Maack, 4020–30. http://ils.unc.edu/callee/p4020-lee.pdf.

Nathan, David (2006). 'Thick interfaces: mobilising language documentation.' In *Essentials of Language Documentation*, edited by Jost Gippert, Nikolaus P. Himmelmann and Ulrike Mosel, 363–79. Berlin: Mouton de Gruyter.

Nathan, David (2010). 'Archives 2.0 for endangered languages: from disk space to MySpace.' *International Journal of Humanities and Arts Computing* 4(1–2): 111–24.

Nathan, David (2011a). 'Digital archiving.' In *Handbook of Language Documentation*, edited by Peter K. Austin and Julia Sallabank, 255–73. Cambridge: Cambridge University Press.

Nathan, David (2011b). 'Archives as publishers of language documentation: Experiences from ELAR.' Paper presented at the Second International Conference on Language Documentation and Conservation, University of Hawai'i, Manoa, 12 February. http://hdl.handle.net/10125/5223.

Nathan, David (2012). 'Archive fever: Making languages contagious, or textually transmitted disease?' Paper presented at Charting Vanishing Voices: A Collaborative Workshop to Map Endangered Oral Cultures, University of Cambridge, 30 June.

Nathan, David (2013). 'Access and accessibility at ELAR, a social networking archive for endangered languages documentation.' In *Oral Literature in the Digital Age: Archiving Orality and Connecting with Communities*, edited by Mark Turin, Claire Wheeler and Eleanor Wilkinson, 21–40. Cambridge: Open Book Publishers.

Nathan, David and Meili Fang (2014). 'Reimagining documentary linguistics as a revitalization-driven practice.' In *Keeping Languages Alive: Documentation, Pedagogy and Revitalization*, edited by Mari C. Jones and Sarah Ogilvie, 42–55. Cambridge: Cambridge University Press.

Nathan, David and Peter K. Austin (2005). 'Reconceiving metadata: Language documentation through thick and thin.' In *Language Description and Documentation, Volume 2*, edited by Peter K. Austin, 179–87. London: SOAS.

Rice, Keren (2012). 'Ethical issues in linguistic fieldwork.' In *The Oxford Handbook of Linguistic Fieldwork*, edited by Nicholas Thieberger, 407–29. Oxford: Oxford University Press.

Schwiertz, Gabriele (2012). 'Online presentation and accessibility of endangered languages data: The general portal to the DoBeS Archive.' In *Potentials of Language Documentation: Methods, Analyses, and Utilization*, LDandC Special Publication No. 3, edited by Frank Seifart et al., 126–28. Honolulu: University of Hawai'i Press.

Terras, Melissa (2012). 'Using social media to promote your own open access research.' Presentation at *Open Access Week 2012: Opening Research and Data*, Birkbeck College, London, 22 October. http://tiny.cc/2012-oa-terras.

Wilbur, Joshua (2014). 'Archiving for the community: Engaging local archives in language documentation projects.' In *Language Documentation and Description, Volume 12*, edited by David Nathan and Peter K. Austin, 85–102. London: SOAS.

Wittenburg, Peter, Ulrike Mosel and Adrienne Dwyer (2002). 'Methods of language documentation in the DOBES project.' *Proceedings of the Third International Conference on Language Resources and Evaluation (LREC 2002)*, edited by Manuel González Rodríguez, Suárez Araujo and Carmen Paz. http://www.lrec-conf.org/proceedings/lrec2002/pdf/221.pdf.

Woodbury, Anthony (2014). 'Archives and audiences: Toward making endangered language documentations people can read, use, understand, and admire.' In *Language Documentation and Description, Volume 12*, edited by David Nathan and Peter Austin, 19–36. London: SOAS.

Part 2
Enriching the archive

4
KinOath Kinship Archiver: genealogical and social relations

Peter Withers

Anthropologists and other researchers often study kin and other social relationships. There have been numerous applications that have tried to meet the needs of researchers in this area. However, there remain numerous gaps in either the functionality, usability or affordability of existing software. Some of these needs may be as simple as quickly creating diagrams. Some are more complex, such as statistical analysis of large sets of data. Interoperability is also a crucial factor, so that data collected in one application can be transferred to another. Linking resource files or archived material to genealogies also gives the opportunity to tie together all the data that might be available – finding individuals in a genealogy or matching a given affiliation pattern, such as matrimonial rings or other kinship patterns. Finding archived material associated with an individual or with a given affiliation pattern can also greatly assist the research process.

With these issues in mind, KinOath Kinship Archiver is a recently written application for the collection of kinship data and the subsequent exploration of that kinship data. The primary goal of this appli-

Withers, Peter (2015). 'KinOath Kinship Archiver: genealogical and social relations.' In *Research, Records and Responsibility: Ten Years of PARADISEC*, edited by Amanda Harris, Nick Thieberger and Linda Barwick. Sydney: Sydney University Press.

cation is to be flexible and culturally nonspecific, so that the complex facets in kinship and other social structures can be adequately represented. Beyond this, the application is designed to connect kinship data with archived data, such as audio data, video data or written resources. Kin type strings – notations for describing kinship relations – are used throughout the application for constructing and searching data sets. The representation and recording of kin terms is also integrated into the application, allowing comparative diagrams of kin terms across cultures or parallel kin term systems within the same culture. Graphical representation of the data is an important part of the application and the diagrams produced are intended to be flexible and of publishable quality.

The structure of this paper is as follows. Following consideration of some background issues behind KinOath, we discuss the internal data structure used and methods of data entry, and the various uses of kin type strings and the diagram types that are available. We then discuss methods of searching through the kinship data, the importing and exporting of kinship data, and the plugins framework that can allow extensions to be made for the application. Methods of doing statistical analysis on the data from KinOath are considered, as are the future possibilities of archiving with kinship data and the visualisation of the kinship data and the graphics used in KinOath. The conclusion includes discussion of future directions of the application.

Background

The following section describes the initial development stages of KinOath, its intended users, the relevance of kinship data to archiving, and existing applications.

Initial development

KinOath Kinship Archiver was developed by the author, Peter Withers, at the Language Archive (TLA), funded by the Max Planck Society and the Berlin-Brandenburg Academy of Sciences and Humanities. The needs assessment phase of development was done by Withers with the assistance of researchers at the Max Planck Institute for Social Anthropology and the Max Planck Institute for Psycholinguistics.

Intended users

The intended users of KinOath are any researchers that collect data in a context of social relations, which could be, for instance, genetic, religious, monetary or political. Potential users could include anthropologists, linguists, ethnomusicologists, or any researcher that collects field data on interconnected individuals. The application could also be of use when the social context (e.g., social relations, genealogical relations, religious relations, ownership) is pertinent to the data collected or investigated. Geneticists may find it useful in recording the genealogical structures of a community when they are collecting genetic samples. Field data that has been collected with the inclusion of kinship relations can then be aggregated to form a stronger corpus by combining the data from each of these different fields in an aggregated kinship-based search.

Relevance of kinship data

Kinship data is often not systematically included in the metadata of archives and hence it could be asked: why is the kinship data relevant to archiving? When interpreting data, the context of that data can assist its interpretation. If the data collected comes from a context with social and genetic relations, then that context can be very relevant to the interpretation of the data. Even if such relevance is not immediately obvious, there may be no other opportunity to collect that information. Some of the contextual information might seem obvious at the time of collection, but to researchers interpreting that data at a later date it might not be so clear. Yet, without that social context, the data can be of reduced value or just much harder to find. By having the kinship data associated with the field data as it is archived, or preferably as it is collected, it will be possible to do archival queries based not only on the immediate metadata but also to perform kinship-based archive searches that include relatives or community members associated to that initial data point of interest.

Existing applications

There are many existing kinship applications available. However, many of these will be out of financial reach of students or under-resourced researchers, while others will not be able to describe the cultural facets of interest. In relation to archived material, some metadata records used in archives can record kinship information, albeit in a very granular and unconnected way, such as a free text description. However, for the kinship data to be stored in such a way in an archive, this lack of structure will limit the ability to retrieve data based on the social structures. For instance, when two metadata records refer to an individual, it might not be clear in retrospect if one individual is referred to or two individuals with the same or similar names.

Many of the existing kinship applications force a culturally specific structure onto the data being collected. This cultural specificity is also reflected in the main file format used in many genealogy applications, the Genealogical Data Communication (GEDCOM) format. This format has a rich syntax for the cultural features specific to the authors of the format (The Church of Jesus Christ of Latter-day Saints). However, it can be limiting for other social structures. One example is gender, for which the GEDCOM format allows only 'male', 'female' and 'undetermined' (Family History Department 1999, 61). There are many examples of societies with more than two gender categories, with genders like *fa'afafine* in Samoa (Macpherson 2001) and *hijra* in India (Sharma, 1989; Talwar 1999). Another example is that 'unions' in GEDCOM can at most represent the union of one female and one male spouse (Family History Department 1999, 25), whereas many other types of relationships exist, even in Western societies, such as polygamy, polyamory, same-sex relationships, and sperm/egg donors.[1] These restrictions limit what can reliably be recorded, and do not offer an unbiased way to represent the variety of unions possible. If a culture being documented has any features that cannot be described in the software used, then these features will either not be recorded or a non-standard record must be

---

1   While the ASSO tag could be used to create other union types, it is intended only as an 'indicator to link friends, neighbours, relatives, or associates of an individual' (Family History Department, 1999, 84).

created. This will result in missing or non-interoperable records, leading to an avoidable modulation in the data collected for that culture.

Data structure and data entry

In this section we discuss the flexibility of the data structure and relations used in KinOath and the methods used to keep the resulting kinship data interoperable with other datasets. We also discuss the underlying technologies and some methods of working with the data in KinOath.

KinOath, kinship and social relations

KinOath is designed to be flexible and culturally nonspecific. This means that the data fields, such as name, date or clan, for each entity or individual are flexible, and, if required, customisations can be defined in an XML schema file. For most users the default settings will be quite adequate. However, when needed, this flexible metadata can be defined and then processed by the application via custom configurations by the user. These configurations determine, for instance, the symbol used on the diagram to represent a given gender. All of these customisations are stored in the diagram and/or in the project configuration. In order to keep the meaning of this flexible data clear, each custom field can be linked to an entry in the Data Category Registry (Broeder et al. 2010), which semantically links concepts in such a way that data can be shared across disciplines. One of the intentions of this is that data collected in different specialisations can be aggregated or shared across different fields of research, despite specialised terminologies being used, while at the same time providing a flexible structure from which specialised kinship data and diagrams can be constructed.

Underlying technology

The internal data used by KinOath is a directed graph with the primary data stored in XML files, with each entity having a separate XML file as its record. Currently this data is accessed via XQuery[2] from a BaseX

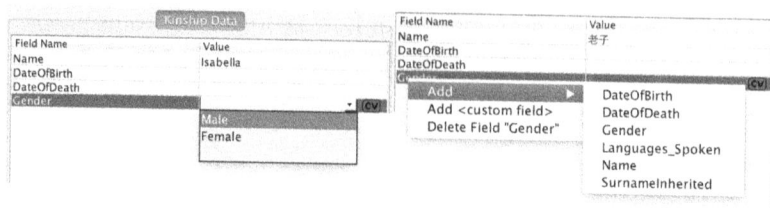

Figure 4.1 Example default fields and custom fields. Left: The default fields for a person entity. Right: Adding a new field to an entity without a profile.

database.[3] All graphics are initially generated in SVG format[4] and this is also used as the diagram storage format.

Custom data fields

By default, person entities have the fields 'Name', 'DateOfBirth', 'Date-OfDeath' and 'Gender'. These fields for each entity can be customised, either by simply adding fields as needed (Figure 4.1) or by using the Clarin[5] Component Registry[6] to create a profile and adding it to the project settings (Figure 4.2). This means that you can specify the data fields that you need for your project. When using a Clarin profile the meaning of each field such as 'name' or 'clan' can also be defined via the ISOcat Data Category Registry.[7] This registry provides a way to disambiguate the intended meaning of each field. It may also clarify when field names are equivalent; for instance, one dataset could use 'human' while another uses 'person', and in a given context these meanings might be equivalent. Within a Clarin profile it is also possible to de-

---

2 http://www.w3.org/TR/xquery-30.
3 http://docs.basex.org.
4 http://www.w3.org/Graphics/SVG.
5 'CLARIN is a large-scale pan-European collaborative effort to create, coordinate and make language resources and technology available and readily useable.' http://www.clarin.eu/content/about-clarin.
6 http://catalog.clarin.eu/ds/ComponentRegistry.
7 http://www.isocat.org/.

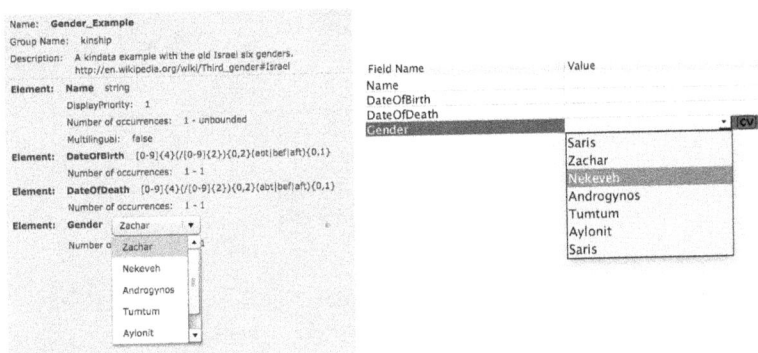

Figure 4.2 Example custom person profile. Left: Example of adding genders via the Clarin Component Registry. Right: Resulting entity with the controlled vocabulary listing the genders.

fine controlled vocabularies for each field, for instance, 'gender', which might have simply 'male' and 'female' or any number of entries as required.

Custom relation types

Representing kinship systems in tree-based genealogies will necessarily exclude many aspects of kinship (Bouquet 1996). There are many different relation types other than genealogical ones that need to be represented to cover the various facets of a kinship system. For this reason the relation types in KinOath can also be customised to suit the needs of the system being recorded. This can be done in the 'diagram settings' under 'relation type definitions' in the settings panel of the diagram. These customisations are stored in the diagram but can also be saved in the default diagram for a project. When defining a custom relation, the custom name, type and display style can to be entered. This new relation type will then be available to create relations between entities. The following are two examples: suckling relation (Giladi 1999), as exemplified by Figure 4.3; and song inheritance, as exemplified by Figure 4.4.

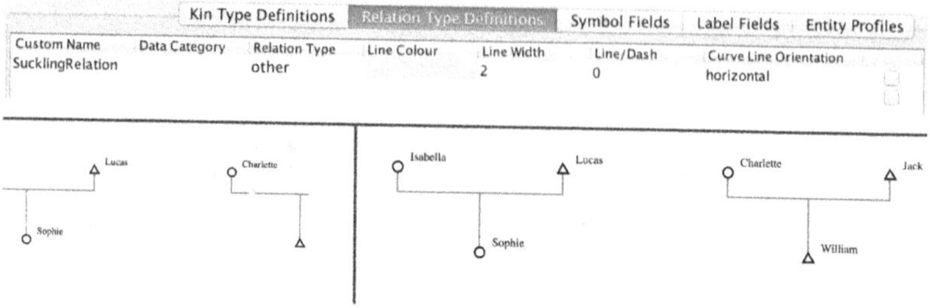
Kin Type Definitions
Relation Type Definitions
Symbol Fields
Label Fields
Entity Profiles
Custom Name
Data Category
Relation Type
Line Colour
Line Width
Line/Dash
Curve Line Orientation
SucklingRelation
other
2
0
horizontal
Lucas
Sophie
Isabella
Lucas
Charlette
Jack
Sophie
William

Figure 4.3 Example custom relation configuration. Top: Definition of a custom relation in the diagram settings. Bottom left: Example of creating a relation via the relation handles. Bottom right: Resulting diagram showing the custom relation in place.

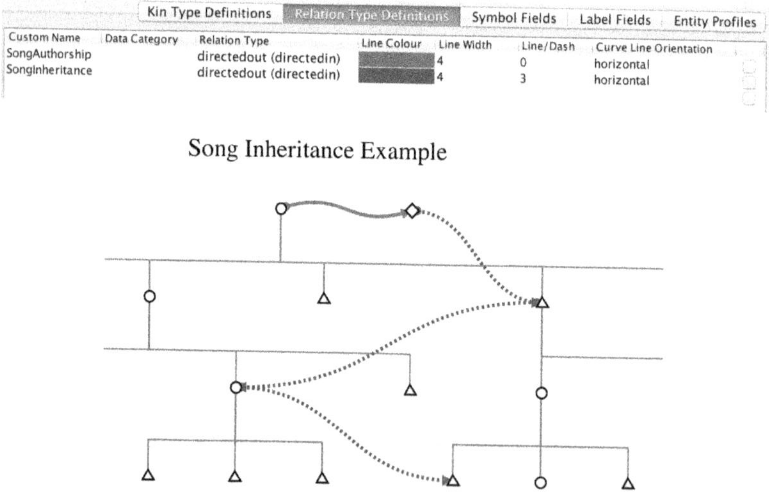
Kin Type Definitions
Relation Type Definitions
Symbol Fields
Label Fields
Entity Profiles
Custom Name
Data Category
Relation Type
Line Colour
Line Width
Line/Dash
Curve Line Orientation
SongAuthorship
directedout (directedin)
4
0
horizontal
SongInheritance
directedout (directedin)
4
3
horizontal
Song Inheritance Example

Figure 4.4 Example custom directional relations used to represent song inheritance.

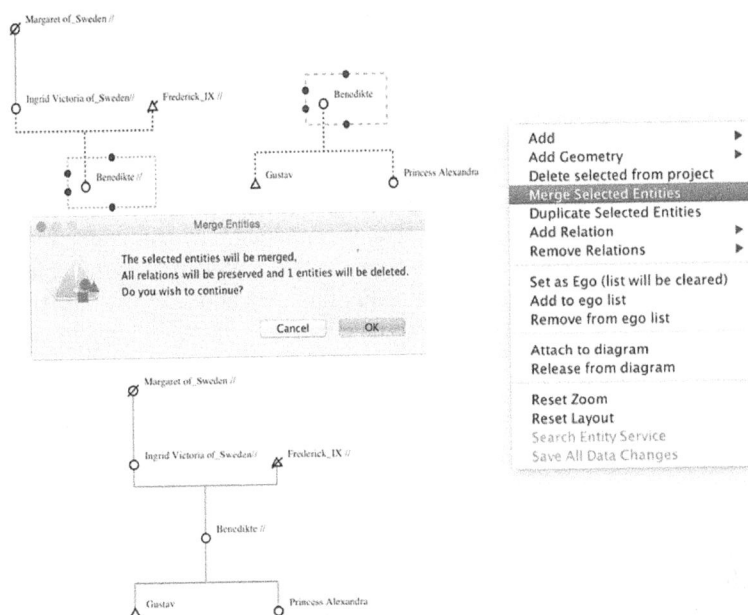

Figure 4.5 Example of merging selected individuals. Top left: Initial diagram with two individuals selected. Right: Context menu for merging the selected entities. Centre left: Verification message shown before merging. Bottom left: Resulting diagram with the two individuals merged with all relations maintained.

Merging and separating entities

When collecting data, it can be useful to merge two entities into one (Figure 4.5), or to separate one entity into two (Figure 4.6). For example, in the case of field data of genetic relations, it may be years until it is realised that two records are of the same person, or that one record refers to two separate people. In this example, it would be necessary to select two records and merge them into one, or to expand one record out into two distinct records. KinOath keeps a journal of changes made to the project data by the user, which could be used to trace back to when a change was made. Merging or duplicating records is not stored by the current version of the application, but this may be added in the future.

Kin type strings and diagram types

During the needs assessment phase of KinOath, it was determined that kin type strings can be used extensively throughout the application. One example usage of kin type strings in this application is the ability to quickly construct freeform kin diagrams by entering the kin type strings that describe the required diagram. Another is using kin type string queries to search for related individuals within a dataset. Creating diagrams from queries and generating freeform diagrams are core features of KinOath. However, these features would be of limited use if the resulting diagram could not be published. Hence, the ability to create diagrams of publishable quality is also a core feature of this application. All diagram types can be exported to JPG, PDF and SVG. In the case of SVG, the information required to generate the diagram, such as customisations and queries, can also be saved within the file, making it self-contained. If the SVG diagram contains the queries and other information required to generate the diagram, it becomes easier to replicate the results shown on the diagram, which may be crucial to support any published claims.

In the following sections we look at what kin type strings are and how they are used in this application. We also look at the various diagram types available in KinOath and the way each of them can be used.

Kin type strings

Kin type strings are notations used to describe kinship relations. For example, with 'E' signifying the individual to which the relation pertains (ego), 'M' signifying 'mother', and 'F' signifying 'father', then the relation 'maternal grandfather of ego' can be represented by 'EMF' (i.e., Ego's Mother's Father). KinOath offers, by default, variations on notations of the same relations. For instance, 'mother' can be notated as either 'M' or 'Mo'. In addition to the default notations, the user can also

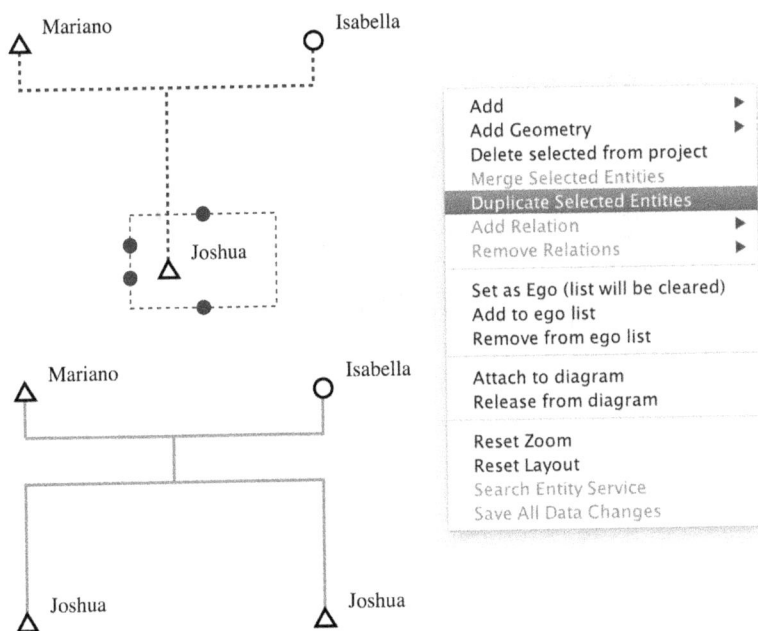

Figure 4.6 Example of duplicating an individual. Top left: Initial diagram with one individual selected. Right: Context menu for duplicating the selected entity. Bottom left: Resulting diagram with the two resulting individuals with data on all relations maintained in both.

add, delete, or change the notations used to suit his or her needs. Kin type strings are used throughout the application to search kinship data and to generate diagrams. These kin type strings can be edited in the diagram settings (see Figure 4.7) and each kin type can use any string, any relation type and any symbol. These kin types are defined and stored in each diagram file but they can also be stored in the default diagram of a project.

Kin Type String	Relation Type	Symbol Type	Display Name
Br	sibling	triangle	Brother
Ch	descendant	triangle, circle	Child
Da	descendant	circle	Daughter
Ef		circle	Ego Female
Em		triangle	Ego Male
Fa	ancestor	triangle	Father
Hu	union	triangle	Husband
Mo	ancestor	circle	Mother
Pa	ancestor	triangle, circle	Parent
Sb	sibling	triangle, circle	Sibling
Si	sibling	circle	Sister
So	descendant	triangle	Son
Sp	union	triangle, circle	Spouse
Wi	union	circle	Wife
*	ancestor, descendant, union, sibling	<any>	Any Relation
B	sibling	triangle	Brother
C	descendant	triangle, circle	Child
D	descendant	circle	Daughter
E		square	Ego
F	ancestor	triangle	Father
f		circle	Female
G	sibling	triangle, circle	Sibling
H	union	triangle	Husband
M	ancestor	circle	Mother
m		triangle	Male
P	ancestor	triangle, circle	Parent
S	descendant	triangle	Son
W	union	circle	Wife
x		square	Undefined
z	sibling	circle	Sister

Figure 4.7 The default kin type definitions displayed in the settings panel.

Freeform diagrams

Freeform diagrams have no kinship data records and all the data required is stored in a self-contained diagram. The kin type strings or kin term definitions entered into the diagram are the only source data for these diagrams. These freeform diagrams can be created by simply entering kin type strings, with the resulting diagram showing all the entities and relations described in that string. The intention with this functionality is for the user to be able to quickly generate a diagram, which correctly describes the relations they have in mind. This supports the construction of diagrams containing matrimonial rings and specifying names and dates for individuals. This provides a very interactive way to learn how to use kin type strings or how to visualise kinship relations on a diagram. When eliciting data from a consultant, this provides a way to quickly annotate the kin structure described.

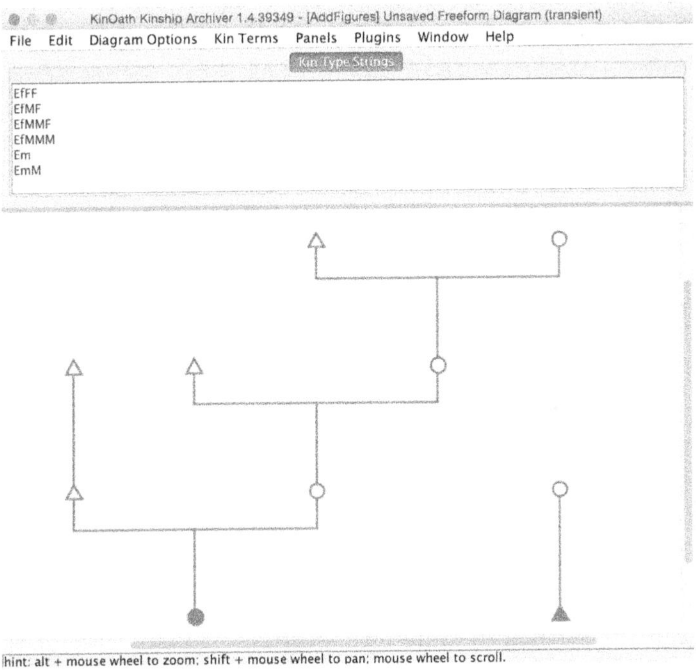

Figure 4.8 Application layout when editing a freeform diagram.

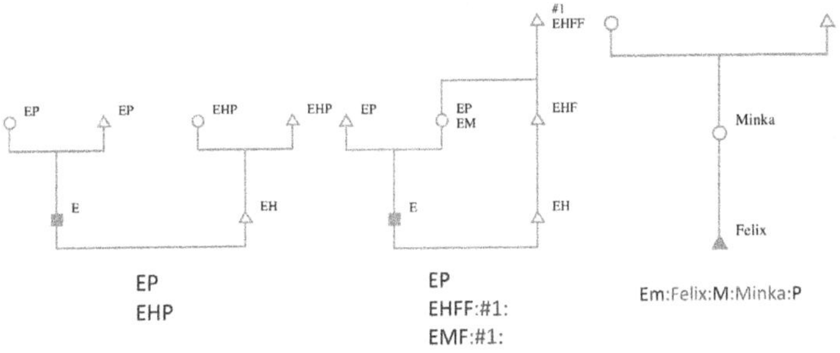

Figure 4.9 Three examples of freeform diagrams.

<Kintype>:<id>;<label>;<label...>;<DOB>-<DOD>:<Kintype...>

EM:#1:Jane;1721-1803:

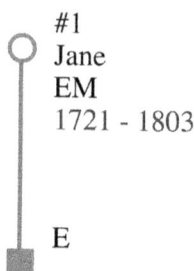

#1
Jane
EM
1721 - 1803

E

Figure 4.10 The syntax used to generate a freeform diagram. Top: Generalised syntax showing all the optional elements. Middle: Syntax used. Bottom: Resulting diagram.

Project diagrams

Projects are different from freeform diagrams in that each project has its own database of entities, which can be used by any number of diagrams. Project diagrams display and query kinship records from a given project (Figure 4.11). There is a data file for each entity, which can, for example, be a person, thing, place, affiliation, kin term or event. This database can be queried to find, for example, people born after a given date or affiliations of a given type, and the result can then be shown on the diagram. Data can be imported into these projects from GEDCOM or CSV and exported to CSV. In a project diagram the changes to the kin data of a project are reflected on all diagrams using that project. This is intentionally like a database-driven drawing program.

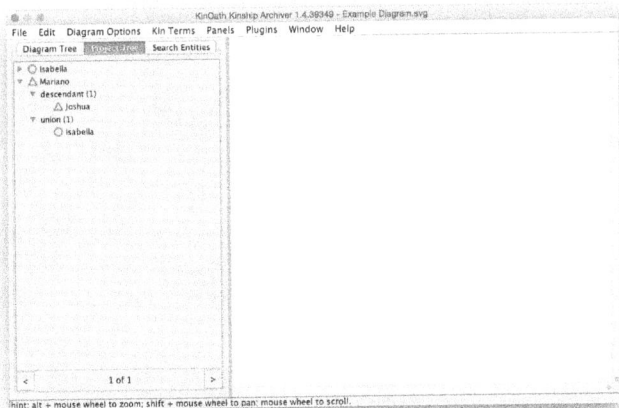

Figure 4.11 Application layout when editing a project diagram.

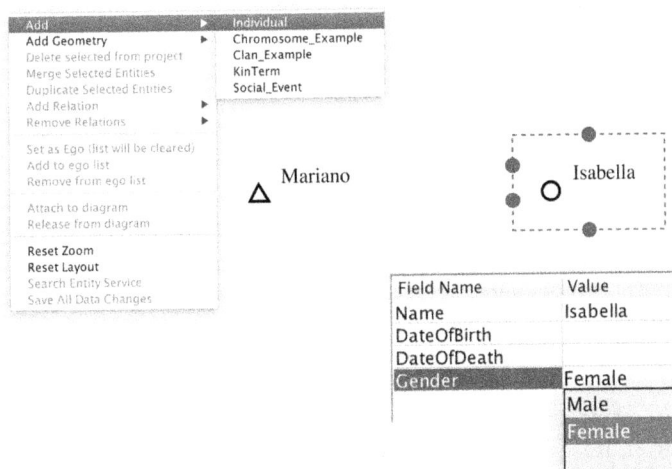

Figure 4.12 Adding an entity via the context menu and editing the name and gender.

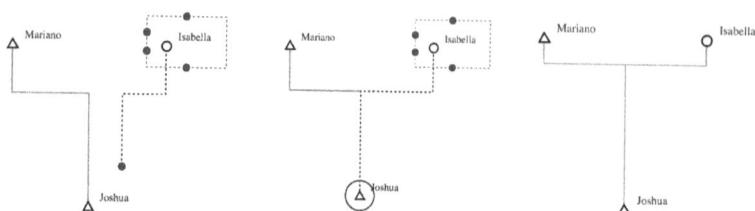

Figure 4.13 Creating relations by dragging the handles from one entity to another. Left: Selecting the relation handle (dotted) on the first entity (top = ancestor, bottom = descendant). Centre: Dragging to the second entity. Right: The resulting relation.

In a project diagram new entities are added by right clicking on the diagram and selecting the type required from the 'add' submenu (Figure 4.12). Once added, details can be entered such as name, date of birth, gender etc. The default fields can be used or custom fields added as required.

Relations can be created either by selecting a number of entities and choosing the relation type via the context menu (Figures 4.13 and 4.14), or by dragging the dots from one individual to another. There will be a coloured dot for each relation type available.

Kin terms diagrams

Having an effective way to visualise the kin terms used in a language can help to understand and document their structure. This application currently provides two methods to do this. The first way is via a kin terms diagram where each kin term is listed in a table with the kin type string from ego (e.g., paternal grandmother EFM). This will generate a freeform diagram from the listed kin terms (Figure 4.15). This table of kin terms can currently only be overlayed on a freeform diagram; however, it is planned to extend this to project diagrams in future releases. The kin terms can be organised in groups and can be imported and exported to CSV format. There are a number of example kin term diagrams available in the application. The second way is to use a project diagram and create an entity for each kin term with directed relations

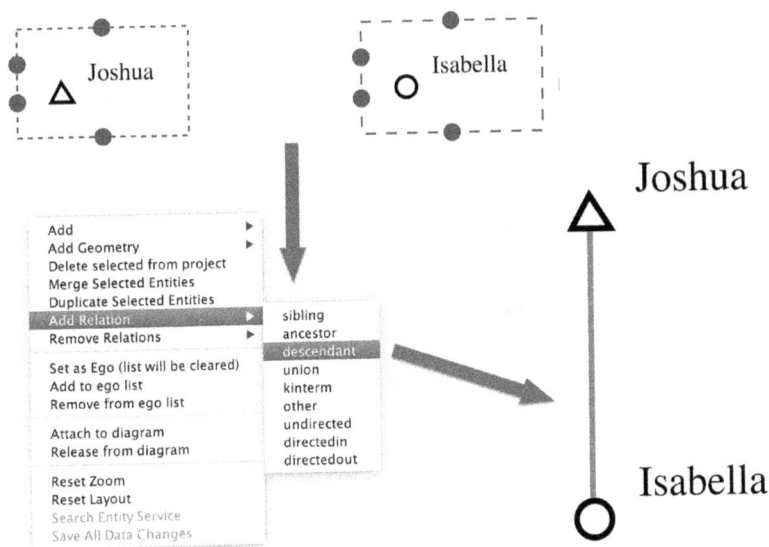

Figure 4.14 Creating relations via the context menu after selecting the relevant individuals on the diagram.

to the ego and referent (Figure 4.16). This method links kin terms to specific individuals rather than the former method, which shows terms in relation to a common ego.

There are cases where ego and referent is inadequate; for instance, triangular kin terms – these are kin terms which, in order to be properly described, require a 'propositus' (or 'anchor') to be defined in addition to defining the referent and ego (Evans 2003, 34). One such example from Gundjeihmi is illustrated in Figure 4.17. These triangular kin terms can be entered using the second method described, on a project diagram with custom relations linking the relevant individuals to the kin term.

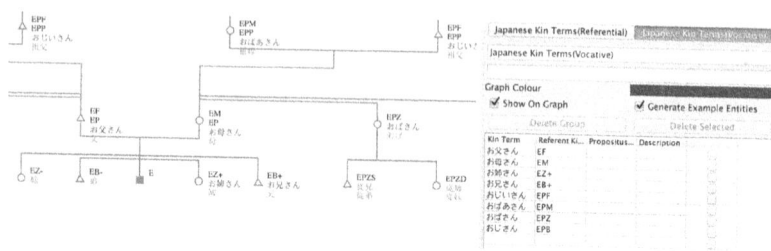

Figure 4.15 Example freeform kin term diagram with the kin terms entered in the table on the right in two groups, referential and vocative.

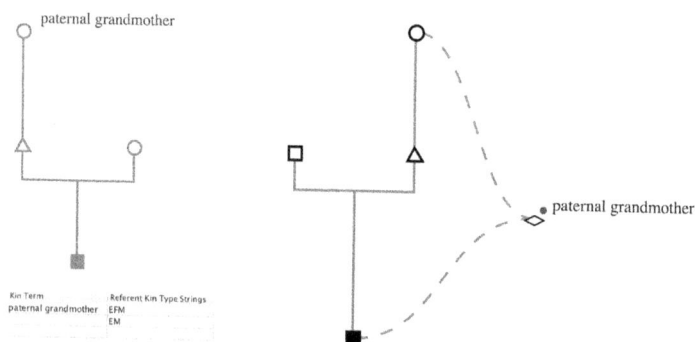

Figure 4.16 Example kin term when used in a project diagram.

Searching data in KinOath

There are a number of ways to query the data in a KinOath project. In this section we cover simple searches that can be done, for instance, to find individuals, and more complex searches that span relations between individuals or other entities in the project.

Kin type string queries

The kinship data stored in projects can be queried by simple keyword searches and the results then selectively added to a kin diagram. A more powerful search can be done via the kin type strings; for instance, to

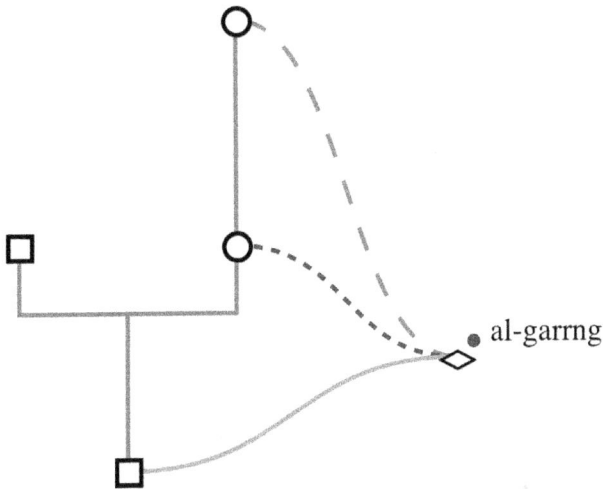

al-garrng, "the one who is your mother and my daughter, given that I am your mother's mother", in the Gundjeihmi language (Evans, 2003: 34)

Figure 4.17 Example triangular kin term when used in a project diagram.

find an individual matching a textual query (Figures 4.18 and 4.19), then based on kin type strings select relations of that individual that match another textual query. This makes it possible to query, for instance, all individuals who are trilingual and whose great-grandparents lived in mountainous regions (providing that information has been collected and recorded with links to relevant archive metadata/data). Multiple queries can be used per kin type and each condition in the query can use the following comparators: = contains; == exact match; > greater than; < less than.

Search panel

Project diagrams also have a search panel (Figure 4.20), which takes a free text search string and shows the results in a browsable tree. This

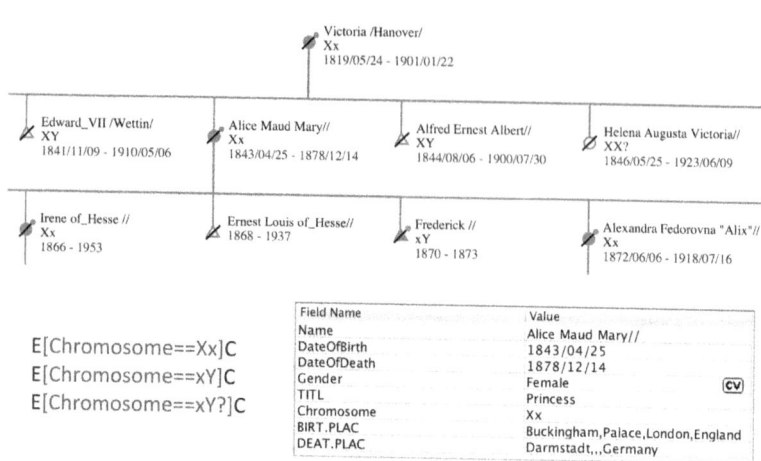

Figure 4.18 Example of kin type string queries. Top: Resulting diagram. Bottom left: Query used. Bottom right: Data of one individual selected by the query.

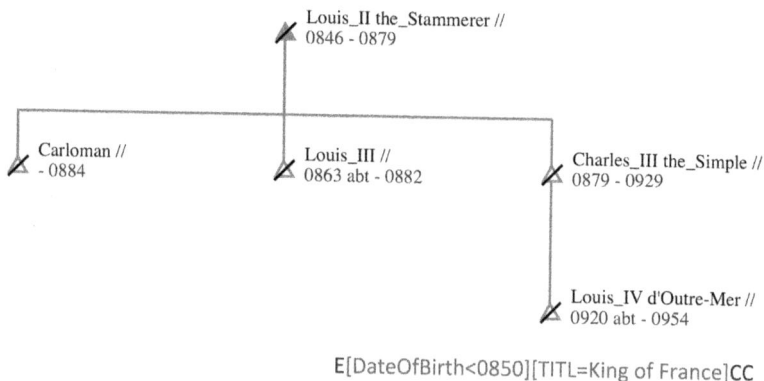

Figure 4.19 Example of kin type string queries with multiple comparators. Top: Resulting diagram. Bottom: Query used that matches by date of birth and title.

search type uses fuzzy matching so that similar or misspelt names can be found. These search results can be browsed hierarchically in the tree so that immediate relations can be seen. If 'graph selection' is enabled, the selected results will be shown on the diagram, and enabling 'expand selection' will also show relations matching the kin type string entered. This allows the results of the search to be inspected on the diagram in context.

If the data contains time data such as event dates, this can be used to filter the information shown on the diagram. Currently this can only be done based on entities. However, it is intended to extend this functionality to also filter on specific relations. In Figure 4.21 there are three individuals, one social group and three events causing affiliation between the social group and the individuals. The events are dated 1701, 1705 and 1791. The state of this relation network can then be shown for various dates by attaching the group and the individuals to the diagram; for instance, by dragging them from the project tree onto the diagram and then querying the events by date.

Export, import, plugins and interoperability

This section covers interoperability in the context of import/export, importing updates to previously imported data, the plugin structure that is available for extending functionality and the export of data in order to perform statistical analysis.

Interoperability

Data can be imported from CSV, TIP[8] and GEDCOM formats. Data can be exported to CSV but not to GEDCOM, because the constraints of the GEDCOM format limit the social structures that can be recorded without simplification. If the user has chosen to use the Data Category Registry entries for each field, the resulting kinship data will be more accessible to other software such as for aggregated searches.

---

8 http://kintip.net/kinship-network-formats-topmenu-54.

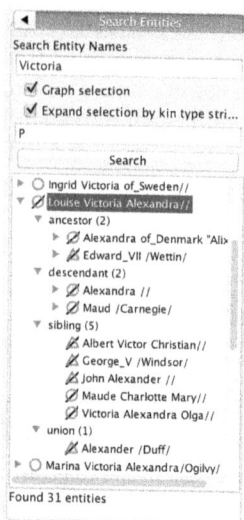

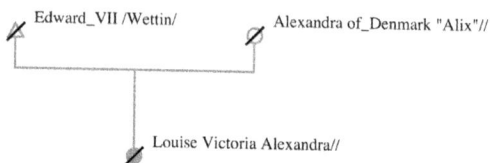

Figure 4.20 Example of search panel results. Left: Search tree showing results with browsable relations. Right: Selected result expanded by kin type 'P' shown in the diagram.

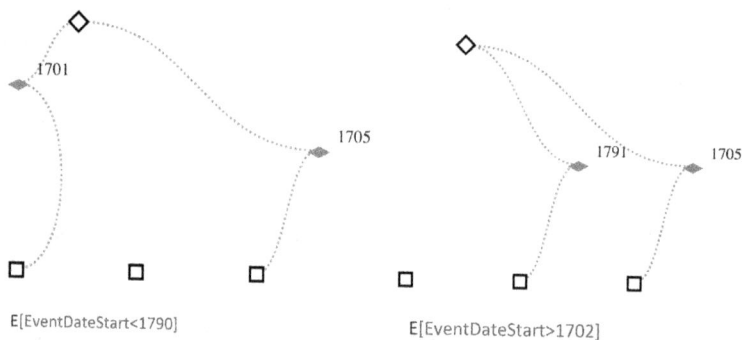

Figure 4.21 Example time-based query.

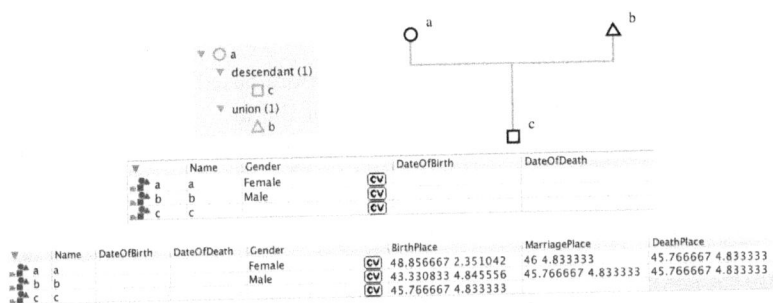

Figure 4.22 Example of updating existing data via a CSV import. Top left: Individuals to be updated in the project tree. Top right: Individuals to be updated on the diagram. Centre: Data of the individuals before the update (see Appendix B). Bottom: Resulting data for the individuals after the update via CSV (see Appendix C).

Importing updates

When a project needs to be synchronised with an external data source, it can be updated via a CSV import, providing the ID fields are the same for each individual in both the update and original CSV import files (Figure 4.22). This could also be used to insert columns generated via R[9] or other external processing methods or for adding new information when it becomes available from a third party such as lab results.

Plugins

KinOath has been designed so that plugins can be written for specific tasks that are outside the scope of the main application. There is an existing import-export plugin, which could be extended if other formats are needed. This provides potential for extended features, such as custom graph sorters or alternative data sources, to be written without needing to modify the main application. This is an area for future development and potential collaboration.

---

9 http://www.r-project.org.

Statistical analysis

Being able to do statistical analysis on corpora based on the social and genealogical relations is potentially one of the most fruitful results of integrating archived data/metadata with kinship data. Because there are already good tools for doing statistics, KinOath focuses on integration with these tools rather than reinventing them. Integration with R and SPSS[10] is achieved in the desktop application by exporting to appropriate CSV and TXT files that can be used as data sources. This data can be used in R for instance (Figure 4.23) with the standard 'read.table()' which results in a data frame that can be further processed and analysed.

Interoperability and archiving

In the following section we discuss the topic of linking resources and archived material, followed by the potential use of kinship data to search archived material.

Links to external resources

It is possible to link external resources to entities in a project. This can be done within the application or during the import of data. There are also archive resource linking features in the application, which provide some integration with Arbil,[11] which is a metadata management application. While the integration with Arbil was added early on in the development of KinOath, this integration is incomplete and will need further work in the future. Features of the application used to create external links to IMDI metadata[12] resources have been held back in the current stable version due to the need for a technical agreement on how to persistently link kinship individuals to the IMDI format. However,

---

10 http://www-01.ibm.com/software/analytics/spss.
11 https://tla.mpi.nl/tools/tla-tools/arbil.
12 https://tla.mpi.nl/imdi-metadata.

```
|id momid dadid  sex ego dob dod label_0 symbol_triangle symbol_blackstrikethrough  symbol_redmarker  symbol_circle  UniqueIdentifier
1  21 42  1 0 1900 1904  Henry //  1  1  1  0  iid_1abe7dabd1c70628f07963e95f9eb0f3
2  37 43  2 0 1846/05/25 1923/06/09 Helena Augusta Victoria//  0  1  0  1  iid_ed611b28b31aaec4c49801aab67955c5
3  17 44  1 0  Son_2 //  1  0  1  0  iid_f165b998134ee9c87fcf7f77afcdcb30
4  21 42  1 0 1889 1945  Waldemar //  1  1  1  0  iid_01af3ba990cdf7c5f099c99663310fb5
5  37 43  2 0 1857/04/14 1944/10/26 Beatrice Mary Victoria//  0  1  1  1  iid_d573d6fdbe6bc99b0dee7584a73f1c4c
6  29 45  2 0 1897/06 1918/07/18 Tatiana Nicholovna //  0  1  0  1  iid_61f27021af082a3ae38Sfa409ae578ad
7  14 46  1 0 1870 1873  Frederick //  1  1  1  0  iid_o8a378106e81dd1a93587099ed2140d9a
8  32 47  1 0 1907 1938  Alphonso of_Cavadonga //  1  1  1  0  iid_b79466e3fda64b430682cf359d3e989f
9  37 43  1 0 1841/11/09 1910/05/06 Edward_VII /Wettin//  1  1  0  0  iid_15cfe4ec699efd384eb3892d68164be4
10 37 43  1 0 1850/05/01 1942/01/16 Arthur William Patrick//  1  1  0  0  iid_55158ffef1ef49fb5e03dcc7c97e856b
11 37 43  2 0 1848/03/18 1939/12/03 Louise Caroline Alberta//  0  1  0  1  iid_04c5146f7a9f5602148fe498a2719272
12 32 47  2 0 1911  Maria Christina //  0  0  0  1  iid_38fe23e9e9198f80ec2bea370315527d
13 29 45  1 0 1904/08/12 1918/07/18 Alexis Nicolaievich /Romanov/  1  1  0  0  iid_67530193a6b8b2c0a1033446c23b55fe
14 37 43  2 0 1843/04/25 1878/12/14 Alice Maud Mary//  0  1  1  1  iid_7b6f6a6d2514f5ea6a2c0133f6481faf
15 14 46  2 0 1874 1878  Mary "May" //  0  1  0  1  iid_c7be01fab14a0b30a944cfbc7b1af370
16 5 48  1 0 1889 1922  Leopold //  1  1  1  0  iid_076ea3ded22a12f1dddf4bee9d9f5cd2
17 49 41  2 0 1883 1981/01 Alice of_Athlone //  0  1  1  1  iid_49c88dd77a2264b6aa613021e236eb84
18 5 48  1 0 1886 1960/02/23 Alexander of_Carlsbrooke //  1  0  0  0  iid_7b59019be9dc376171a1eba6080225a
19 14 46  1 0 1868 1937  Ernest Louis of_Hesse//  1  1  0  0  iid_42b0e4a05d3ed02b29c62a3df8d29482
20 32 47  1 0 1914 1934  Gonzalo //  1  1  1  0  iid_d5699a66a887d30bb18939c592c88d62
21 14 46  2 0 1866 1953  Irene of_Hesse //  0  1  1  1  iid_2297e359f40o11761ca4a82o4a49f5a0
22 21 42  1 0  Child_#3 //  1  0  0  0  iid_cfab646cc3dff46971e79f0c3b0a853f
23 37 43  2 0 1840/11/21 1901/08/05 Victoria Adelaide Mary//  0  1  0  1  iid_d0e1f42101710cd32d6ae07940f3169e
24 32 47  1 0 1913/06  Don Juan of_Spain//  1  1  0  0  iid_76a8b10d50c99d531a226f479ca8c3d0
25 29 45  2 0 1901/06 1918/07/18 Anastasia Nicholovna /Romanov/  0  1  0  1  iid_cefe73aa656fef02c994ac13ec32e453
26 37 43  1 0 1844/08/06 1900/07/30 Alfred Ernest Albert//  1  1  0  0  iid_439671a86d8cf7ef7b646063d17c045c6
27 14 46  2 0 1864 1918/07/17 Elizabeth "Ella" //  0  1  0  1  iid_c0a0255ad17cb3b3f7ceef79a562c98fa
28 29 45  2 0 1899/05 1918/07/18 Maria Nicholovna /Romanov/  0  1  0  1  iid_2cf36745e277a718028035c9547243d8
29 14 46  2 0 1872/06/06 1918/07/16 Alexandra Fedorovna "Alix"//  0  1  1  1  iid_8719d4e8c7f5f343aa17007ee4ad4c59
30 5 48  1 0 1891 1914  Maurice //  1  1  0  0  iid_7b00f979e251465c17088bf0d190a6aa
31 14 46  2 0 1863 1950  Victoria Alberta of_Hesse//  0  1  1  1  iid_6ef08317358fc7605bba50ba947c5fa1
32 5 48  2 0 1887 1969  Victoria Eugenie "Ena"//  0  1  1  1  iid_f270191b0089852dc55227521319af9
33 32 47  1 0 1908 1975  James //  1  1  1  0  iid_92724995a7618cec9cff9c8d177b0b5a
34 32 47  2 0 1909  Beatrice //  0  0  0  1  iid_f236828d50909413df16564a9c44ba10
35 29 45  2 0 1895/11 1918/07/18 Olga Nicholovna /Romanov/  0  1  0  1  iid_5e6b6b2dbaa03bf4544a255deecec69a
36 17 44  2 0 1906  May Cambridge //  0  0  0  1  iid_87b865a0d336994f9f24654fdb214c71
37 50 51  2 0 1819/05/24 1901/01/22 Victoria /Hanover/  0  1  1  1  iid_7efe2ede2b0df488c46bc7d6f8b11779
38 49 41  1 0 1884 1954  Charles Edward //  0  1  1  0  iid_3dcede17c537c1aa8d74aa0a4aadf972
39 32 47  1 0  Don Jamie //  1  1  0  0  iid_8b561f64886573a2b5164f687dd02a24
40 17 44  1 0 1928  Rupert //  1  1  1  0  iid_72fd2eb4dded4353125894161fcfc8dc
41 37 43  1 0 1853/04/07 1884/03/28 Leopold George Duncan//  1  1  1  0  iid_72fd2eb4dded...
```

```
dataFrame <- read.table("KinOathDemoR/exportedData.tab",header=T)
# get all affected parents ids
affectedIds = dataFrame$id[dataFrame$symbol_redmarker == 1]
# get all children of affected
childrenOfAffected = dataFrame[dataFrame$momid %in% affectedIds || dataFrame$dataid %in% affectedIds]
# print names of affecteds' children
childrenOfAffected$label_0
```

Figure 4.23 Example of processing exported data in R based on the haemophilia in European royalty. Top: Example extract of exported data for use in R. Bottom: Example R script to process the data exported from KinOath.

despite the limitations to creating external links to resources, once created they will be maintained when importing and exporting data.

Utilising external links

Currently external and resource links can only be viewed in the table when working in KinOath (Figure 4.24). Alternatively, when a diagram is saved as an SVG and viewed in a web browser, these links will be available as hyperlinks. For the intended potential of these links to be available, more work needs to be done within KinOath to better make use of these resources, and the kinship data produced in KinOath needs to be supported by archiving services. KinOath was originally intended to have a web interface for the purpose of providing an archive search facility. However, this web application has not been completed at this stage. The issues of privacy and access to both the data and kinship records will need to be adequately addressed by the archive when such search facilities are completed. As a desktop application, KinOath does not apply permissions to the data in a project, but, if required, fields can be defined to indicate what permissions would need to be applied once the data is archived.

Visualisation and graphics

This section discusses the graphics format used in KinOath and the possible customisations that can be made.

Graphics format

The diagrams produced by KinOath use the SVG (scalable vector graphics) format and other formats, such as PDF and JPG, can be exported. Prior to publication, these diagram files can also be edited in other graphics programs, such as InkScape, Gimp, Illustrator or Photoshop, for instance.

Custom symbols

In order for the application to be truly flexible, it is necessary that custom symbols can be added and assigned to individuals and entities on the graph (Figure 4.25). This includes, but is not exclusive to, symbols indicating the gender or caste of an individual. There are a number of symbols provided in the application by default, but users can manually edit the SVG to add more specific symbols if required (Figure 4.28). These symbols can consist of graphical and/or textual elements. Once a custom symbol is defined in the diagram it can then be assigned based on features in the data for an individual. In addition to these base symbols, an overlay symbol can be applied in the same manner. For in-

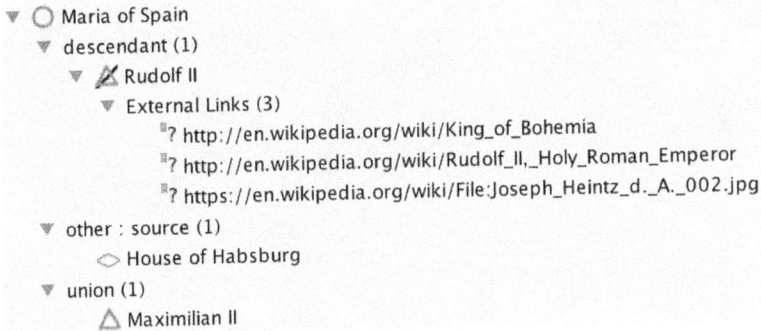

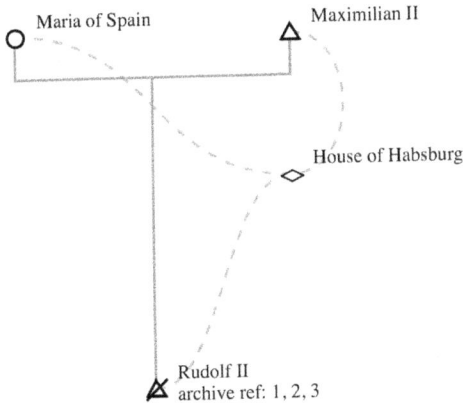

▼ ◯ Maria of Spain
  ▼ descendant (1)
    ▼ ⊿ Rudolf II
      ▼ External Links (3)
        ? http://en.wikipedia.org/wiki/King_of_Bohemia
        ? http://en.wikipedia.org/wiki/Rudolf_II,_Holy_Roman_Emperor
        ? https://en.wikipedia.org/wiki/File:Joseph_Heintz_d._A._002.jpg
  ▼ other : source (1)
    ◇ House of Habsburg
  ▼ union (1)
    △ Maximilian II

Figure 4.24 Example of external links in data imported from a GEDCOM file (see Appendix A). Top: External links shown in the project tree. Bottom: External links shown on the diagram.

stance, when a metadata record contains a date of death, an overlay of a strike-through symbol is appended to the symbol of that individual.

The default symbols in this application are circle for female, triangle for male and square for unknown. Another common use of symbols is square for male and circles for females. This is easily configured in the diagram settings.

The overlay symbols could be used, for instance, to indicate known data on an individual. For instance, states like *affected, unaffected, un-*

known, asymptomatic, obligatory or *adopted* can be indicated by the default markers or custom markers could be manually added (Figure 4.27).

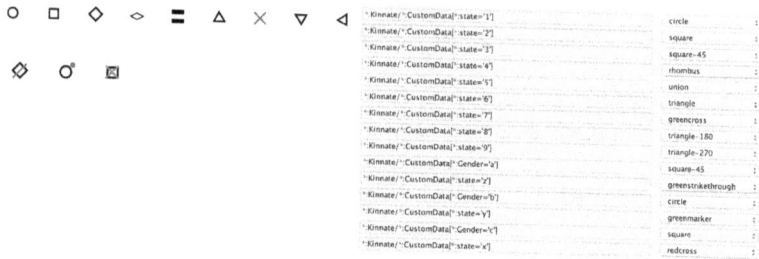

Figure 4.25 Example custom symbol configuration. Left: The top line shows 9 of the 30 symbols currently available by default. The second line shows an example of overlay. Right: Assigning symbols to features.

Figure 4.26 Example configuration with square representing male and circle representing female.

Figure 4.27 Example overlays configured for affected, unaffected, unknown, asymptomatic, obligatory and adopted.

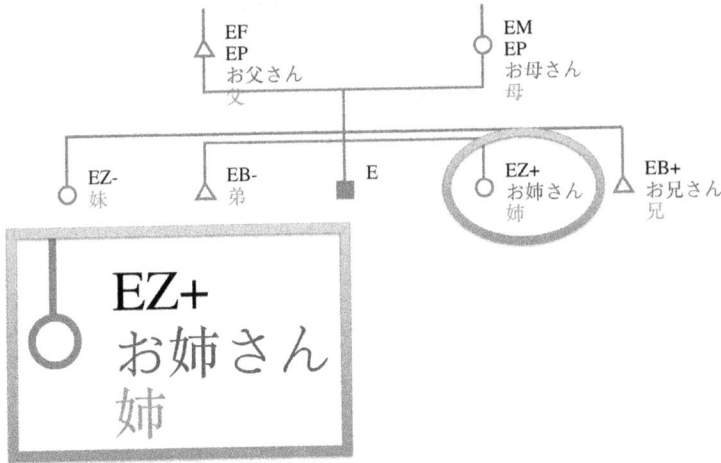

Figure 4.28 Example of the SVG diagram that KinOath produces.

Conclusion and future directions

There have been numerous applications which have tried to meet the needs of anthropologists and other researchers who frequently study kin and other social relationships. However, there are shortcomings in either the functionality, usability or affordability of this earlier software. The development of KinOath has been a recent attempt to address some of the needs of researchers, with a flexible application that can be used in conjunction with existing specialised tools. The use of kin type strings as a query language has provided a simple way of creating quick kin diagrams and a flexible way of querying kinship data. Interoperability with existing tools has provided a path to performing complex statistical analysis and the ability to migrate data from one application to another. Linking resource files and archived material to genealogies can be done, but more work needs to be done to fully explore the potential and the issues with archiving and kinship data.

KinOath is an open source project under General Public License (GPL). The current version of the application and related software can be downloaded from: http://tla.mpi.nl/tools/tla-tools/kinoath/.

KinOath is currently maintained by Peter Withers on GitHub[13] and there are many areas in which the application could be further developed as funding allows. There are currently plans to collaborate with the KinSources[14] and PUCK[15] projects, which will involve sharing code and functionality between these projects. KinOath has been developed with a plugin structure intended to allow third-party developers to provide extended functionality to KinOath and for the functionality of KinOath to be provided to other applications. This modularity could allow for custom graph sorters, importers, exporters, symbol design and data processing. Another benefit of this structure is that new features do not need to have such an impact on the core application's stability. There is also potential for a subset of features to be provided as an application for web, mobile and tablet use, particularly in the case of crowdsourcing kinship data. KinOath already offers a lot of functionality and flexibility. However, for the full potential of this application and its use in archival searches, there will need to be further work done. Despite this, it still operates as a stand-alone application for kinship data collection and exploration.

Works cited

Bouquet, Mary (1996). 'Family trees and their affinities: The visual imperative of the genealogical diagram.' *The Journal of the Royal Anthropological Institute* 2(1): 43–66.

Broeder, Daan, Mark Kemps-Snijders, Dieter Van Uytvanck, Menzo A. Windhouwer, Peter Withers, Peter Wittenburg and Claus Zinn (2010). 'A data category registry- and component-based metadata framework.' *Proceedings of the Seventh International Conference on Language Resources and Evaluation (LREC 2010)*, edited by Nicoletta Calzolari et al. Malta: European Language

---

13 https://github.com/KinshipSoftware/KinOathKinshipArchiver.
14 https://www.kinsources.net.
15 http://kintip.net.

Resources Association (ELRA). http://www.lrec-conf.org/proceedings/
lrec2010/index.html.

Evans, Nicholas (2003). 'Context, culture, and structuration in the languages of
Australia.' *Annual Review of Anthropology* 32: 13–40. doi: 10.1146/
annurev.anthro.32.061002.093137.

Family History Department of the Church of Jesus Christ of Latter-day Saints
(1999). *The GEDCOM Standard Draft Release 5.5.1*. Salt Lake City: The
Church of Jesus Christ of Latter-day Saints.
http://phpgedview.sourceforge.net/ged551-5.pdf.

Giladi, Avner (1999). *Infants, Parents and Wet Nurses: Medieval Islamic Views on
Breastfeeding and Their Social Implications*. Leiden: Brill.

Macpherson, Cluny, Paul Spoonley, and Melani Anae (2001). *Tangata o Te Moana
Nui: The Evolving Identities of Pacific Peoples in Aotearoa/New Zealand*.
Wellington: Dunmore.

Sharma, Satish Kumar (1989). *Hijras: The Labelled Deviants*. Washington: APA
Books.

Talwar, Rajesh (1999). *Third Sex and Human Rights*. New Delhi: Gyan Publishing
House.

Appendix A: Example file imported to produce Figure 24

example.ged
```
0 HEAD
1 NAME House of Habsburg
0 @I1@ INDI
1 NAME Rudolf II
1 SEX M
1 TITL Holy Roman Emperor
1 BIRT
2 DATE 19 JUL 1552
2 PLAC Vienna, Austria
1 DEAT
2 DATE 20 Jan 1612
1 BURI
2 PLAC St. Vitus Cathedral, Prague
2 PLAC Prague, Bohemia
1 FAMC @F1@
1 OBJE
2 FILE http://en.wikipedia.org/wiki/Rudolf_II,_Holy_Roman_Emperor
```

```
1 OBJE
2 FILE http://en.wikipedia.org/wiki/File:Joseph_Heintz_d._%C3%84._002.jpg
1 OBJE
2 FILE http://en.wikipedia.org/wiki/King_of_Bohemia
0 @I2@ INDI
1 NAME Maximilian II
1 SEX M
1 FAMS @F1@
0 @I3@ INDI
1 NAME Maria of Spain
1 SEX F
1 FAMS @F1@
0 @F1@ FAM
1 HUSB @I2@
1 WIFE @I3@
1 CHIL @I1@
0 TRLR
```

Appendix B: Example file imported to produce the first part of Figure 22

import.csv
```
ID,Name,Gender,DateOfBirth,DateOfDeath,Mother,Father
315791,a,Female,,,,
315792,b,Male,,,,
315793,c,,,,315791,315792
```

Appendix C: Example file imported after the file in Appendix B to produce the second part of Figure 22

update.csv
```
ID,BirthPlace,MarriagePlace,DeathPlace
315791,48.856667 2.351042,46 4.833333,45.766667 4.833333
315792,43.330833 4.845556,45.766667 4.833333,45.766667 4.833333
315793,45.766667 4.833333,,
```

5
Shoehorning complex metadata in the Living Archive of Aboriginal Languages

Catherine Bow, Michael Christie and Brian Devlin

The Living Archive of Aboriginal Languages is making endangered literature in Australian Indigenous languages publicly available online (Bow et al. 2014). Like any other project attempting to package a vastly complex body of work into an accessible repository, this project has grappled with a number of complex issues. Wrangling a variety of text types, languages, locations, digitisation processes, metadata and other issues into an accessible online repository requires a great deal of shoehorning. While straightforward decisions can be made simply, a number of decisions require complex solutions, and are readily dumped into an expanding 'too-hard basket'. Accordingly this paper – informed by Christie's work on Aboriginal knowledge traditions and digital technologies (2004, 2005), and picking up on many of the issues identified in Nakata (2007) on Indigenous digital collections – explores some of the 'too-hard basket' issues emerging from the Living Archive project, and various attempts to resolve them. This is not to suggest that the solutions reached within this project should be seen as normative or appropriate for other projects, but rather to explore and describe some

Bow, Catherine, Michael Christie and Brian Devlin (2015). 'Shoehorning complex metadata in the Living Archive of Aboriginal Languages'. In *Research, Records and Responsibility: Ten Years of PARADISEC*, edited by Amanda Harris, Nick Thieberger and Linda Barwick. Sydney: Sydney University Press.

of the decision-making processes and the impact of these solutions and compromises on the overall project.

The initial aim of the Living Archive project was to collect materials created in Australian Aboriginal languages of the Northern Territory for schools with bilingual education programs, and to create digital versions of these materials for both preservation and access (Christie et al. 2014). Copies of the books were sourced, collected (from the schools themselves, or from libraries or private collections), catalogued, and digitised in both preservation and presentation formats. With the permission of the original creators, both the metadata and the digital objects were uploaded to a digital repository at the Charles Darwin University Library. A web-based interface was developed to facilitate open access to the materials, with a restrictive Creative Commons licence.[1] The data was stored in a MySQL database, with the metadata catalogued according to library standards, using both Metadata Object Description Schema (MODS) and Open Language Archives Community (OLAC)[2] schemas. These standardisation practices and recommendations serve as the basis for many of the decisions made in the establishment and structure of the Living Archive, in order to conform to best current practice for the digital archiving of language resources so as to facilitate discoverability and interoperability (Bird and Simons 2003).

The focus on published texts is a key point of difference between the Living Archive and a number of other related archives, such as PARADISEC (Thieberger and Barwick 2012), the collection at AIATSIS[3] and others listed at http://www.language-archives.org/. While the addition of audio, video and other materials would enhance the archive significantly, uncertainty about ongoing funding limits these options. Despite the impression that the focus on published texts should make the creation of metadata simple and unambiguous (cf. Nathan 2013),

1   Creative Commons Attribution-NonCommercial-NoDerivs 3.0 Australia: https://creativecommons.org/licenses/by-nc-nd/3.0/au.
2   The Metadata Object Description Schema is an XML-based bibliographic schema developed for library applications. The Open Language Archives Community is an international partnership of institutions and individuals creating a global virtual library of language resources.
3   http://www.aiatsis.gov.au.

this paper demonstrates some of the complexities involved in creating useful metadata. As the archive is designed as both a research tool and a community resource, good metadata is vital to accessibility. Engaging different kinds of users in appropriate and interesting ways (e.g., Woodbury 2014; Trilsbeek and König 2014) requires that the contents of the archive be easily discoverable, searchable and navigable. Mediation (Holton 2014) may be required to assist users to navigate the complexity of the materials, so that users do not feel 'lost in a thicket' (Woodbury 2014, 22). The act of inviting community members to participate in the collection and correction of metadata of existing resources (Garrett 2014) is an important form of engagement that assists in bringing the archive to life.

While the complexity of the collection and its 'standardisation' into a usable archive inevitably leads to disagreement and error, it also allows for – and even requires – engagement with local authorities (Linn 2014). Community leaders and language authorities are well placed to review the information available and make decisions about metadata, categorisations, inclusion or exclusion of items and other key components of the archive. An important feature of this process has been negotiating the conflicting demands of standardisation with the often heterogeneous nature of the materials while taking account of the requirements of the various users. While sharing the load of such activities as forms of 'crowdsourcing' (cf. Birch 2013; Bird 2013) has the potential to capture the utility of digital distribution and the power of social networking, it is important not to neglect the value of sitting with community leaders 'offline' to perform such tasks. Further development of the archive will involve consultation with community members and this is expected to challenge some of the requirements of the standardised system, and to open up a number of interesting empirical and theoretical questions.

Three clusters of issues are raised in this paper: (1) naming or identification conventions (as applied to languages, places, people and book titles); (2) categorisation practices (the use of controlled vocabularies, grouping into communities and linking related items); and (3) determining whether to include or exclude materials (including photo books, and annotated versions).

Naming/identification

Languages

Language identification should ordinarily be a straightforward issue, especially since the majority of books in the collection clearly name the language used. In some cases, the language could be unambiguously assumed given the item's publication site; for example, all the books published on Bathurst Island are in the Tiwi language, while Yipirinya School published books in four different languages, each of which is clearly identified in the metadata. The wider collection raised a few challenges in this area.

The current recommended international standard for language identification (ISO 639-3) allocates a three-letter code to all languages listed in its database,[4] in order to assist with consistent language identification and to facilitate discoverability of resources. While such an international standard is useful, mapping the languages in this archive to this specification can be quite complex, as the codes did not always match the nomenclature used in the communities or in the books themselves. Where there was a direct mapping from language identification to language code, these were used (e.g., the code [mph] identifies the Maung language); however, in many cases the language name is listed as an alternative name or dialect in ISO 639-3 (e.g., Wubuy, discussed below).

A particularly complex case is in the Yolŋu area of north-east Arnhem Land (Christie 1993), where the different levels of clan affiliations and moiety distinctions are not incorporated into the ISO 639-3 codes. For example, Yolŋu people often classify their languages by the word used for 'this', which yields a set of eight related language groups: Dhuwal, Dhuwala, Djaŋu, Djinba, Djinaŋ, Dhaŋu, Dhay'yi, and Nhaŋu (Schebeck, 2001). Each language contains a pair of corresponding dialects (*matha*), which are categorised by moiety and linked to clans (*mala*). So people of the Djambarrpuyŋu *mala* speak a version of Dhuwal which is often referred to by their clan name, Djambarrpuyŋu, while the closely related Gupapuyŋu people speak Dhuwala (although

---

4 http://www-01.sil.org/iso639-3/codes.asp.

the books are listed as being in Gupapuyŋu language). The use of clan names to differentiate 'dialects' is not incorporated in the ISO 639-3 system. A book in the Wangurri language should ideally be identified as Wangurri, Dhaŋu and Yolŋu, but this is currently not permissible using the ISO 639-3 system.

The ISO 639-3 codes are also subject to change, which needs to be monitored; for example, in 2012 a request to change the name of the Dhangu language [dhg] to Djangu (with the same three-letter code) was accepted by the ISO,[5] requiring a change in metadata for the Living Archive. In 2013, a further request resulted in that change being reversed, reflecting the distinction between the Dhangu and Djangu languages. Consequently the ISO 639-3 situation needs to be regularly monitored to identify and process any further changes to the system.

A further example of the complexity of language nomenclature involves the book *Jatdi Na-yahwurt* ('The little frog', Galmur 1994) (Figure 5.1). The cover indicates that the book is in Mayali language; however, ISO 639-3 has no code for Mayali, listing it only as an alternative name for Gunwinggu [gup], along with Kuninjku, Kunwinjku and Gunwinjgu.[6] Garde (2014, personal communication) states that Mayali is a variety that is distinct from Kunwinjku, Kuninjku and Gundjeihmi, and notes that Evans (2003) recommends the term 'Bininj Gun-wok' as a collective name for this dialect chain. Other books in the Living Archive collection are identified as Kuninjku and Kunwinjku, but none use the ISO 639-3 name of Gunwinggu. A compromise was required for the Living Archive in order to conform to ISO 639-3 codes for discoverability, while still respecting community usage and the printed identification of the language by the book's creators. This was achieved by creating an additional metadata field labelled 'Language note' to allow for clarification of otherwise potentially confusing information. In the case of this book, the metadata displays the language as Kuninjku (linked in the background to ISO code [gup]) and the language note specifies 'Mayali language'.[7] While such a solution is less than satisfac-

5 http://www-01.sil.org/iso639-3/chg_detail.asp?id=2012-047&lang=dhg. Here the ISO 639-3 spellings are used without special characters.
6 http://www.ethnologue.com/language/gup.
7 http://laal.cdu.edu.au/record/cdu:31258/info.

tory, it aims to meet both the demands of standardisation and the local preferences of the community.

Another means of managing these discrepancies was the establishment of a synonym list which linked the ISO 639-3 codes (and AUSTLANG codes,[8] another system commonly used for identification of Australian languages, though not compliant with OLAC standards) with the language names as used in the Living Archive, and allowing discoverability via both the official ISO names or common alternative names. For example, the Numbulwar community calls their language Wubuy, while ISO 639-3 and many other sources retain the label Nunggubuyu. Simply listing Nunggubuyu in accordance with ISO 639-3 standards may prevent people finding Wubuy materials, or alienate users more familiar with the name Wubuy. The synonym list allows searches for both Nunggubuyu and Wubuy to return the same results, and while Wubuy is retained as the preferred language name in the archive, it is directly connected to Nunggubuyu as the ISO standard name. In some cases selecting the language names was uncontroversial (e.g., Warlpiri, Tiwi) but in many it was necessary to shoehorn complex information into a simplified structure.

Places

While the majority of items were clearly identified as coming from a specific Literature Production Centre based within a school, the naming of place was not always straightforward. Over the four decades of literature production, the official names or spelling of some locations changed. Some places had changed name (e.g., Oenpelli is now known as Gunbalanya), and some are known by both a Western and an Indigenous name (e.g., Docker River is also known as Kaltukatjara). The use of the synonym list mentioned above for language identification included alternative names (or spellings) of place names to return appropriate search results.

In addition, OLAC conventions allow for the inclusion of location information beyond place of publication, such as 'geographical origin'

---

8   http://austlang.aiatsis.gov.au/main.php.

(used for the setting of a story – for example, the story *Kapirdi-langu-patu* (Martin 2011), published at Yuendumu in Warlpiri language, is based on a Dreaming belonging to the Gundungurra people from the Blue Mountains in NSW) and 'origin of story' (used if a story told in the book originated from a location different from the one indicated by the language or location of the publication). An example of this is the Maung story of a mother turtle (Kurrunama and Margalgala no date), which lists Warruwi as the origin of the story, was translated into Burarra language in Maningrida and into Djambarrpuyŋu language in Galiwin'ku. These details are particularly useful for an audience which is consciously aligned to place; however, for non-Indigenous staff entering data in the Living Archive database, it was sometimes difficult to clearly identify and categorise these additional locations as either geographical origin or story origin. This gives further opportunity for local users to validate and enhance the metadata of these objects, especially where some of the metadata fields are optional or not relevant, while more detail allows for greater enrichment and complex searchability.

People

Identification of people can become complex given the use of different Aboriginal naming practices (Christie 1993), such as changing names due to marriage or death, different spelling conventions, the use of both Indigenous and non-Indigenous names, each person having a number of different personal names, and the emergence of surnames in some places. The challenge is to link records to a single person, if the name appears differently in different books. For example, one author has books attributed to her by a number of different names and alternative spellings, including Ampi, Margaret Ampi, Margaret Umpi, Margaret Ampi Poulson, and Margaret Poulson. The infrastructure on which the Living Archive is built allows for authors (and other contributors) to be allocated a unique four-digit code. Using this, each record displays the name of the contributor as it is listed in the book metadata, and is also linked to any records of the same contributor identified by any alternative name. All books by the above author can be viewed together by clicking on any variant of her name, while the integrity of the metadata for each individual record is maintained.

Nonetheless, community knowledge is required to identify these connections and correct any errors. For example, in the Gunbalanya collection, two names were given separate codes until a local contact identified the two names as referring to the same person. Such errors are often identified, and there are undoubtedly additional errors like this in the existing archive, exposing another area where local input is needed to identify problems and correct errors. A strategy is being developed to allow and enable community members and appropriate stakeholders to identify and rectify these situations.

Different community practices raise different issues with regard to attribution of authorship. A series of Maningrida readers includes no mention of authors, yet local people know exactly who wrote them. This information can then be supplemented in the metadata in the archive using square brackets. Also in Numbulwar, a conscious decision was made at the time many books were produced not to include the names of authors, so most items are listed as written or illustrated by 'Numbulwar Community Education Centre'. Since the project team is asking creators for permission to make the books public (Bow et al. 2014), this creates a problem, and identification of authors risks negating the original reason for their exclusion. Such questions can best be answered at the local level, yet involve wider legal and ethical implications.

Titles

While the identification of a book's title is generally unproblematic, some of the materials in the Living Archive do not conform to standard practice in this area. There are a small number of books which have no clear 'title' on either the cover or a title page, and even some books with no words, for which titles had to be devised. In other cases the distinction between a title, a subtitle or a series title was unclear. In a few cases there are discrepancies between the title as it appears on the title page and on the cover, such as 'Kukaku Anu' which on the cover is listed as 'Kukaku Yanu' (Raggett 1979). Such problems are not unique to this collection, although they may be more difficult in this case as some of the materials are in languages not understood by the people developing the archive.

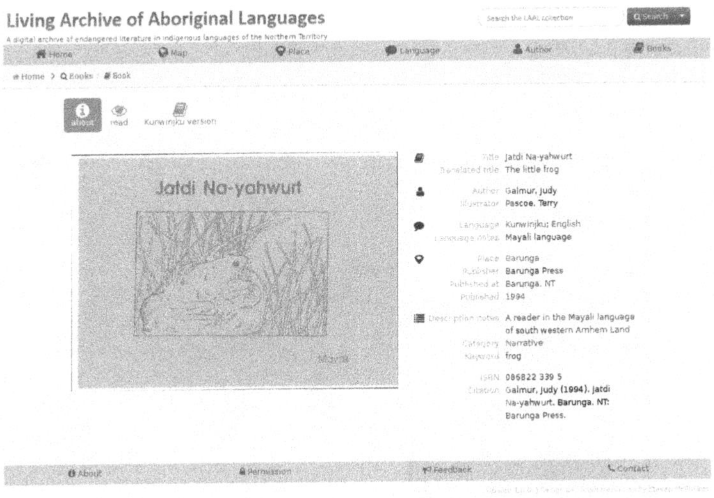

Figure 5.1 'The little frog' by Judy Galmur. http://laal.cdu.edu.au/record/
cdu:31258/info/.

Categorisation

Library cataloguing is a carefully managed process, with strict protocols
addressing a range of possible scenarios. The books produced in
Literature Production Centres do not consistently conform to these
standards, making it sometimes difficult to shoehorn them into the
required categories, leaving many in a nebulous 'too-hard basket'. In
the Living Archive this has led to additional metadata fields which may
only be relevant for a small number of books each. While this enhances
the granularity of the archive and allows for complex searching and
sorting, it also requires careful decisions for data entry. Questions such
as 'Should this be a description note or an abstract?', 'Should this be
considered a series name or a subtitle?', 'How do we catalogue this book
which has a different title on the cover and on the title page?' were
regularly discussed within the project team and with a librarian with
expertise in metadata. Where some questions were outside the standard
metadata practice, new solutions had to be identified.

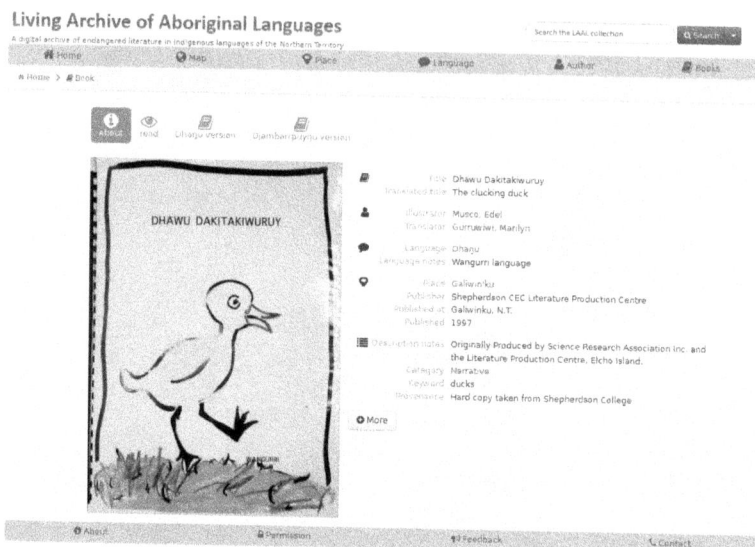

Figure 5.2 'The clucking duck'. http://laal.cdu.edu.au/record/cdu:31310/info/.

Controlled vocabularies

Use of controlled vocabularies is a standard feature of many database programs, forcing the use of a set of pre-defined terms, rather than free text. Limiting this range of options enforces a consistency which aids manageability – for example, avoiding spelling errors, and grouping like with like. In the Living Archive, controlled vocabularies are used in a number of metadata fields (category, type of resource, scan source, etc.), each with its own set of compromises, such as those involved in using controlled vocabularies for language names outlined above.

The use of a 'category' field assists end users to navigate through a huge range of materials. However, categorising Aboriginal literature into Western-style literary genres can create more problems than it solves, because it undermines traditional classifications of modalities (Christie 2005). Currently the archive lists seven genres or categories: traditional, instruction, language instruction, map, memoir, narrative and song. While it may be helpful to distinguish between a text of language instruction and a memoir, or a song and a narrative, these distinctions are not always transparent, and often depend on the perspective of the person inputting the data. Putting things into such categories is useful for navigation, yet grossly oversimplifies the issue. Further discussion and community engagement is desirable to further explore appropriate categories, and these will most likely be quite different in different communities. Already community feedback has prompted a change, where what was once categorised as 'folktale' according to library standards was changed to 'traditional' (i.e., traditional story) in response to a request from community members who thought the word folktale devalued the significance of traditional stories.

Most of the materials in the Living Archive are books; however, a limited selection of additional related materials, such as audio files, videos, and other multimedia files (e.g., ebooks) is included in the archive. Using the controlled vocabulary of 'Type of resource' to classify all records using MODS categories Text, Sound, MovingImage and InteractiveResource allows for a search that simply retrieves the appropriate type. This expands the infrastructure of the archive to incorporate more materials as they may emerge.

Digitisation of materials in the Living Archive has been distributed across a number of different sites. Using a controlled vocabulary for the metadata field 'Scan source' allows easy access to data sets from these different locations, whether digitised at Charles Darwin University Library, by staff at Australian National University (which is a project partner), on scanners or multi-function printers at schools or Literature Production Centres as part of previous digitisation projects (such as at Barunga School), by Department of Education staff in Alice Springs (for materials from a number of desert communities), or those created digitally at Literature Production Centres, which required no scanning. This is an example of refining metadata fields to assist in project management as distinct from using metadata to facilitate access or discoverability.

Using these controlled vocabularies is an attempt to simplify the database from both a data-entry and an end-user perspective (i.e., allowing faceted browsing); however, this disguises much of the complexity behind each of these issues.

Grouping into communities

The initial grouping of materials was complex due to a lack of one-to-one mapping between a language and a place. Some languages were linked to several places (e.g., Warlpiri language materials came from Yuendumu, Lajamanu and Willowra; Kunwinjku materials from Gunbalanya, Maningrida and Barunga), while some places produced materials in several different languages (e.g., Maningrida produced a large number of Burarra and Ndjébbana materials, plus smaller numbers of Kunwinjku, Gurrogoni, Djinaŋ, etc.; Yipirinya School produced materials in Warlpiri, Luritja, Central Arrernte and Western Arrernte). In fact, one-to-one mapping was rare (only Nguiu for Tiwi language materials and Wadeye for Murrinh-Patha[9]). Even apparently simple cases had some degree of complexity (e.g., Warruwi Literacy Centre only produced Maung language materials, but these were mostly published in Maningrida, as Warruwi had no printing facilities). Even if one location produced materials in only one language, another location producing anything in the same language removed the possibility of any 1:1 mapping (e.g., Santa Teresa only produced Eastern Arrernte materials, but Yipirinya School also produced items in this language among others). From a project management perspective it was helpful to create functional groupings that allowed for materials to be located in a single 'collection', even if they overlapped with another group. As a result, 16 collections were formed, based on either a language or a location. This, however, is not transparent in the resulting online archive, as the browse options are currently limited to either language or place. This is yet another example of the careful thinking needed about how the archive would be used, and how this would be affected by decisions made at the project management level.

9   Materials from the Wadeye bilingual program are only in Murrinh-Patha language; however, materials in other languages are likely to emerge as the search expands beyond these school sources.

Related items

The Living Archive includes materials that connect with one another in various ways. There are examples of books which have translations into different languages; others appear in various versions (whether with varying layout, such as 'big books' and 'instant readers', or in different editions, such as updated or revised versions), and some which have related multimedia objects. In other cases the relationship is more along the lines of membership of a series. In order to facilitate discovery and access to these related items, additional fields were included in the metadata to enable links to be made visible. Two types of related items were explicitly addressed: those linking to multimedia formats and those linking to other versions. The first category allows for audio or video files to be uploaded and linked directly to the book to which they refer – for example, an audio file and an epub version of *Ŋalindiy bumara yolŋunha mala* ('The moon killed people', Djäwa 1975). The second category allows for the different 'versions' noted above, with translations distinguished by including a language field, while alternative versions are in the same language. An example is *Dhäwu Dakitakiwuruy* (Figure 5.2) ('The clucking duck', literally 'A story about ducks', Unknown 1977) which has an original version in Djambarrpuyŋu language from 1977, linking to an updated A4 sized version from 1997, as well as translations in two varieties of what ISO 639-3 refers to as Dhaŋu language (Wangurri and the combined Gälpu/Golumala/ Ŋaymil version). Other relationships are accessible through hyperlinking specific fields, such as contributor names and categories, as well as place and language.

Inclusion and exclusion

The wide range of materials in the archive meant that the project team needed to decide which items should be prioritised for inclusion, which should be excluded, and which left in the 'too-hard basket' – a receptacle noted for its ever-growing capacity. For example, at Yirrkala a series of workshops with traditional elders and school children exploring facets of culture and teaching led to the production of books. These 'Galtha Rom' books remain a valuable repository of traditional knowledge and experience. The community had already been through a process of deciding which ones could be shared – made accessible in the community through the school library, for example – and which should be protected from view. However, these decisions needed to be reconsidered in light of internet technology, which has the potential to take the materials beyond the community to a much wider public, and so gives questions about accessibility broader significance. These books stand in a separate category as their authorship is complex, so it is almost impossible to find all those involved in their creation and request permission from everyone concerned or their families for the materials to go online. Decisions about whether such materials belong in an open access repository such as the Living Archive must be made by the community. A scanner was provided to the school to enable them to digitise materials themselves as required, ensuring preservation, but leaving open the question of access. In a number of situations, items may escape digitisation because appropriate permissions for such complex (and often quite politically charged) material may be simply too hard to get given the funding, time and personnel available.

Photographic books are another potential hotspot, and caveats about Indigenous people not displaying images of deceased people are well known. However in some communities these rules are loosening, and people enjoy seeing photos of relatives. Also photos of those who are still alive may be contentious, especially with certain sensitivities surrounding images of children. While the creation of the books incorporated parental permission for including photos of the children in various settings (often on school excursions or involved in school or community activities), those permissions did not explicitly include (or preclude) any publication of the images on the internet. Many of those children are now adults and may want a say in whether or not their images may be reproduced for the world to see. Similarly, many books in the collection are made up of stories and pictures produced by school children as part of a class activity. The effort to track down each child and ask permission for the material to go online is beyond the capacity of the current project. Economies of scale make it difficult to address each individual item in the collection with the appropriate authorities, and so it is the easy cases which make their way to the front of the line. Further development will enable community-level enrichment and enlargement of the archive to provide an opportunity for some of these issues to be resolved authoritatively and decisively. An online feedback form is already available[10] and offline feedback is regularly sought, particularly with Indigenous community members.

The books in the archive were created for classroom and community use, and consequently some hard copies bear signs of wear and tear. While attempts were made to select the 'best' copy for digitisation, there are many examples of marked, defaced, and damaged artefacts in the collection, as well as some with careful annotations. In some cases it was possible to digitally enhance the original documents; however, there is still some merit in retaining the evidence of use, showing that the books have been handled and engaged with by various users. Annotated copies present a different challenge, particularly when it is not known who made the annotations (often spelling modifications, changes in diacritic use or punctuation) and therefore if they are to be accepted. At the current stage of development, the archive only allows a single plain text version to accompany the scanned PDF files. However, a solution whereby different textual variants can be included is desirable.

Conclusion

The materials created for bilingual education programs in remote Indigenous community schools over a number of years represent a wealth of knowledge, experience and skills. They belong to a specific context of time, place, people and situation, which cannot be retained when bringing digital versions to life in an online archive. The vastly different array of possibilities for dissemination and access to materials were unimaginable when the programs began, and so the resources take on a new identity in this environment. While Western knowledge systems force certain requirements on today's archiving standards, traditional knowledge systems should still be respected. In the Living Archive project, the development of the archive has seen compromises and solutions drawing on both traditions, yet sometimes satisfying nei-

---

10   http://laal.cdu.edu.au/feedback.

ther. Such is the nature of a project such as this one, in managing a wide range of material in various categories, with a number of cases not fitting neatly into established protocols. This 'too-hard basket' is where some of the most interesting and complex issues reside, and much is lost in the oversimplification (or shoehorning) of rich and complex data.

Works cited

Birch, Bruce (2013). 'The Ma! Project: Crowdsourcing software for language documentation.' Presented at Research, Records and Responsibility (RRR): Ten Years of the Pacific and Regional Archive for Digital Sources in Endangered Cultures, The University of Melbourne, 2–3 December. http://hdl.handle.net/2123/9858.

Bird, Steven and Gary Simons (2003). 'Seven dimensions of portability for language documentation and description.' *Language* 79(3): 557–82. http://tiny.cc/2003-7dim-birdsimons.

Bird, Steven, Florian Hanke and Haejoong Lee (2013). 'Collaborative language documentation with networked smartphones.' Presented at Research, Records and Responsibility (RRR): Ten Years of the Pacific and Regional Archive for Digital Sources in Endangered Cultures (PARADISEC), The University of Melbourne, 2–3 December. http://hdl.handle.net/2123/9857.

Bow, Catherine, Michael Christie and Brian Devlin (2014). 'Developing a living archive of Aboriginal languages.' *Language Documentation and Conservation* 8: 345–60.

Christie, Michael (1993). 'Yolngu linguistics.' *Ngoonjook: A Journal of Australian Indigenous Issues* 8: 56–77.

Christie, Michael (2004). 'Computer databases and Aboriginal knowledge.' *Learning Communities: International Journal of Learning in Social Contexts.* 1 (February), https://www.cdu.edu.au/northern-institute/lcj/learning-communities-journal-archive.

Christie, Michael (2005). 'Aboriginal knowledge traditions in digital environments.' *The Australian Journal of Indigenous Education* 34: 61–66.

Christie, Michael, Catherine Bow, Brian Devlin and Jane Simpson (2014). *The Living Archive of Aboriginal Languages.* Darwin: The Northern Institute, Charles Darwin University.

'Dhäwu Dakitakiwuruy' (1997). Translated by Marilyn Ganyinurr. Galiwin'ku: Shepherdson CEC Literature Production Centre. http://laal.cdu.edu.au/record/cdu:31310/info.

5 Shoehorning complex metadata

Djäwa (1975). *Ŋalindiy Bumara Yolŋunha Mala*. Milingimbi: Milingimbi Bilingual Centre. http://laal.cdu.edu.au/record/cdu:31730/info.

Evans, Nicholas (2003). *Bininj Gun-wok: A Pan-dialectal Grammar of Mayali, Kunwinjku and Kune*. Canberra: Pacific Linguistics.

Galmur, Judy (1994). *Jatdi Na-yahwurt*. Barunga: Barunga Press. http://laal.cdu.edu.au/record/cdu:31258/info.

Garrett, Edward (2014). 'Participant-driven language archiving.' *Language Documentation and Description* 12: 68–84.

Holton, Gary (2014). 'Mediating language documentation.' In *Language Documentation and Description* 12: 37–52. London: SOAS.

Kurrunama, Rosemary and Maggie Margalgala (n.d.). *Inyarlgen*. Warruwi: Warruwi Literacy Centre. http://laal.cdu.edu.au/record/cdu:31684/info.

Linn, Mary S. (2014). 'Living archives: A community-based language archive model.' *Language Documentation and Description* 12: 53–67.

Martin, Margaret (2011). *Kapirdi-langu-jarra*. Translated by Shirley Martin Napanangka, Tess Ross Napaljarri and Serena Shannon Nakamarra. Yuendumu: Bilingual Resources Development Unit.

Nakata, Martin (2007). 'Indigenous digital collections.' *Australian Academic and Research Libraries Journal* 38(2): 99–110.

Nathan, David (2013). 'Access and accessibility at ELAR, a social networking archive for endangered languages documentation.' In *Oral Literature in the Digital Age: Archiving Orality and Connecting with Communities*, edited by Mark Turin, Claire Wheeler and Eleanor Wilkinson, 21–40. Cambridge: Open Book Publishers.

Raggett, Obed (1979). *Kukaku Anu*. Papunya: Papunya Literature Production Centre. http://laal.cdu.edu.au/record/cdu:31914/info.

Schebeck, Bernhard (2001). *Dialect and Social Groupings in Northeast Arnhem Land, Australia*. Munchen: Lincom Europa.

Thieberger, Nick and Linda Barwick (2012). 'Keeping records of language diversity in Melanesia: The Pacific and Regional Archive for Digital Sources in Endangered Cultures (PARADISEC).' In *Language Documentation and Conservation, Special Publication No. 5: Melanesian Languages on the Edge of Asia: Challenges for the 21st century*, edited by Nicholas Evans and Marian Klamer, 239–53.

Trilsbeek, Paul and Alexander König (2014). 'Increasing the future usage of endangered language archives.' *Language Documentation and Description* 12: 151–63.

Woodbury, Anthony C. (2014). 'Archives and audiences: Towards making endangered language documentations people can read, use, understand, and admire.' *Language Documentation and Description* 12: 19–36.

6

Reviewing, reconstructing and reinterpreting ethnographic data on musical instruments in archives and museums

Jennifer C. Post

> To realise its function as a sound-producing device, a musical instrument requires the intimate touch of players, whose absence becomes all the more keenly felt when they depart and the music they played is lost. Accordingly, a historical musical instrument of this sort, especially one played at a former imperial court, becomes the perfect metaphor for the inevitable vanishing of the past; yet as a fragile physical object that has survived against all odds it is also a perfect metonym for the resilience of the past and a symbol of cultural and national continuity. (Zeitlin 2009, 397)

Considering a centuries-long journey and the ultimate survival of the pear-shaped Little Hulei, a two-string plucked instrument called *huqin* in 8th century China, Zeitlin references the instrument as an object and sound producing device. In her article, she explores its ties to players, its repertoires and its embodiment of history, which can encompass both a sense of loss and evidence of – and potential for – cultural resilience. It is surprising how easy it is to relate Zeitlin's discussions about a highly

Post, Jennifer C. (2015). 'Reviewing, reconstructing and reinterpreting ethnographic data on musical instruments in archives and museums.' In *Research, Records and Responsibility: Ten Years of PARADISEC*, edited by Amanda Harris, Nick Thieberger and Linda Barwick. Sydney: Sydney University Press.

valued, finely made musical instrument to other instruments that may not have been made for longevity, connected to well-documented dynasties, or produced in long-established instrument workshops. Over the centuries, musical instruments have travelled along trading routes, with touring performers, with musicians experiencing forced or voluntary migration, and due to the actions of collectors representing museums, archives, academic disciplines, or building personal collections. During the travels of a musical instrument from place to place, or from one time period to another, as object, image, document or memory, it takes on new meanings. At the same time, the instrument leaves behind a trail that includes a heritage community with historical, emotional, and conceptual connections to it as object and source for musical sound.

Musical instruments, and ethnographic documentation about production and use, retain valuable historical, social and environmental data, even when kept outside source communities in storage or on display in archives, museums and private collections. In traditional archival and museum practice, musical instruments have been preserved and presented as objects with geographic tags, measurements, and identifying names and numbers in accordance with organology, the academic study of musical instruments that for generations has framed an approach to their collection, storage, research, and display. As objects defined primarily by their descriptions, dimensions, classification and sounds, the wealth of information about their social lives is absent. Musical sounds, photographs, drawings, narrative information and interpretative material preserved in archives, while often products of an earlier scholarly era, in fact are rich resources that can animate musical instruments so that they can be used in current and future research and shared with source communities. Expanding our view of instruments at the collection and documentation level, and maintaining broad awareness of their social lives, will contribute to recovering relationships between people and instruments, and between instruments and the social and geophysical environments they came from. This will play a significant role in reframing local community members' relationships to historical practices and scholarly connections to music.

This chapter focuses on musical instrument-related data produced by anthropologists and ethnomusicologists during scholarly fieldwork and deposited in archival and museum collections. Representing topics ranging from overviews of musical practices to detailed studies of individual musical instrument types, research materials are preserved in audio and video recordings with supporting documentation, in field-notes and diaries providing contextual information about music and social life, and in acquired musical instruments and instrument parts. Left in the care of archivists and curators, many unaware of their value to local community members (the donors and their relatives) and to current scholarship, some musical instrument information may be inadequately identified and indexed, or even overlooked. An essential difference between musical instrument collections made by collectors and those by ethnographers relates to the quantity and type of documentation gathered in support of their collections. Of particular note is the data on human–object relationships and on social and cultural production typically found in ethnographic data. How can ethnographic materials gathered during an earlier scholarly era be connected to contemporary musical instrument research? And what actions are needed in order to share documentation on musical instruments with both source community members and scholars?

The multi-format collections of ethnomusicologist John Blacking at the University of Western Australia and Queen's University, Belfast present useful examples of the importance of providing better access to musical instrument information. Resources drawn from the archives can be used to illustrate how musical recordings and descriptive and visual information about musical instrument design and function, as well as production and use, have the potential to contribute to knowledge about cultural, economic and ecological vulnerabilities, adaptation, and resilience through their sounds, images, and stories.[1] The internationally recognised ethnomusicologist John Blacking spent 15 years based in South Africa (1954–69) where he worked at the International Library of African Music and studied, then taught, at the University of the Wit-

---

1 The data for this study is largely drawn from the University of Western Australia John Blacking Collection housed in the Callaway Centre in the School of Music, where the author worked from January to December 2013. The author has also examined the John Blacking Collection at Queen's University in Belfast and many of the issues noted are shared by both collections.

watersrand. During his tenure in Africa he collected music and musical instrument data in South Africa, Zambia, Uganda and Mozambique.[2] The historical data in the Blacking archives represent documentation primarily from the period 1955–65, yet these resources can be effectively used for contemporary research as well. Archivists and museum personnel, in conjunction with scholars in ethnomusicology and other music-related disciplines, can make materials available so that younger scholars might use them in conjunction with newer ethnomusicological approaches. This includes social advocacy projects and research that engages community members in discussions about musical production and instrument making. Practical and interpretive information compiled by ethnographers such as Blacking, housed in archival and museum collections, offers knowledge for the source communities and provides opportunities for data sharing among all peoples impacted by cultural and material loss.

Ethnographic information on musical instruments

Most published ethnographic research conducted by ethnomusicologists and anthropologists is backed by an abundance of field data. Using publications to identify collections with musical instrument data can be difficult, though. While many ethnographic studies that focus on musical practices have been published during the last 60 years, in-depth ethnomusicological studies that concentrate on musical instrument production and use are surprisingly scant. At the same time, field data compiled by ethnomusicologists since the mid-20th century, now housed in archives and personal collections around the world, demonstrate that ethnographers amass considerable information about musical instrument production and use during their research.[3] Data

---

2 During the period that Blacking was in Africa, Zambia was known as Northern Rhodesia and Mozambique was Portuguese East Africa.
3 For example, recordings with documentation held in the British Library Sound Archive (London) show in-depth evidence of musical instrument use in Uganda from the 1940s through the 1990s in collections by ethnomusicologists Klaus Wachsmann, Kenneth Gourlay and Peter Cooke. Similar examples can be found in other national archives holding music-based collections such as the Archive of

collected may include instrument tuning systems, playing styles, musical repertoires, as well as musical instrument construction and materials use. In addition, ethnomusicological queries also offer information on human–object relationships, such as between musical instruments and players, ritual construction and use of instruments, and the role of instruments in identity formation.[4]

The cultural study and the social life of musical instruments represent two key areas that frame new research methods driven especially by scholars redefining and redesigning relationships to musical instruments.[5] In 2001, Dawe encouraged the museum community to

---

Folk Culture, Library of Congress (Washington, DC); institutional archives such as the Archives of Traditional Music (Indiana University), the Archive of Māori and Pacific Music, University of Auckland in New Zealand, the UCLA Ethnomusicology Archives, University of the Philippines Center for Ethnomusicology Archives in Manila, the World Music Archives at Wesleyan University (Middletown, CT); and other collections such as the Australian Institute of Aboriginal and Torres Strait Islander Studies (AIATSIS) (Canberra), Archives and Research Centre for Ethnomusicology (ARCE) (Delhi, India), and the International Library of African Music at Rhodes University (Grahamstown, South Africa). Other small and large archives in locations around the world hold collections of ethnographic data that contain field recordings, many with written documentation providing detailed information on musical instrument production and use.

4 Some of the focused ethnographic studies on musical instruments since the 1960s include an account of the process of constructing a drum among the Bala (Basongye) in the Democratic Republic of the Congo by Alan Merriam (1969), the Shona *mbira* in Zimbabwe and the relationship between player and instrument by Paul Berliner (1978), the Mediterranean *mijwiz* as a culturally and physically interactive entity by Ali Jihad Racy (1994), the cultural and social meanings of *sarangi* and experiences of *sarangi* players in North India and Pakistan by Regula Qureshi (1997, 2000), and the structural and social development of *tanbur* and *dutar* in Afghanistan by John Baily (1976, 2006). Since 2000, other instrument-centered research includes studies of the *duduk* and Armenian identity by Andy Nercessian (2000), crafting the sacred *tanbur* of western Iran by Navid Fozi (2007), ethnographic studies of the *lyra* in Greece and the guitar in Turkey by Kevin Dawe (2007, 2013), local fiddles and fiddling in West Africa by Jacqueline DjeDje (2008), musical instruments, gender and fertility in the Bolivian Andes by Stobart (2008), on the ceremonial use of musical instruments on the Vanuatu islands (Ammann 2012), and *tabla* design and construction in India by Alan Roda (2012, 2013).

engage more ethnographically when he challenged readers of the *Galpin Society Journal* to shift away from older organological approaches to view musical instrument study more broadly, arguing that musical instruments are 'objects existing at the intersection of material, social and cultural worlds' increasingly entangled in transnational industries and engaged in political activities (Dawe 2001, 220). Dawe notes musical instruments 'are one way in which cultural and social identity (a sense of self in relation to others, making sense of one's place in the order of things) is constructed and maintained' (Dawe 2011, 195).[6] Eliot Bates reflects this in his 2013 article on musical instruments when he explores their social lives as independent objects encouraging object–object as well as human–object social relationships to be valued in ethnographic research on musical instruments (Bates 2012, 364). Both Dawe and Bates express concern about the loss of agency experienced by instruments in museum collections, expressed by Bates when he refers to museums as 'mausoleums, places for the display of the musically dead, with organologists acting as morticians, preparing dead instrument bodies for preservation and display' (Bates 2013, 365).[7]

Musical instruments are not only trapped in museum collections; instruments and their contextual data are hidden, and sometimes imprisoned, in archives. Most musical instrument collections in museums are developed and maintained for historical preservation and for display, and their archives do not support musical 'objects' with the in-depth contextualisation valued in ethnographic research. Even museums that hire ethnomusicologists to provide documentation typically

---

5   The development of new relationships can be traced in ethnomusicological literature published during the last 30 years by Dournon (2000), DeVale (1990), Kartomi (1990, 2005), Dawe (2001, 2011), Bates (2012) and Roda (2014).
6   Calling for a more holistic approach to instrument study, Dawe encourages archivists, museum professionals and scholars to utilise ideas and theories from diverse academic disciplines. He says, 'As sites of meaning construction, musical instruments are embodiments of cultural based belief and value systems, as artistic and scientific legacy, a part of the political economy attuned by, or the outcome of, a range of associated ideas, concepts and practical skills' (Dawe 2011, 195).
7   Similarly, Dawe says, 'like animals in a zoo or pinned butterflies in specimen drawers, musical instruments in collections and displays are *out of place*' (2011, 222).

support limited field journeys to gather display-focused information on objects and their relationships to the people that play them. Ethnographic archives in university, public and personal collections, on the other hand, sometimes accumulate papers, recordings, images, and even instruments from ethnographers and other collectors who have spent extended periods in the field. Ethnographers, frequently seeking answers to multiple research questions, rarely are able to fully complete documentation projects and their multi-format collections are seldom well organised. Overburdened archivists are not in a position to devote time or skilled personnel, such as subject specialists, to find connections among all the data that would benefit scholarly research today. Most importantly, incomplete and poorly organised musical instrument data limits its association with local peoples and landscapes who might provide in-depth understanding of an instrument's history and use, and limits opportunities to initiate and maintain relationships with those most invested in the objects: source community members.

John Blacking and musical instrument study

The ethnographic materials on music and dance in Africa in the 1950s and 1960s amassed by John Blacking and preserved in two university collections are focused on his work in southern and eastern Africa. The largest collections include audio, visual and manuscript data on music collected in South Africa, especially among the Venda, between 1956 and 1958, in the Valley Tonga and Nsenga in Zambia in 1957 and 1961 respectively, and from diverse groups in Uganda during a series of weekend field excursions in 1965.[8] The most in-depth information on

---

8   Educated at King's College, Cambridge, Musée de l'Homme in Paris, and the University of the Witwatersrand in Johannesburg, South Africa, John Blacking conducted fieldwork with support from various African and European institutions and organisations. His research on Venda children's music and dance practices and on initiation ceremonies are his most widely known African studies. Blacking was expelled from South Africa in 1969 and joined the faculty at Queen's University, Belfast, where he remained until his death in 1990. The John Blacking Collection, representing the contents of his home office, is housed in the Callaway Centre, University of Western Australia. The collection comprising the contents of his

music in Africa is on Venda practices, reflecting the 22 months Black-ing spent in the field with Venda communities.[9] Blacking began his studies in Africa working at the International Library of African Music with Hugh Tracey, a collector with a particular interest in document-ing musical instruments and instrumental performance. Conducting research more independently by mid-1956, some of Blacking's collect-ing continued to replicate, complement, and contribute to Tracey's, at least through 1957.[10] Blacking continued his own fieldwork during the following years with an ear and eye for music, dance, as well as mate-rial culture, including musical instruments. Considering images, diary entries, film clips, and written research, Blacking's interests revolved around specific instrument types in all the regions of Africa in which he worked. His fieldnotes reference musical bows, xylophones and lamel-laphones, end- and side-blown flutes, side-blown horns, and drums. He provided descriptive data on instruments, their names, tunings and note naming conventions, construction processes and materials used, makers' names, repertoires, and he completed aural and visual documents on performance practice, in different quantities depending on the specific social and research circumstance. Blacking also oc-casionally took the time to record detailed information on processes connected to building and tuning instruments.[11] The data exemplifies information that is hidden away in institutional and private collections,

---

university office is held at Queen's University, Belfast, in the School of History and Anthropology.

9 In addition, Blacking also took other short field excursions in Africa. His collection of recordings and images includes documentation of Chopi music in the southern coastal areas of Mozambique, Venda, Pedi, Zulu, Sotho, Tswana, and Tsonga music in Limpopo and KwaZulu Natal, South Africa, Valley Tonga and Nsenga performance in the Zambezi River valley and Petauke districts of Zambia, and music of indigenous groups in Uganda collected during a series of weekend field excursions to record Ganda, Adhola, Acholi, Toro, Kiga, and Karamajong music.

10 For example, Blacking went to visit Valley Tonga musicians in Gwembe, Zambia (Northern Rhodesia at the time) and produced a documented set of recordings, possibly in conjunction with Hugh Tracey's work. Tracey travelled to the same region several months later and produced another related set of recordings (some of Tracey's documentation for these recordings is housed at the University of Western Australia).

difficult to access by contemporary researchers, who are unaware of its depth and breadth, and generally completely unknown to source communities. It also demonstrates that there are areas where collections would benefit from follow-up work in order to compile more complete records on cultural production and tell a more comprehensive tale about a particular practice, or a musical instrument and its life experience.

One of the key issues for researchers or source community members who might benefit from one or both of the John Blacking Collections is that detailed information on musical instruments in his audio recordings, fieldnotes and images has not been well indexed. In fact, neither Blacking nor institutional personnel recognise that in order for musical instruments to have agency, and more importantly in order for the instruments to communicate effectively back to their heritage places, they need to be offered a voice: to be given a chance to be both heard and contextualised. Once connections are made between written accounts and musical sounds, the opportunities for using more fully contextualised recordings, and for connecting with communities, increase considerably.[12]

Sociality of musical instruments

Blacking offers descriptive data as well as social information on musical instruments in his fieldnotes and publications. He demonstrates that during his research in South Africa, Zambia and Uganda, musical instruments were well integrated in the social lives of each community he studied. Indeed, his notes also provide evidence that instruments had social lives of their own and were engaged in both human and object relationships (Bates 2013). Blacking's documentation on Venda *tshikona*

---

11   Some of Blacking's descriptive information on these processes reflects the published ethnographic report produced by John Merriam on Bala drum-making in 1969 based on fieldwork in 1959 and 1960 (Merriam 1969). Blacking completed his fieldwork a few years before Merriam did.
12   Some indexing was completed at the University of Western Australia archive in 2013.

practices offers an example of how instruments were integrated into social life and carried social power. *Tshikona* is a dance form in which performers play the single-note *nanga* (pipe or flute) in hocket style (individual flutes, each playing a single note, contribute alternately to a shared melody). Blacking called *tshikona* the 'national dance' of the Venda (1973); Kruger later explored its relationship to both social ritual and local politics (2007). The social lives of the bamboo *nanga* and the *khwatha* (side-blown animal horn) are illustrated in narrative information recorded in a diary identified with one of Blacking's translators, Alfred Tshibalanganda. The diary documents preparations for a *bepha* (musical expedition in which youth visit neighbouring communities and engage in *tshikona* competition).[13] The narrated story features roles for *nanga* and *khwatha* as well as *ngoma* drums.

The narrator recounts *bepha* preparation and performance in 1954 in the Gaba district of Limpopo (South Africa). Local children trained for *tshikona*, and to earn an opportunity for *bepha*, by playing the flute and dancing as they laboured each day for the local chief. In one passage, when the headman managing their activities commended the children for dancing nicely, the narrator wrote, 'When we boys heard that, flutes were blown in such a way that if possible they can crack'. This expression of their excitement established the *nanga* and bamboo as extensions of their bodies and emotions, and expressed an independent relationship of the bamboo to its environment; that of the human–object relationship between the breath and the bamboo, and the object–object relationship between the bamboo and its environment. Both human and non-human entities (performer and *nanga*/bamboo) contributed to that event. While rehearsing *tshikona*, *nanga* playing by the youth was essential to the performance of *tshikona*, but it was the sound of the *khwatha* that called their attention, and they were directed by the *khwatha* to stop their *nanga* playing and pay attention when there was news to share. When the children asked the headman at what time they needed to return to work in the morning, 'He said the *khwatha* will tell you. I will blow it.' In the morning 'we heard the

---

13   See Blacking's 'Musical expeditions of the Venda' (Blacking 1962) for more information on the *bepha* tradition. The *bepha* diary discussed in this section is unsigned, but it is likely that Alfred Tshibalanganda is the author.

sound of *khwatha*, but before the *khwatha* blower came to us, we started dancing our *tshikona*. The narrative shows musicians and musical instruments ascribed specific social roles which are reinforced by their presence and sounds at work parties and other *bepha* preparations, at rehearsals and at *tshikona* performances. They are actors in social networks with agency that is expressed through the intersections of sound, substance, performance and social position.

Musical instrument makers, agency and action

Blacking documented musical instrument making in different locations, naming builders, drawing and diagramming instruments, and providing written information on processes and transmission of knowledge. Working with the Valley Tonga in Northern Rhodesia (now Zambia) in 1957, Blacking noted details on building specific instruments, especially *mutetule* and *nenda* flutes (obsolete by 1957), the *kalumbu* musical bow, *nkolenkole* xylophone,[14] and *nyele* antelope horns. His fieldnotes offer information on some construction techniques, and he names woods and other materials used and sometimes provides step-by-step construction procedures. Figure 6.1 shows Blacking's notation of the process one instrument maker used to build a four-key *nkolenkole* xylophone using wood of the *musigili*[15] (Natal mahogany tree) and *mwingili*[16] (white raisin bush) trees.[17] In addition to *musigili* woods, he noted that the maker used *mukonzo* (*Triplochiton zambesiacus* or Zambezi-oak), *mukololo* (*Lonchocarpus capassa* or raintree) or *mutondo* wood.

---

14 This is possibly the instrument Tracey called *chikorekore*.
15 *Trichilia emetic.*
16 *Grewia flavescens*. Reynolds also notes the wood is used for axe handles and drum sticks (Reynolds 1968).
17 This information is reproduced as noted in Blacking's field notebook. He demonstrates his interest in the amount of time it took to complete work, referring in his notes to time (recorded as four-digit numbers) and to the actual time it took to complete tasks.

12/8/57

2nd XYLOPHONE
made by Jeremiah Tshisoa

Jeremiah brings 4 pieces of musigili – lengths 64.2 (diam 7.4-8.0)
62-8 (6.4-7.4), 55.6 (6.5-7.1), 55.0 (5.0-5.6)
0930

1. Takes the longest piece
2. Holds it up vertically on a block & cuts down the inside edge with an axe (mbezyo), taking off bark & making almost st. [straight] edge.
3. Then he hammers the bark with the wooden haft of the axe. Removes bark.
4. Holds wood, inside edge upwards. Begins to cut down into the wood, to make a triangle 'trough.'
5. Turns wood round, cuts other side & eases out the cut wood. His general technique is to hack – edge out, hack – edge out.
6. Triangular slit now cut
7. 0950 Begins pointing ends.
8. 0955. Lays aside piece with ends partly pointed.
9. Begins hammering bark of 2nd piece   0956
10. Tears off bark 0957, but has to rehammer some parts, as the bark will not come off readily.
11. 0958 Begins cutting down inside edge. He laid it on his knees to test for fell & for symmetry.
12. Begins cutting triangular trough. He strikes with the axe in short sharp strokes from a height of about 1 ft–1 ft 6".
13. 1003 Tears off rough piece & begins second cut deeper.
14. 1005 Tears off second piece & begins vertical slicing of triangular trough. Alternates this with horizontal cutting.
15. 1006 Begins pointing ends. Also pays more attention to the triangular trough.
16. 1009 ½ Lays 2nd slat aside.
17. 1010 Take 3rd piece of wood (i.e. 55.6 length) & begins hacking straight edge on inside.
18. 1011 Hammers the bark & tears it off.
19. 1012 ½ Returns to inside edge & begins △ trough
20. 1015 ½ Tears off first piece. Continues hacking. He hacks down into the apex of the △ & either eases with the axe blade away from him or towards him, depending on side of triangle he is working. Lays on legs for feel.
21. 1018 ¼ Begins hacking corner, 1'30"
22. 1020 2nd corner Occasional pause as he works to look up and say something. 1'15"
23. 1021 ½ - Begins hacking inside edge of smallest piece
24. 1022 ¾ - Begins hammering bark with haft. 57" -- completed.
25. 1024 – Returns to back st. edge, & begins hacking out △ trough, and pulls out strip 2'34"
26. 1027 – Continue on △ trough (NB there is always 2nd cut, digging deeper than the 1st cut) After 2'30" he begins the vertical shaving of the sides of the △ 3'45" whole process.
27. 1030 ½ Begins pointing one end. Complete 2'19" (NB a little conversation)
28. 1033 Begins pointing other end. 1'12"
29. 1034 General touch up & test for tune, including a little repointing 55"
30. 1035 Laid last slat aside & said "Finish."

We go to look at musigili tree & then cut 2 beaters from mwingili.
Then Jeremiah tests out the keys for sound & arranges them on his knees in the order 4, 3, 2, 1 – 4 being nearest J's body.

Always carves biggest key first & smallest last. The four keys came from 4 branches. Can be cut from one branch if there is a sufficiently long one.

Figure 6.1 Excerpt from John Blacking's dairy entry on Jeremiah Tshisoa's nkolenkole making (continues next image).

Preference for woods:
1. Musigili   2. Mukonzo   3. Mukololo   4. Mutondo

Jeremiah said that if he cut any more the wood would crack when the slats dried. He said that they would sound
O.K. when the wood dried. At present, 4 sounds about 75 cents below 2, although considerably smaller. The
relative intervals between all keys are in fact very slight: e.g.

Tunings: 1. Largest 380
            2. 416
            3. 464
            4. (smallest 400)

(He showed me how to cut the pieces of wood to the correct lengths, Jeremiah stretched out his arm and
touched the tip of his shoulder & a part nearer the neck. In fact the 2 lengths of the pieces coincided with the tip
of his shoulder & a part further down his arm)

Systematic information on materials and their sources is useful for current scholars but, more importantly, the narrative information recorded
by Blacking for this instrument and others is of greatest potential value
to the communities he studied, especially those who may no longer
have access to knowledge about constructing some of their valued historical instruments.

Ecological data and asset protection

Ethnographers studying instrument production and use during their
research have often focused on performance practice and on social, political and economic issues related to production and use. Sometimes
simple questions regarding the specific materials used for building instruments are neglected. It is fortunate that Blacking had a particular
interest in naming woods and skins for the instruments.[18] His field documents note names of resonant woods, plants, valued skins and other
materials, offering researchers and local community members a more
complete description of a musical object's identity. This information
can also be a source for measuring ecosystem health, including environmental degradation and loss. Knowledge of issues identified with

18   Among his papers are notebooks (housed at Queen's University, Belfast)
detailing trees in the Magidi region of Limpopo during the mid-1950s.

local ecologies can even contribute to an explanation for the loss of, or change in, musical instrument practices.

Blacking's detailed fieldnotes on xylophones and on lamellaphones (which he called 'hand pianos') frequently listed woods used for the bars and soundboards. For the Venda *mbila mutondo* xylophone the resonant wild teak wood (*kiaat* in Afrikaans),[19] called *mutondo* in Venda, was the only wood used for the bars.[20] While Blacking recorded a few performances on film and tape and took photos of the *mbila mutondo*, the instrument was rare even in the 1950s. In contrast, Blacking recorded a number of *mbila dza madeza* and *mbira tshipai* lamellaphone[21] performances and provided detailed diagrams, tunings, and note names for the instruments in his notebooks (see Figure 6.2). The wood preferred for the soundboard for this instrument was also *mutondo*.[22] Even during the period that Blacking was in the field in South Africa the government had restricted the use of this popular wood, probably due to its vulnerability to overharvesting for timber. In a 1956 diary entry he noted that 'people can be arrested if found with a piece of *mutondo*'.

Similarly, Blacking noted that the Venda *nanga* flutes used for *tshikona* were made from the stem of *musununu* or bindura bamboo,[23] a species that has been difficult for local residents to source for several generations. Blacking reported that the bamboo was grown in a 'sacred grove' in the eastern region of the province (Byron 1995, 136) and was 'cut exclusively by the male members of one family' (Blacking 1967, 20).

---

19 *Pterocarpus angolensis.*

20 Information on the instrument is preserved in Blacking's images of performance and instrument making as well as recordings and film clips; it was rare even in the 1950s. Between 1956 and 1965, Blacking made recordings of *mbila mutondo* duets in just two days in the field (in 1956 and 1957), with six pieces and five performers represented.

21 The *mbila dza madeza* and *mbila tshipai* had keys typically made from locally sourced metal, such as bicycle spokes. For the *mbila dza madeza*, resonation for the instrument was frequently provided by an added large gourd or paraffin tin (often with attached shells or bottlecaps).

22 He recorded other woods used as well, including *muzere, suringa, muvanghu, minesenga, mutokota,* and *muvangazi*. Blacking noted that the same kind of wood was also used by the Valley Tonga in Zambia for their lamellaphones.

23 *Oxytenanthera abyssinica.*

13

MBILA MADELA. - 23 note. MULEMBA player.
The wooden frame = gondelo   Calabash with snail shells
                                tied round (Kumba)
Andries Ramaro, mutupo - Boba

Lives here at La-Ramaro. He is responsible for killing
cattle.
Photo + I I , 27.
The mbila was made by his father, who lived wherever
Chief Rasempane lived.
Plays mbila at any time, especially during Phalemba Malombo.
He does not make mbila. There is no one who makes
them near here -
NB 2 finger-holes L & R.
Made of mutondo wood. 21.7 x 18.6 x
        The back is curved & there is a "well" under-
neath the notes - usual design.
Are they in tune? - Dzo elelwa na?
        23 musical
1 = $\boxed{216 \times 2}$ & swears this is   11 = 308   21 = 344 × 2
               in tune.
    2 = 260   12 - 308/2   22 = 380 × 2
3 = 412 (slightly sharp)   13 - 412/2   23 = 412 × 2
    4 = 228   14 = 412/4 (slightly sharp)
5 = 380   15 = ⓞ260
    6 = 380/2   16 = 412
7 = 344   17 = 228 × 2
    8 = 344/2   18 = 244 × 2
9 = 280   19 = 280 × 2
    10 = 280/2   20 = 308 × 2

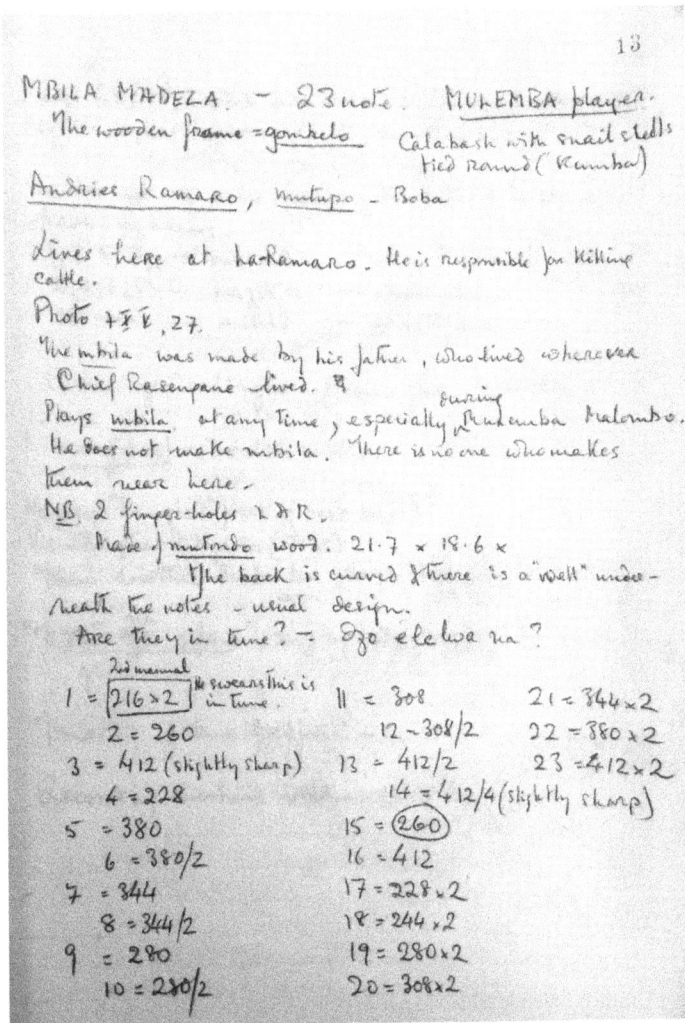

Figure 6.2 John Blacking diary excerpt on *mbila madeza*.

Figure 6.3 Venda *tshikona* performer uses a pram handle to replace the *nanga* flute during a performance, c. 1957. Photo by John Blacking.

In fact, in the early 1960s Blacking reported that the flutes in the urban areas were made of materials such as metal tubing, hosepipe, curtain rods and pram handles (see Figure 6.3). While he did not specify the reason, this was likely due to limited access in the cities to the valued bamboo.

Musical instruments are not only entangled in relationships with musicians; their materials are intertwined with people who have uses for them outside of music, sometimes restricting access by instrument makers. Increasingly, resonant woods are of interest to international industries, leading to species degradation and loss. Community protection of assets as a strategy to address both social, cultural, economic and ecological needs and the consumption and trade of natural resources has been documented in various regions of southern and eastern Africa (Shackleton and Shackleton 2001; Ipara et al. 2005).[24] Among the Venda in South Africa, the *mutondo* tree not only offers a valued musical wood, but is also used for woodcarving (Shackleton 2005) and has links to spiritual healing (Mugovhani 2009, 52). Mugovhani also reports that the bark of the *muonze* tree used for *mbila mutondo* mallets[25] is also valued for traditional medicine (2009).[26] And the Venda protection of bamboo for *nanga* flutes through their social systems, documented by Blacking in his fieldnotes and by other researchers (Kruger 2007), demonstrates community protection of assets even as national and provincial government practices, and increasingly international industries, are placing people and their cultural assets in jeopardy. Addressing one such issue directly, Blacking quoted a Venda resident in an undated diary entry: 'Who is going to look after the reed flute grove if people are moved by the government?' Blacking then commented him-

24 In Kenya, clan-based collective conservation of plants and animal life has occurred due to their connections to medicinal, religious, or other socio-cultural events (Ipara et al. 2005, 650).
25 *Spyrostachys africana.*
26 Similarly, the *kichipichipi* tree (*Erythrina abyssinica*), that Alan Merriam noted was the highly valued source for making drums among the Bala in the Democratic Republic of the Congo, continues to be used in central and east Africa for drums and harps, but it has also been used for medicinal purposes. In Kenya communities conserve this tree due to its sacred status. Today in western Uganda it is one of the key plants used to treat HIV/AIDS patients (Tabuti et al. 2010).

self, 'People have already been moved in other places and they are afraid that the same will happen here.'

Linking sounds and musical instruments

Blacking's field recordings include sounds from a wide range of musical instruments in South Africa, Zambia and Uganda. Recordings and notes on performances demonstrate his interest in repertoire, but instrument tunings and brief discussions about musical compositions and musical events are also preserved in recordings. His audio recordings of Nsenga music in 1961 show an ongoing interest in the *kalimba* lamellaphone, among other instruments.[27] Recordings include compositions and tunings for specific instruments. Fieldnotes offer drawings of the *kalimba* with other detailed descriptive information (see Figure 6.4). Blacking did publish an article using this research, but it draws from only some of the collected information now preserved in the archives (Blacking 1961). Blacking also notated and recorded tunings for Venda flutes. In the archives, recordings and fieldnotes are located in separate files and there is currently no link between information on sound and musical instruments used in a performance. Similarly, a group of flutes that Blacking collected, probably in the mid-1950s, is housed in the University of Western Australia archives. The flutes are unlabelled and are not linked to documentation of any kind. This makes it difficult to identify a potentially significant relationship between the object (instruments) and the references in Blacking's fieldnotes on the flutes.

Linking audio and descriptive information, including images and drawings, that address playing style, repertoire and other aspects of performance practice, connects an instrument to social life. It also indi-

---

27   It is important to note that Hugh Tracey had a particular interest in lamellaphones in Africa and completed instrument collections and research on the instrument-type, especially in southern regions of the continent. His son Andrew Tracey carried on his work and completed a number of publications on musical instruments, including one on African lamellaphone history, 'The original African mbira?' (Tracey 1972).

vidualises sound and provides agency for music, musician, maker and instrument by making clear connections between audio recordings and particular instruments by specific makers or performances by named musicians.

Collaborative documentation on musical instruments

When collecting musical instrument information is not the primary goal of a research expedition, instrument-related data is generally incomplete. In some cases, Blacking's notes on music and musical instruments are brief, providing valuable but fragmented pieces of information. During a short visit to Nabweyo near Namasale in Uganda in 1965 Blacking recorded Lango musicians Laban Okao and his son playing six tuned drums (*myel bul*) that Okao had carved himself (see Figure 6.5). In his notes, Blacking revealed that Okao learned the instrument-making craft from his older brother, who in turn had learned from his mother's brother. While Blacking did not specify the woods used, he did note that the double-headed drums were covered on the top with antelope skin and on the bottom with crocodile.[28] The drum songs (also called *myel bul*) accompany Lango *ikoce* dance events, especially around harvest time.

Scholars who have conducted more in-depth research on Lango music in Uganda have recorded information about this relatively rare drum-chime (Cooke 1999; Wachsmann 1965), although their documents offer little additional information on the instrument's construction.[29] Combining fragments of information from different ethnographers who may have gathered contextual information during the same period will inevitably offer more in-depth understanding of each instrument and its social scenes.

---

28   He also noted that a single-headed drum, *atimo*, was covered with monitor lizard skin.
29   The British Museum holds a set of drums attributed to the Lango people, collected in 1915. The accompanying annotations note that the drums were made of yago wood (*Kigelia africana*), known in English as the sausage tree (Acquisition number: Af1915,0309.4). The information is available online at http://www.britishmuseum.org/research.aspx.

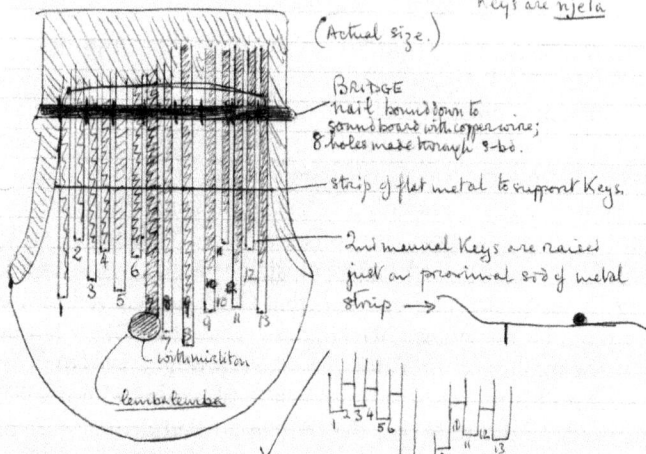

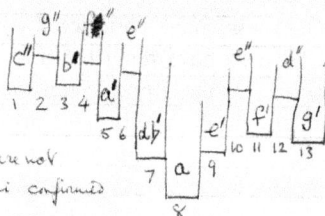

Figure 6.4 John Blacking's 1961 diary entry on a 13-note Nsenga *kalimba* found near Petauke, Zambia.

Figure 6.5 Laban Okao and his son play *myel bul* in Nabweyo, Uganda, 1965. Photo by John Blacking.

Conclusion: animating archives and museum collections, making connections

It is timely to consider how musical instrument data collected by ethnographers can be made more useful, especially to promote cultural and ecological sustainability in heritage communities, but also for scholarly research and education. Institutions and individuals housing musical instruments and their documentation have opportunities to share information more widely, effectively and creatively. This knowledge, now separated from source communities, once part of lively musical practices that were well integrated into the social, cultural, economic and ecological landscape, can become part of a contemporary discourse on musical instruments and their social lives. The instruments – their materials, playing styles, relationships to performers and to the landscape – are represented in archival images, diagrams, local stories, film clips, sounds and in the instruments themselves. Together they can contribute to an ongoing dialogue about music, sociality, and the physical environment within local communities, about instruments and social meaning and the complexity of materiality in our understanding of musical performance in scholarly realms. With histories in local environments, they tell tales about human and non-human entities and relationships, including the health of local economies and ecologies. For ethnomusicologists and musicologists who have embraced new organological approaches, musical instruments are not just objects to be measured and classified. Structurally and socially they are the result of decision making by individuals and social groups over time, reflecting social relationships in the workshop and performance spaces and representing social and economic patterns in production (Dawe 2011; Connor 2013). Instruments are also 'vibrant matter', things made of substances that respond to the environment independently, with lives as objects that have changed over time (Bennett 2010). They exhibit an association with their own materials, the people who make and play them, and the sounds that emerge from their strings, air columns, membranes and woods (Bates 2013; Roda 2013).

Some of the current scholarly ethnomusicological fieldwork that focuses on a musical instrument as a social and cultural entity, with materials that play multiple roles in communities, will ultimately be deposited in archives or museums. Making plans for managing this influx of new musical information is critical. The John Blacking Collection, and its links to makers and designs, repertoires and socio-ecological issues, demonstrates that even historical ethnographic material can be a resource for beginning a process of identifying key sources of information on musical instruments in our archives and developing strategies for making it more accessible. Cultural geographers Dwyer and Davies refer to 'animating' archives as a process of engaging with their 'material and documentary properties' through collaborative work, especially in creative collaborations between artists and material culture (Dwyer and Davies 2010, 89). This artistic action between objects and people that animates archival data can be applied to musical instruments and their documentation. An historical instrument without the musician that made or played it, and the community that supported it, is of limited use to scholarship or to the instrument. Musicians from a source community can still enliven it, though, and need to be given the opportunity to do so. Similarly, recorded data in connection with musical instrument study – the sounds, measurements, materials, tunings and structures, as well as beliefs and behaviours – can provide opportunities for source communities to connect with the musical information in their current lives, in their own way.

When local musicians and musical instrument makers work with archivists, curators and ethnomusicologists to develop models for information management and sharing, the proactive and collaborative archiving processes revitalise the collections even as they embrace the unique characteristics and needs identified with musical instrument practices (Landau and Fargion 2012; Vallier 2010). Creatively constructed community-driven knowledge management, shared digitally (Srinivasan 2004) or face-to-face (Lobley 2011), offers opportunities for scholars, archivists and source communities to benefit during the process. In 2007 and 2008, Lobley explored animation of sound archives connected to Hugh Tracey's work in Africa, especially to consider the long-term value of archived sound recordings and how they can benefit the local communities they were drawn from. Taking the sounds to the communities and giving individuals and groups opportunities to establish their own ways of responding to and utilising the musical information offers new ideas for management, promotion and interpretation of audio data (Lobley 2011, 2012). In the same way, ethnographic materials tied to musical instruments, including sound files, but also drawings, diagrams, images, film footage and narrative information, involve local communities with rights to and interests in the materials held outside of their reach, and can be valuable sources for them as they (re)consider their own heritage.

Returning to Zeitlin and the plucked lute in China referenced at the beginning of this chapter, musical instruments offer opportunities for reconstructing histories and for contributing to a sense of continuity in relation to cultural and national identity, as tangible objects that embody knowledge, memory and 'ownership' of a practice that may no longer be in place, yet remains in the cultural memory of a community. Ethnographic process and the information that is gathered during fieldwork can offer in-depth knowledge that may be useful to researchers and source community members even long after the musical traditions represented have been supplanted by new ones. As Lobley shows so effectively, local community responses to archival data once caught up in colonialist institutions can be unexpected, and, within the same community, range from indifference to complete engagement (Lobley 2011). It is critical that archivists and others managing musical data provide opportunities for collaboration and creative animation of musical instruments and their documentation, currently hidden away in archives and museum collections.

Works cited

Ammann, Raymond (2012). *Sounds of Secrets: Field Notes on Ritual Music and Musical Instruments on the Islands of Vanuatu.* Berlin: LIT Verlag.

Baily, John (1976). 'Recent changes in the dutār of Herat.' *Asian Music* 8(1): 29–64.

Baily, John (2006). 'John Blacking and the "Human/Musical Instrument Interface": Two plucked lutes from Afghanistan.' In *The Musical Human: Rethinking John Blacking's Ethnomusicology in the Twenty-First Century,* edited by Suzel Ana Reily, 107–23. Aldershot: Ashgate.

Bates, Eliot (2012). 'The social life of musical instruments.' *Ethnomusicology* 56(3): 363–95.

Bennett, Jane (2010). *Vibrant Matter: A Political Ecology of Things.* Durham: Duke University Press.

Berliner, Paul (1978). *The Soul of Mbira: Music and Traditions of the Shona People of Zimbabwe.* Chicago: University of Chicago Press.

Blacking, John (1961). 'Nsenga kalimba music.' *African Music* 2(4): 26–43.

Blacking, John (1962). 'Musical expeditions of the Venda.' *African Music* 3(1): 54–78.

Blacking, John (1964). *Black Background: The Childhood of a South African Girl.* New York: Abelard-Schuman.

Blacking, John (1973). *How Musical Is Man?* Seattle: University of Washington Press.

Blacking, John (1967). *Venda Children's Songs: A Study in Ethnomusicological Analysis.* Johannesburg: Witwatersrand University Press.

Byron, Reginald (1995). *Music, Culture and Experience: Selected Papers of John Blacking.* Chicago: University of Chicago Press.

Connor, Will (2013). 'The role of the instrument maker in popular music studies.' Blog. *Ethnomusicology Review.* http://tiny.cc/2013-connor-music.

Cooke, Peter (1999). 'Fieldwork in Lango, Northern Uganda, Feb–Mar 1997.' *African Music* 7(4): 66–72.

Dawe, Kevin (2001). 'People, objects, meaning: Recent work on the study and collection of musical instruments.' *Galpin Society Journal* 54: 219–32.

Dawe, Kevin (2007). *Music and Musicians in Crete: Performance and Ethnography in a Mediterranean Island Society*. Lanham: Scarecrow.

Dawe, Kevin (2011). 'The cultural study of musical instruments.' In *The Cultural Study of Music: A Critical Introduction*, 2nd ed, edited by Martin Clayton, Trevor Herbert, and Richard Middleton, 195–205. New York: Routledge Press.

Dawe, Kevin (2013). 'Guitar ethnographies: performance, technology and material culture.' *Ethnomusicology Forum* 22(1): 1–25.

DeVale, Sue Carole (1990). 'Organising organology.' *Selected Reports in Ethnomusicology* 8: 1–34.

DjeDje, Jacqueline (2008). *Fiddling in West Africa: Touching the Spirit in Fulbe, Hausa, and Dagbamba Cultures*. Bloomington: University of Indiana Press.

Dournon, Geneviève (2000). *Handbook for the Collection of Traditional Musical Instruments*, 2nd edition revised and enlarged. Paris: UNESCO.

Dwyer, Claire and Gail Davies (2010). 'Qualitative methods III: Animating archives, artful interventions and online environments.' *Progress in Human Geography* 34(1): 88–97.

Fozi, Navid (2007). 'The hallowed summoning of tradition: Body techniques in construction of the sacred tanbur of western Iran.' *Anthropological Quarterly* 80(1): 173–205.

Ipara, Hellen I., Joshua J. Akonga, John S. Akama (2005). 'The Tenure factor in wildlife conservation.' *International Journal of Environmental Studies* 64(6). 643–53.

Kartomi, Margaret (1990). *On Concepts and Classifications of Musical Instruments*. Chicago: University of Chicago Press.

Kartomi, Margaret (2005). 'On metaphor and analogy in the concepts and classification of musical instruments in Aceh.' *Yearbook for Traditional Music* 37: 25–57.

Kruger, Jaco (2007). 'Singing psalms with owls: A Venda 20th century musical history part two: Tshikona, beer songs and personal songs.' *African Music* 8(1): 36–59.

Lamorde, Mohammed, John R.S. Tabutic, Celestino Obuad, Collins Kukunda-Byobonae, Hindam Lanyerod, Pauline Byakika-Kibwikaa, Godfrey S. Bbosa, et al. (2010). 'Medicinal plants used by traditional medicine practitioners for the treatment of HIV/AIDS and related conditions in Uganda.' *Journal of Ethnopharmacology* 130(1): 43–53.

Landau, Carolyn and Janet Topp Fargion (2012). 'We're all archivists now: Towards a more equitable ethnomusicology.' *Ethnomusicology Forum* 21(2): 125–40.

Lobley, Noel (2011). 'Recording the vitamins of African music.' *History and Anthropology* 22(4): 415–29.

Lobley, Noel (2012). 'Taking Xhosa music out of the fridge and into the townships.' *Ethnomusicology Forum* 21(2): 181–95.

Merriam, Alan (1969). 'The ethnographic experience: Drum-making among the Bala (Basongye).' *Ethnomusicology* 13: 71–100.

Mugovhani, Ndwamato George (2009). 'Mbilamutondo music and instruments in Venda culture.' *South African Journal of Arts and Humanities* 24(3): 45–54.

Nercessian, Andy (2000). *The Duduk and Armenian National Identity.* Lanham: Scarecrow Press.

Qureshi, Regula (2000). 'How does music mean? Embodied memories and the politics of affect in the Indian sarangi.' *American Ethnologist* 27(4): 805–38.

Qureshi, Regula (1997). 'The Indian sarangi: Sound of affect, site of contest.' *Yearbook for Traditional Music* 29: 1–38.

Racy, Ali Jihad (1994). 'A dialectical perspective on musical instruments: The East-Mediterranean mijwiz.' *Ethnomusicology* 38(1): 37–57.

Reynolds, Barrie (1968). *The Material Culture of the Peoples of the Gwembe Valley.* Manchester: The University of Manchester Press.

Roda, Allen (2012). 'Local makers, global players: Tabla design and construction in an international marketplace.' Paper presented at the Annual Meeting of the Society for Ethnomusicology, New Orleans, 1–4 November. http://allenroda.com/conference-papers.

Roda, Allen (2013). 'What tablas do: An exploration of non-human agency and human relations in banaras or why tabla makers worry about the weather.' Paper presented at the Annual Meeting of the Society for Ethnomusicology, Indianapolis, 14–17 November. http://allenroda.com/conference-papers/what-tablas-do.

Roda, Allen (2014). 'Tabla tuning on the workshop stage: Toward a materialist musical ethnography.' *Ethnomusicology Forum* 59(2): 315–36. doi:10.1080/17411912.2014.919871.

Shackleton, Charlie M., Sheona E. Shackleton and Ben Cousins (2001). 'The role of land-based strategies in rural livelihoods: The contribution of arable production, animal husbandry and natural resource harvesting in communal areas in South Africa.' *Development Southern Africa* 18(5): 581–604.

Shackleton, Sheona E. (2005). 'Bowls, spoons, and other useful items: The kiaat woodcrafters of Bushbuckridge, South Africa.' In *Carving Out a Future: Planning for Woodcarving in the 21st Century,* edited by Bruce Campbell et al., 81–102. London: Earthscan.

Srinivasan, Ramesh (2004). 'Knowledge architectures for cultural narratives.' *Journal of Knowledge Management* 8(4): 65–74.

Stobart, Henry (2008). 'In touch with the earth? Musical instruments, gender and fertility in the Bolivian Andes.' *Ethnomusicology* Forum 17(1): 67–94.

Tracey, Andrew (1972). 'The original African mbira?' *African Music* 5(2): 85–104.

Vallier, John (2010). 'Sound archiving close to home: Why community partnerships matter.' *Notes* 67(1): 39–49.

Wachsmann, Klaus (1965). 'Some speculations concerning a drum chime in Buganda.' *Man* 65: 1–8.

Zeitlin, Judith (2009). 'The cultural biography of a musical instrument: Little Hulei as sounding object, antique, prop, and relic.' *Harvard Journal of Asiatic Studies* 69(2): 395–441.

Part 3
Communities and the archive

7

Repatriating childhood: issues in the ethical return of Venda children's musical materials from the archival collection of John Blacking

Andrea Emberly

In ethnomusicological research, children are often conceptualised as the next generation of culture bearers who must be entrusted with valuable cultural materials to be sustained into the future. This conception, whether from cultural insiders, invested outsiders, or those in-between, often positions childhood as a place for re-embedding so-called 'endangered musical traditions'. Understanding children as the next generation of culture bearers informs the ways we approach the research process surrounding the documentation, archiving, and repatriation of musical cultures.

Although archival practices and collections may sometimes seem somewhat irrelevant when presented to children, it is important to consider issues that impact children in terms of repatriation of musical materials. Through collaborative research with children and young people, we can examine best archival practices and the ethics and values of the repatriation of collections that may hold meaning for children and young people. This paper will explore some of the issues that surround

Emberly, Andrea (2015). 'Repatriating childhood: issues in the ethical return of Venda children's musical materials from the archival collection of John Blacking'. In *Research, Records and Responsibility: Ten Years of PARADISEC*, edited by Amanda Harris, Nick Thieberger and Linda Barwick. Sydney: Sydney University Press.

exhibiting and repatriating materials from John Blacking's historic research with children and young people in Venda communities from
1956 to 1958. Significant shifts in methodological approaches to research with children have framed how the repatriation of Blacking's
work highlights issues particular to working with children and young
people.

Research with children and young people

There have been few comprehensive ethnomusicological studies of children's musical cultures and perhaps even fewer discussions of the vested
and active interest children have in the sustainment and perpetuation
of their musical traditions (see Emberly 2004, 2009, 2013; Minks 2002;
Wiggins and Campbell 2013 for some examples). Moreover, a movement to engage children in the research process raises issues of intellectual property, informed consent, accessibility and ownership. In
addition, given the 1989 UNCRC (United Nations Convention on the
Rights of the Child) definition of a child as anyone under the age of
18, most Institutional Human Ethics Review boards mandate that any
research with children is considered high risk – making it challenging for researchers to obtain ethical clearance for research that engages
children directly in the research process. Therefore, conducting ethnomusicological research with children and young people requires a
delicate balance that considers the unique ethical issues of working with
children and the need for further research *with* children rather than research *on* and *about* children and young people.

At present, researchers who work with children are faced with
complex ethical issues to consider, including: questions of consent from
children; children's ability to understand the long-term ramifications
of documenting music including video and audio recordings; issues
of children being documented at significant (and perhaps vulnerable)
events in their lives where music is central such as during initiation
ceremonies; issues surrounding children driving the research decisions
and conducting research with other children in terms of snowballing
consent, particularly when the researcher is not present; and issues of
positionality and cultural understandings of the adult–child dichotomy.

Figure 7.1 Young boys using video cameras to film each other making music videos, Tshakhuma village, Limpopo, South Africa, 2012.

These ethical considerations challenge researchers to consider children's participation in the research process and how to shift away from tokenistic representations of children to informed, child-directed and child-initiated research participation, while balancing issues of consent, access and dissemination (see, for example, Alderson and Morrow 2011; Greig 2013).

With most children eager to engage in technology in terms of video recording, photography, music editing and audio recording, it has rarely been problematic to engage children in the physical practice of collecting and, to some extent, analysing materials. In South Africa in particular, over the course of my own research with Venda communities in the last ten years, children have become engaged in my research and in the process of 'doing' the research themselves. When children are asked to document and analyse the role of music in their own lives, they become an integral part of the research process – as filmmakers, collaborators, and investigators. As such, it is important to understand how documenting, archiving, and in this instance repatriating, sits within this movement of engaging children and young people in the research process. This raises significant questions in terms of ethics, methodologies and long-term goals that will be discussed through a case study of the John Blacking archival materials.

John Blacking and Venda materials

From 1956 to 1958, anthropologist John Blacking conducted ethnographic research with Venda communities in Limpopo, South Africa. His archival collection and publications from this research period are comprised of audio and video recordings, photographs, song transcriptions and analysis, and detailed field notes (see, for example, Blacking 1964, 1967, 1973, 1980, 1988). Blacking focused on Venda children's songs and on girls' initiation ceremonies in particular, including the great *Domba* – a year-long ceremony that is the final stage for young women before marriage (Blacking 1969, 1980). After teaching for several years at the University of the Witwatersrand, Blacking left South Africa in 1969 and took a post at Queen's University, Belfast, where he stayed until his death in 1990.

After Blacking's death his widow, Zureena Desai, donated selected materials from his home office to the Callaway Centre at the University

South African Provinces

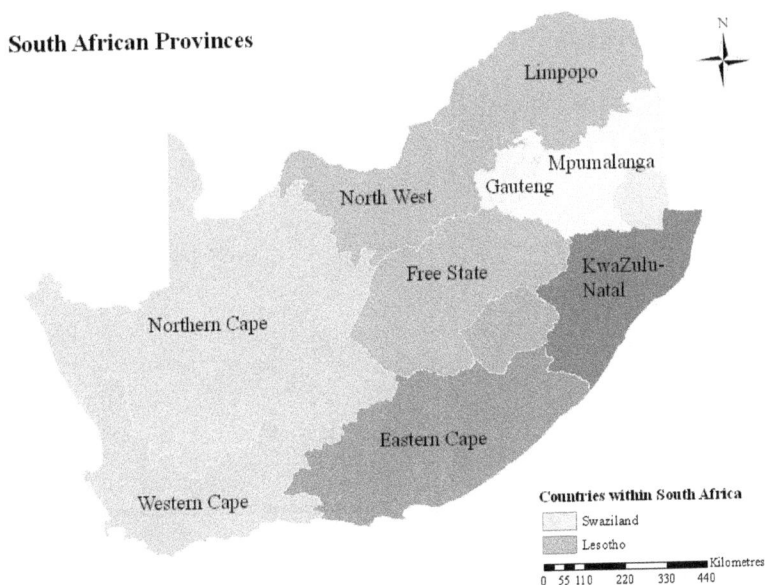

Figure 7.2 Map of South African provinces.

of Western Australia (UWA). The materials remained untouched until a limited selection of materials was digitised in 2003. In 2007 the remaining 16 boxes were officially unpacked, processed and shelved in the Callaway Centre (see also Post, this volume). The collection is comprised of print, sound and image with a mix of ethnographic materials from across the African continent and beyond, including limited recordings from personal and work travel. This collection raises issues surrounding archival recordings as outlined by Lobley and Jirotka (2011) who note that 'archival sounds have often travelled far from the areas where they originate, retaining no ongoing connection with their source community'. This is the case with the materials in the Callaway Centre, which have travelled far from Limpopo and have held no connection with their source community. This provokes the question, 'What purpose do archives serve?' (Seeger and Chaudhuri 2004; Lobley and Jirotka 2011).

Limpopo Districts

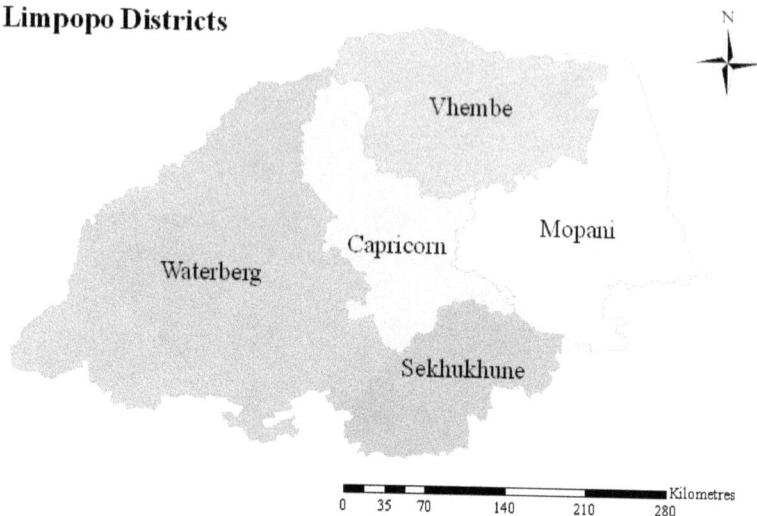

Figure 7.3 Map of Limpopo districts. Blacking conducted his research with Venda communities in what is now Limpopo province and the Vhembe district.

What purpose does the Blacking Collection held at the Callaway Centre serve and how might we consider issues of connection to source community that might further enrich the collection and contribute to its ongoing relevance? Questions posed by Nannyonga and Weintraub (2012, 224) in their Music of Uganda Repatriation Project are extremely relevant in this context, for example: 'Where is knowledge located? Where can music of the past be experienced? Whose interests are served by repatriation?' These questions are central to examining issues surrounding childhood and the repatriation of the Blacking Collection. Although it is apparent that there is no single answer to these questions, there are a number of possibilities to consider in relation to this rich collection. These considerations will be discussed below with regard to collaboration with Venda communities and connection between historical representations of children in the Blacking Collection and contemporary cultures of Venda childhood.

In addition to the Blacking Collection housed at the Callaway Centre Archives, a second collection of Blacking's materials, comprised of the contents of his work office, is housed at Queen's University, Belfast. Although there has been limited discussion between the two institutions who house the collections, there has been no significant analysis of the contents of both collections, although crossover and duplication between the two is apparent as well as incongruities. What is relevant for this discussion is that neither collection is available for general access and there has been little or no access to materials by the communities of origin. Although a review of Blacking's film *Domba* notes that the film was reviewed in Thohoyandou in 2000 (Farigon 2002), beyond this undocumented viewing there has been no significant access to Blacking's original materials by Venda communities.

Blacking and the Callaway Centre, UWA

Since 2009, a team of researchers at UWA has been exploring issues surrounding international collaboration, ethnomusicological archiving practices and frameworks for repatriating selections of the Blacking materials, particularly with regard to the Venda materials (Treloyn and Emberly 2013). One of the outcomes of this collaboration was the curation of a Blacking exhibition – *Music, Dance, Landscape, Image* – which was exhibited at the Lawrence Wilson Art Gallery at UWA in 2013 and included images, sound and video from the Blacking Collection from across the African continent, coupled with Venda instruments and objects from my own research. The next step of this process is an exhibition in Venda communities in Limpopo, where an expanded exhibition will focus solely on Venda materials and will be on display at the University of Venda from July 2014. The exhibition at the University of Venda will be on display in the University Art Gallery which is located in Thohoyandou, a large town in the Vhembe district[1] and an area that connects several of the primary areas where Blacking worked. Through collaboration with the University of Venda Library, Thohoyandou was chosen as a location that was relevant to

---

1 Thohoyandou was the former capital of the Bantustan of Venda.

communities and a place that has central community access. In this way the university functions as a connection between archival materials and community, much in the vein of Du Bois's famous quote:

> The function of the university is not simply to teach bread-winning, or to furnish teachers for the public schools or to be a centre of polite society; it is, above all, to be the organ of that fine adjustment between real life and the growing knowledge of life. (Du Bois 1903, 61)

An additional reason for basing the exhibition at the University of Venda is the late Professor Victor Ralushai (professor emeritus at the University of Venda School of Human and Social Sciences and former vice-chancellor), who was Blacking's primary research assistant and colleague. Ralushai received his PhD in social anthropology from Queen's University, Belfast, under the direction of Blacking, and his ongoing work with Blacking is evidenced throughout the collection. Blacking also referenced his work with Ralushai throughout his publications, in particular Ralushai's work for Blacking's book *Venda Children's Songs*. Therefore, the University of Venda is both a location that is historically relevant and accessible to Venda communities, and an institution that supports the connection between community and materials.[2]

Representations of Venda childhoods

Although limited materials from the Blacking Collection at UWA will be on display in Venda communities (primarily photos, coupled with some sound and video), the curation process is complicated given the subject focus of Blacking's work – children – and a dramatic shift in the ways in which researchers approach research with children and young people today. It is widely recognised at present that research with children and young people must acknowledge children's rights, includ-

---

2   It is recognised that the University of Venda does have access limitations, which are discussed later in this chapter.

ing the right to participate in research and the right to an informed approach that includes archiving documented materials (see, for example, Christensen 2004; Lundy and McEvoy 2011). These rights also include the right to 'have a say about things that concern them' (Thomson 2008, 1), which, in the case of repatriating materials surrounding children and childhood, could mean both the rights of those children and young people documented in the materials and the rights of access of children and young people in contemporary Venda communities. As Christensen argues:

> The recognition of children's social agency and active participation in research has significantly changed children's position within human and social sciences and led to a weakening of taken-for-granted assumptions found in more conventional approaches to child research. In order to hear the voices of children in the representation of their own lives it is important to employ research practices such as reflexivity and dialogue. These enable researchers to enter into children's cultures of communication. (Christensen 2004, 165)

Theoretical and methodological changes in research impact the way we view Blacking's materials, but they also impact the ways in which we conceive of and unfold repatriation processes. While this exhibition is a first step in sharing materials from the Blacking Collection with communities of origin, we recognise that access is limited. The University of Venda is a gated institution (as are all institutions in South Africa), meaning that in order to view the collection a person must have a reason to enter the campus and pass through security. As Seeger (2005) points out, the history of the institution may continue to limit access for communities. In addition, the university campus is not typically a place for children and young people, which further limits the benefits of materials focused on children and youth. However, hosting materials from the collection at the University of Venda offers benefits that outweigh issues of limited access, including a safe and secure point of access for community members, as well as access for a large number of young scholars.

The issue of community access to materials is complex and, as Lobley outlines, even materials held at the International Library of

African Music in Grahamstown, South Africa, have 'failed to reach local communities' (Lobley 2012, 182) for many reasons including lack of information about the existence of collections, limited accessibility, and issues of ownership. Access is further complicated by a division of knowledge and access due to the legacy of apartheid. Seeger poses the questions: 'What are the roles of archives in countries that have suffered the kinds of conflict and division created by Apartheid in South Africa? What does it mean for people who could not even enter the door of archives under previous regimes to be able to walk in, read the documents and listen to the voices of both their oppressors and their own people?' (Seeger 2004, 95). Although the Blacking materials have not been deposited in an archive accessible to most people, the materials and the legacy of those materials evoke similar questions raised by Lobley and Seeger. Further complicating access to materials is the role of outsiders – in this case, an ethnomusicologist working as a cultural broker 'between the archive and the relevant heritage community' (Landau and Farigon 2012, 136). In addition to connecting and collaborating with adults, this brokering is unique when working with children and young people as it adds another layer between adults and children. The materials in the Blacking Collection represent Venda childhood in a specific time and place, in the lives of specific people and in specific Venda communities. As such, repatriating childhood is a means both to share records of historical childhoods and to present materials for children and young people today interested in the sustainment of Venda musical arts.

Although many scholars have discussed frameworks and issues surrounding repatriation and the complexities of these processes (see, for example, Lancefield's discussion of the 'changing conceptions of archives' social roles, responsibilities, and opportunities' (Lancefield 1998, 47)), there has been limited discussion focused on materials collected from children and young people. Although many of the issues that arise in this case study can be applied to repatriation of materials in general, discussion around consent and dissemination with regards to the Blacking Collection is particularly relevant due to the focus on children and young people.

As one of the most significant and comprehensive ethnomusicological collections of children's music, Blacking's recordings and scholarly writings tell us more than what we see on the screen and what we read on the page; they represent the quintessential way in which anthropologists and ethnomusicologists have treated the musical culture of childhood – not just in South Africa, but in an international context (Emberly 2004; Minks 2002). Visually and intellectually, Blacking's recordings and writings offer insight into the dynamic and power-based relationship between researchers and children. The researcher, posed in a dominant position with a camera pointed at children, highlights the methodologies that adults have relied on in studying childhood.

When examining and contextualising the Blacking materials, it is important to centralise one of the questions that frame shifting research methodologies in the growing field of childhood studies: 'What is an adult?' (Christensen 2004, 166). That is, what kind of adult is the researcher within the community? When we explore this question with regard to Blacking, we must acknowledge his position within the community at the time. Understanding his role underscores his positionality, which may have affected the collection of materials, and thus their meaning for children and young people today. Therefore, does his position impact the meaning of his materials for those represented in the collection? Furthermore, understanding Blacking's role and his methodologies for collecting research data from child participants leads to greater understanding of the materials produced and their usability for current communities. It is clear from Blacking's materials, his fieldnotes, and through recent discussions with community members that there was some disconnect between adult and child, between researcher and participant. For example, community members who were present at the time have noted that some of the dances recorded and documented were 'practice' dances, that is, because they were recorded during the daytime they are not actual representations of the 'real' dance that Blacking was aiming to record.

As our documentation methods shift, so does the relationship between researcher and participant. Working with children and young people requires additional ethical and methodological considerations. University human-subject review boards require additional documentation for conducting research with children, which, as mentioned previously, is always considered high risk regardless of research subject or

methodologies. As Claudia Mitchell outlines in her chapter aptly titled
'On a pedagogy of ethics in visual research: who's in the picture?':

> The legal and moral components, protection and awareness of the
> vulnerability of children and young people, and new issues in dis-
> semination as a result of social networking sites has made this area
> of ethics one that often seems like a minefield. And although 'doing
> least harm' and 'doing most good' must surely remain as the corner-
> stones of our work as researchers, these clearly are interpretive areas
> in and of themselves. (Mitchell 2011, 15)

Furthermore, while some researchers have attempted to conduct research with children by assuming the 'least adult role'[3] (see, for example, Holmes 1998; Mayall 2000), it is an approach that fails to recognise
or to problematise the social and cultural categories of adult and child
(Christensen 2004, 166). While adults conducting research with children cannot participate as full insiders, methodological approaches
may seek to lessen the divide between adult and child. However, these
approaches have been viewed as problematic given the immense power
differential between adult and child.

The context of Blacking's historical work, coupled with our current
collaborations, creates tension around issues of engagement and children's positionality in the research process. If the children and young
people in Blacking's collection failed to have agency, voice and rights
to informed participation, how does that impact the process of sharing
materials from the collection? In addition, how can we move forward
with collaborations that engage children and young people in the
process and that do not repeat historical processes of disenfranchising
children and young people? These questions underscore our current ex-

---

3 The 'least adult role' often means researchers attempt to enter the culture of
childhood by attempting to disregard their adult role. Blacking himself notes that
he often tried to learn music 'like a child' and would purposely sing songs
incorrectly to children to see when and how they corrected him. At present it is a
widely disregarded practice in the field of childhood studies because it is clear that,
while we may try to act un-adult-like, there is no way to shed the role of adult in
most contexts.

hibition process and will continue to shape the approach of repatriating or sharing materials collected from children and young people.

While this discussion is not intended to criticise Blacking's methodologies, which have roots in the colonial history of our discipline, it does highlight the vast shift in approaches to ethnomusicological research with a focus on children and young people. Differences between approaches in Blacking's time and the present offer insight into the changes in research with children and young people and potentials for creating lasting legacies of children's musical cultures with long-term community impact. While this is the ultimate goal for connecting communities to archival materials, the pitfalls that accompany this process are not overlooked. Researchers are urgently pushing for changes in approaches to working with children and young people;[4] however, the processes themselves are complex in university settings given the tendencies of human ethics review boards to fall on the side of child protection over child engagement. For this reason 'children themselves continue to find their voices silenced, suppressed, or ignored ... and even if they are consulted, their ideas may be dismissed' (James 2007, 261).

Repatriating Venda childhood

The children and young people recorded by Blacking have had no access to the materials collected – none of Blacking's books, films, or written materials have been made widely available in the primary communities in which he worked. In personal discussions with community members there has been repeated reference to the lack of access to any materials from Blacking's historic work, although some people are aware of its existence. Because limited photographic and recorded materials exist from this time period, there is vested interest in the per-

---

4 The movement to change the approaches to research with children and young people is being led by the field of children's and childhood studies, which began primarily in the UK and is currently gaining ground in North America. This field uses ethnographic, qualitative and child-centered approaches to research with children, with a focus on research engagement with children and young people.

sonal representations of childhood that are located in the collection (i.e., people may have no photos of living or deceased relatives who were recorded as children at the time). As such, sharing and collaborating around access to these materials provides access for those individuals represented and to the wider community, while facilitating historical documentation in communities of origin.

Perhaps most significantly, like all research at the time, written consent was not obtained for participation in Blacking's research. Concerns about the repatriation process include obtaining community consent, because individual consent for a collection of this size and age is impossible, given that most of the participants are now elderly, unidentifiable or deceased. However, recognising that materials on display may need to be adjusted due to changing concerns about consent is vital. Some of the materials contain sensitive recordings, photos and/or video and, before public display of these materials, a review by appropriate members of communities must consider the impact of dissemination. Repatriation of materials from the Blacking Collection may address some of these issues by providing access to the relevant materials for discussion and perhaps dissemination, dependent upon community decisions regarding materials.

If researchers have re-evaluated how to approach the study of childhood and youth, then the outcomes of this examination must be applied and considered in relation to repatriation and archival questions that concern materials collected from and by children and young people. One question for the Blacking materials is how to find creative ways to identify children and their families in recordings and photographs. One of the primary goals that has been identified by community members is access to historical photographs of individual people, given the general lack of photos from this period. For the larger prints on exhibition, decisions for display are based primarily on aesthetic choices to complement the theme of Blacking's collection of music, dance and community. In addition to the exhibition materials, large volumes of photos from the Blacking Collection will be shared throughout Venda communities as a means of generating further access to the collection. The volumes include over 1000 laminated images, primarily of children and young people, which people can write on directly (with erasable markers) in an attempt to gather information about photos in order to connect with the children (and perhaps their extended families) represented in the photographs.

These broad themes provide access points to the collection and will hopefully spark further interest in collaborating to provide access to all relevant materials for communities of origin. Because the focus of Blacking's work is children and youth, collaborating with Venda young people is central to considerations of repatriation given the current state of Venda music today, in which many genres of musical traditions are still strong.

Conclusion

What researchers working with children today ask is: can there actually be an anthropology of childhood? (Hardman 1973; Hirschfeld 2002) How do the limitations, methodologies and distinctive features of childhood distinguish themselves from adulthood and what impact does this have on the research process and in turn on the documentation and archival processes? (Lancy 2008; Mead and Wolfenstein 1955; Montgomery 2009) As scholars such as Vallier and Sekula note, 'archives are far from neutral', and protocols for documenting and creating metadata for research with children are less developed (Mitchell 2011, 118). Some questions that researchers might ask include: how can we anticipate what children will feel in the future with regard to documented representations of their lives, and how can we create non-static archival processes that might adapt mechanisms for coding, sharing and retrieving materials that underscore the complex process of documentation? (Mitchell 2011, 118-9) One question that is central to work in rural Venda communities is: what is the community desire to engage in this type of work given the limited access to technology, which is likely to be the source of both historical and current materials? (Mitchell 2011, 132). How might we explore potentials of community-based archives that work across collections, from Blacking's to present-day collections created by Venda young people, to build relevant access that meets the desires of different communities of people?

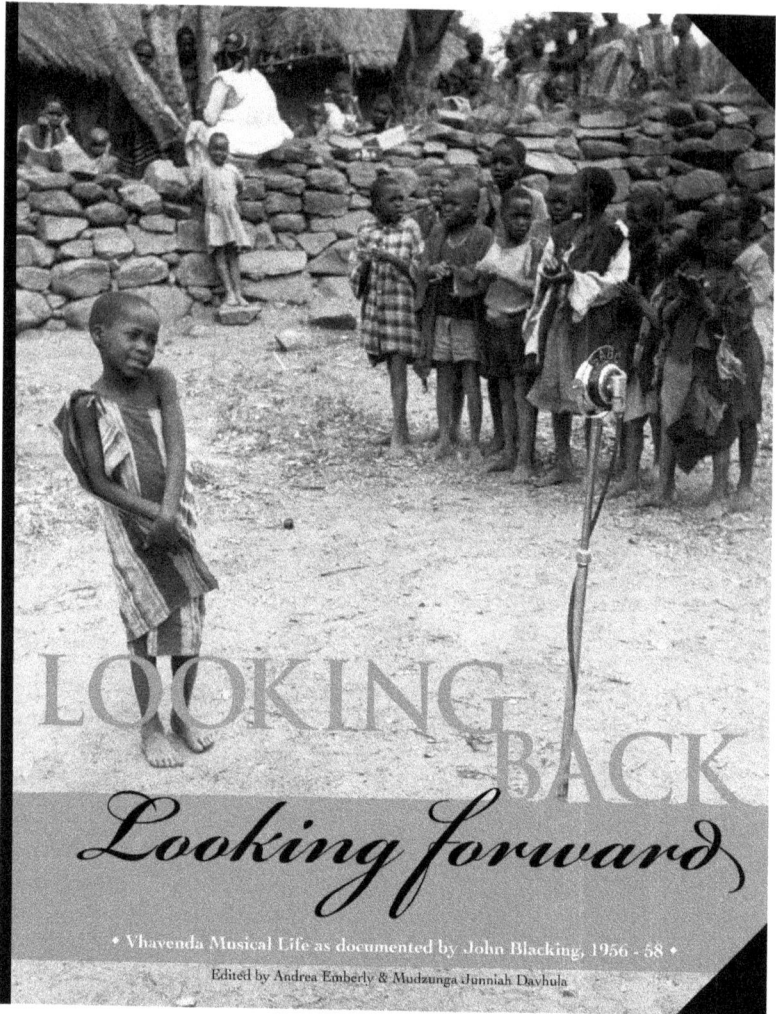

Figure 7.4 Blacking exhibition catalogue, 2014.

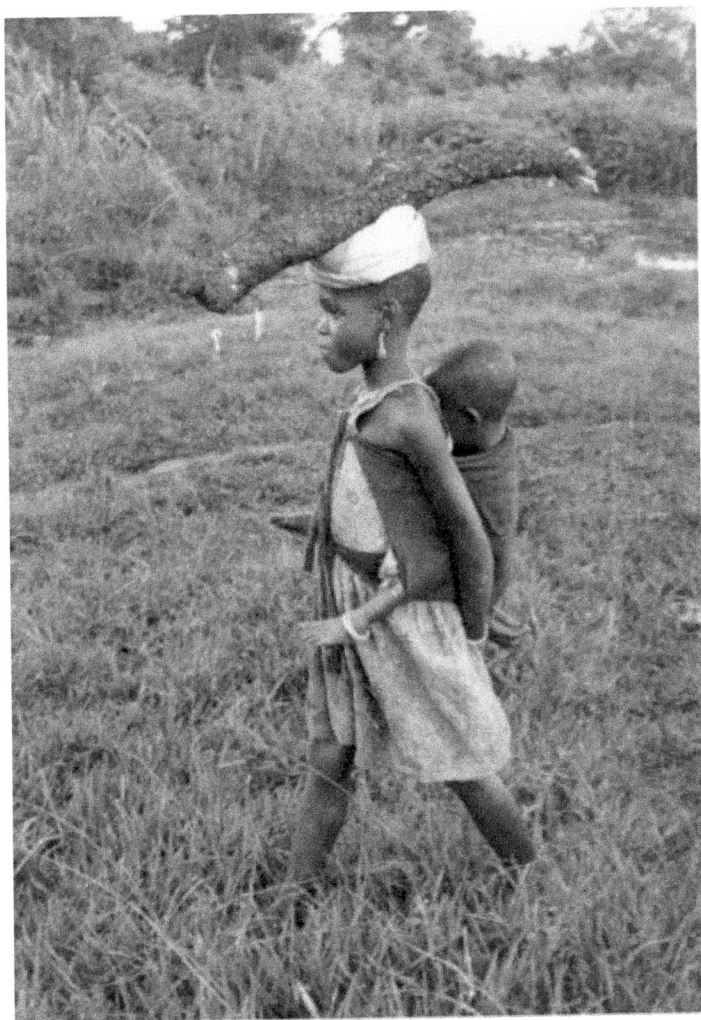

Figure 7.5 Example of a photograph from the Blacking Collection at the Callaway Centre, UWA. A young girl and a baby in a Venda community, names and place unknown. Photo by John Blacking.

Figure 7.6 Venda girls dancing *tshigombela*. Photo by John Blacking from the Blacking Collection, Callaway Centre, UWA.

There is a growing movement among activists and academics to encourage children to 'become active partners and participants in research conducted about them and among them' (Montgomery 2009, 47). By recognising that the culture of childhood can be examined from a unique viewpoint that engages children in the research process, the methodological and theoretical foci of research can benefit children, their local communities, researchers, the international academic community at large and beyond. Engaging in research poses several important questions such as: what is our relationship as ethnomusicologists with community collaborators in terms of audiovisual representation,

Figure 7.7 Venda girls dancing *tshigombela*, Arts and Culture Championship Competition, Maunavhathu Military Base, Limpopo, South Africa, 2009.

and can media be used for purposes such as social intervention? What are the collaborative and reflexive processes that can be used in the production of ethnographic knowledge? What are the ethics of research and documentation in terms of access, ownership and responsibility? In regards to children, these questions become even more significant as children stand to benefit both in terms of immediate skill building and through future engagement with a collection that documents their musical lives and upbringings.

By providing children with tools to represent their own musical lives, the goal, in fields such as childhood studies, is to present a more holistic view of children's musical worlds and to move away from the historical 'othering' of children and their musical communities. As such, access to the Blacking materials provides historical representations of endangered musical cultures; provides representations of children's lives in time and place; provides access to physical documents that are representative of the lives of individuals (who may or may not still be alive, whose families might recognise them, and who may have ideas about public access); provides the opportunity to explore how repatriating materials focused on childhood might have unique impact within Venda communities in terms of education and 'knowledge production' (Vallier 2010, 39); and can provide, as Lancefield suggests, 'help for people to extend their sonic knowledge back to the time of their great-grandparents or before' (Lancefield 1998, 59) or, in the case of the Venda, back to their own histories and those of their parents and grandparents.

At present, many Venda children's songs, such as those documented by Blacking, are in danger of being lost due to shifts in educational frameworks and shifts in children's responsibilities within communities. However, many genres have remained strong since Blacking's time and thus a dichotomy is represented in the Blacking Collection: both the sustainability of musical traditions and a 'quieting'[5] of them (Emberly and Davidson 2011; Emberly and Davhula in prep). Therefore, the Blacking Collection has additional positive value for children and young people, who are at the centre of community action to revive and sustain children's musical traditions. Additionally, contemporary research on Venda children's musical cultures may provide, similarly to Nannyonga and Weintraub's work on sound repatriation in Uganda, 'cultural critique about the work of ethnographic representation' (Nannyonga and Weintraub 2012, 221). And in the case of the Blacking Collection, this critique may centre on the ethnographic representations of children and childhood, thus supporting the notion that repatriation extends far beyond the 'mere return of objects to communities' (Nannyonga and Weintraub 2012, 225). Involving children and young people in the processes of repatriation and collaboration aims to, as Vallier states, 'cradle collections to make them more meaningful, relevant, and resilient' (Vallier 2010, 39).

---

5 A term used in TshiVenda, where the loss of musical tradition is simply referred to as a quieting of certain songs.

Figure 7.8 A young girl recording dancers in Tshakhuma, Limpopo, South Africa, 2012.

Postscript

The exhibition discussed in this article was opened at the University of Venda on July 15, 2014. The exhibition was titled *Looking Back, Looking Forward: Vhavenda Musical Life as Documented by John Blacking 1956–1958* and a catalogue was published by the International Library of African Music (ILAM). The exhibition was opened by the king of Venda with support from local chiefs, the chancellor of the University of Venda, and hundreds of local community members, including several women who were participants in John Blacking's original research. In addition, Professor Ralushai's widow and family members welcomed the collection, as did two of Blacking's children. Further discussions of this exhibition, outcomes, and the ongoing collaboration are forthcoming.

Works cited

Alderson, Priscillia and Virginia Morrow (2011). *The Ethics of Research with Children and Young People.* London: SAGE.

Blacking, John (1964). *Black Background: The Childhood of a South African Girl.* New York: Abelard-Schuman.

Blacking, John (1967). *Venda Children's Songs.* Johannesburg: Witwatersrand University Press.

Blacking, John (1969). 'Songs, dances, mimes and symbolism of Venda girls' initiation schools. Part 1: Vhusha.' *African Studies* 28(1): 3–36. doi: 10.1080/00020186908707300.

Blacking, John (1969). 'Songs, dances, mimes and symbolism of Venda girls' initiation schools. Part 2: Milayo.' *African Studies* 28(2): 69–118. doi: 10.1080/00020186908707306.

Blacking, John (1969). 'Songs, dances, mimes and symbolism of Venda girls' initiation schools. Part 3: Domba.' *African Studies* 28(3): 149–99. doi: 10.1080/00020186908707309.

Blacking, John (1969). 'Songs, dances, mimes and symbolism of Venda girls' initiation schools. Part 4: The great Domba song.' *African Studies* 28(4): 215–66. doi: 10.1080/00020186908707313.

Blacking, John (1973). *How Musical Is Man?* Seattle: University of Washington Press.

Blacking, John (1988). 'Dance and music in Venda children's cognitive development.' In *Acquiring Culture: Cross Cultural Studies in Child Development*, edited by Gustav Jahoda and Iaon M. Lewis, 91–112. London: Croom Helm.

Blacking, John, John Baily and Andrée Grau (1980). *Domba, 1956–1958: A Personal Record of Venda Initiation Rites, Songs and Dances.* Bloomington: Society for Ethnomusicology, 2001, VHS tape and study guide.

Christensen, Pia Haudrup (2004). 'Children's participation in ethnographic research: Issues of power and representation.' *Children and Society* 18: 165–76.

Du Bois, W.E. Burghardt (1903). *The Souls of Black Folk: Essays and Sketches.* Chicago: A.C. McClurg and Co.

Emberly, Andrea (2004). 'Exploring children's Musical culture in ethnomusicology.' Paper presented at the UNESCO Regional Meeting on Arts Education in the European Countries, Canada and the United States of America. Finland.

Emberly, Andrea (2009). 'Mandela went to China ... and India too: Musical cultures of childhood in South Africa.' PhD thesis, University of Washington, Seattle.

Emberly, Andrea (2013). 'Venda children's musical cultures in Limpopo, South Africa.' In *The Oxford Handbook of Children's Musical Cultures*, edited by Trevor Wiggins and Patricia Campbell, 77–95. Oxford: Oxford University Press.

Emberly, Andrea and Jane Davidson (2011). 'From the kraal to the classroom: Shifting musical arts practices from the community to the school with special reference to learning *tshigombela* in Limpopo, South Africa.' *International Journal of Music Education* 29(3): 265–81.

Emberly, Andrea and Mudzunga Junniah Davhula (2015). 'Learning to be musical in Limpopo: Venda children's musical cultures.' (unpublished manuscript).

Greig, Anne (2013). *Doing Research with Children: A Practical Guide*, 3rd edition. London: SAGE.

Hardman, Charlotte (1973). 'Can there be an anthropology of children?' *Journal of the Anthropological Society of Oxford* 4(2): 85–99. Reprinted in 2002, *Childhood* 8(4): 501–17.

Hirschfeld, Lawrence A. (2002). 'Why don't anthropologists like children?' *American Anthropologist* 104(2): 611–27.

Holmes, Robyn M. (1998). *Fieldwork with Children*. London: SAGE.

James, Allison (2007). 'Giving voice to children's voices: Practices and problems, pitfalls and potentials.' *American Anthropologist* 109(2): 261–72.

Lancefield, Robert (1998). 'Musical traces' retraceable paths: The repatriation of recorded sound.' *Journal of Folklore Research* 35: 47–68. http://www.jstor.org/stable/3814785.

Lancy, David F. (2008). *The Anthropology of Childhood: Cherubs, Chattel, Changelings*. Cambridge: Cambridge University Press.

Landau, Carolyn, and Janet Topp Fargion (2012). 'We're all archivists now: Towards a more equitable ethnomusicology.' *Ethnomusicology Forum* 21(2): 125–40.

Lobley, Noel (2012). 'Taking Xhosa music out of the fridge and into the townships.' *Ethnomusicology Forum* 21(2): 181–95.

Lobley, Noel and Marina Jirotka (2011). 'Innovations in sound archiving: Field recordings, audiences and digital inclusion.' Paper presented at Digital Engagement Conference, Newcastle, UK, 15–17 November. http://tiny.cc/2011-lobleyjirotka.

Lundy, Laura and Lesley McEvoy (2011). 'Children's rights and research processes: Assisting children to (in)formed views.' *Childhood* 19(1): 129–44.

Mayall, Berry (2000). 'Conversations with children: Working with generational issues.' In *Research with Children: Perspectives and Practices*, edited by Pia Monrad Christensen and Allison James. London: Falmer Press.

Mead, Margaret and Martha Wolfenstein, eds. (1955). *Childhood in Contemporary Cultures*. Chicago: University of Chicago Press.

Mitchell, Claudia (2011). *Doing Visual Research*. London: SAGE.

Minks, Amanda (2002). 'From children's song to expressive practices: Old and new directions in the ethnomusicological study of children.' *Ethnomusicology* 46(3): 379–408.

Montgomery, Heather and Mary Kellett (2009). *Children and Young People's Worlds: Developing Frameworks for Integrated Practice*. Bristol: Policy Press.

Nannyonga, Sylvia and Andrew Weintraub (2012). 'The audible future: Reimagining the role of sound archives and sound repatriation in Uganda.' *Ethnomusicology* 56(2): 206–33.

Seeger, Anthony (2004). 'New technology requires new collaborations: Changing ourselves to better shape the future.' *Musicology Australia* 27(1): 94–110.

Seeger, Anthony (2005). 'Who got left out of the property grab again: Oral traditions, Indigenous rights, and valuable old knowledge.' In *CODE: Collaborative Ownership and the Digital Economy*, edited by Rishab Aiyer Ghosh, 75–84. Cambridge: MIT Press.

Seeger, Anthony and Shubha Chaudhuri (2004). *Archives for the Future: Global Perspectives on Audiovisual Archives in the 21st Century*. India: Seagull Books.

Thomson, Pat (2008). *Doing Visual Research with Children and Young People*. London: Routledge.

Topp Fargion, Janet (2002). Review of *Domba 1956–1958. A Personal Record of Venda Initiation Rites, Songs and Dances* by John Blacking; John Baily and Andrée Grau. *British Journal of Ethnomusicology* 11(2): 149–50.

Treloyn, Sally and Andrea Emberly (2013). 'Sustaining traditions, collections, access and sustainability in Australia.' *Musicology Australia* 35(2): 1–19.

Vallier, John (2010). 'Sound archiving close to home: Why community partnerships matter.' *Notes* 67: 39–49.

Wiggins, Trevor and Patricia Campbell, eds. (2013). *The Oxford Handbook of Children's Musical Cultures*. Oxford: Oxford University Press.

8
Repatriation and innovation in and out of the field: the impact of legacy recordings on endangered dance-song traditions and ethnomusicological research

Sally Treloyn and Rona Googninda Charles

In 1974 anthropologist Hilton Deakin reported an early example of innovation in the media and modes by which songs were transmitted from person to person in the Kimberley. He described the arrival of a trade package containing a cassette tape of Balga song recordings in the northern Kimberley community of Kalumburu (Deakin 1978). While it is not now known what repertory or repertories of Balga (a genre of dance-song indigenous to Kimberley also known as Junba) this cassette carried, it is clear that the repertory/ies arrived in Kalumburu according to principles of Wurnan – the customary Law and ethos of sharing that underpins the distribution of resources and knowledges throughout the Kimberley. Cultural heritage stakeholders – such as the Wurnan bosses and songmen and women of Kalumburu at the time – established a path for their communities to use new song technologies to learn and teach songs, a pathway that researchers have only in relatively recent times followed. Over the last decade, ethnomusicologists have increasingly become preoccupied with the repatriation of records

Treloyn, Sally and Rona Googninda Charles (2015). 'Repatriation and innovation in and out of the field: the impact of legacy recordings on endangered dance-song traditions and ethnomusicological research'. In *Research, Records and Responsibility: Ten Years of PARADISEC*, edited by Amanda Harris, Nick Thieberger and Linda Barwick. Sydney: Sydney University Press.

of songs and dances to communities of origin for a range of reasons that have been summarised elsewhere (see Treloyn and Emberly 2013; Treloyn, Charles and Nulgit 2013). In Australia, the return and dissemination of audio and video recordings from archival and personal collections to cultural heritage communities has emerged as a primary, and almost ubiquitous, fieldwork method.

Elsewhere, we have provided data that tentatively points towards increases in the quantity and diversity of unique Junba dance-songs and repertories that are performed at unelicited[1] public festivals in the Mowanjum Aboriginal Community in the western Kimberley (see Treloyn, Charles and Nulgit 2013). We suggest that this stimulation of the tradition corresponds to community-led engagement with repatriation and dissemination of legacy records of Junba. In this paper, we provide additional data on the past and present state of the Junba tradition in order to provide further context for and to advance our previous findings. We consider the contexts and ways in which cultural heritage stakeholders across generations use archival and new materials to have an impact upon endangered song traditions, and also consider ways in which the returning materials and community-led dissemination of these materials may continue to influence and innovate fieldwork and research.

Junba legacies

Junba (also known as Balga, Jorrogorl and Jadmi) is one of Australia's richest and oldest performance traditions. Indigenous to almost all of the 30 language groups of the Kimberley region, Junba has been a primary mode of intercultural, interfamily and interpersonal communication since the genre was created by Wanjina ancestors in the *Lalarn* or *Lalai* ('Dreaming', Ungarinyin and Worrorra languages respectively). Junba is a public dance-song genre that is performed during public

---

1   Unelicited performances are here defined as those in which the selection and order of songs is determined by performers and members of the cultural heritage community, rather than by an outside researcher, as may occur in an elicited song documentation session. These performances are also typically danced.

gatherings, in which linguistically and culturally distinct groups come together, with clearly defined roles for insiders and visiting groups. Junba dance-songs and repertories are conceived in dreams by men and women, when an *anguma, agula* or *juwarri* spirit visits a living family member and takes her/him on a journey over the landscape and through history, showing and demonstrating dance-songs and important events. Repertories document and enact the land- and Law-forming actions of Wanjina spirits and other ancestral beings, such as the moiety-heroes Wodoi and Jungun, the travels and activities of various other spirits, and historical and living people. The subjects of repertories and songs are diverse, ranging from songs that celebrate connections between living dancers, deceased family, and ancestral spirits, to Wanjina spirits (see Figure 8.1), to everyday activities such as fishing trips, to historical events such as slavery associated with Captain Cook (see Redmond 2008), Cyclone Tracy in 1974, and the appearance of Spitfire aeroplanes in the sky during World War Two. Today, the practice of Junba on Country and at public cultural events has great significance for the communities that own and maintain these songs and dance traditions, affecting social and emotional wellbeing, and articulating identity in relation to place, family and history (see Treloyn and Martin 2014).

This chapter is concerned with the Junba repertories and practices of communities of people who identify as Ngarinyin (Wilinggin), Wunambal and Worrorra residing in the Mowanjum Community and other communities along the Gibb River Road, which runs through the Kimberley from west to northeast. Members of the three groups join together in maintaining Law ceremonies, and hold, perform and share Junba repertories according to Wurnan. Each Junba repertory comprises approximately 20 to 40 distinct songs. Each song has a unique text that is performed isorhythmically and repeated cyclically, breaking and recommencing at structural melodic points (see Treloyn 2003). The text of a typical Junba song, mixing Ungarinyin and Worrorra languages, is set out in Figure 8.1. The translation and morphological analysis is provided by linguist Thomas Saunders.

Living memories of elder Ngarinyin, Wunambal and Worrorra residing in the town of Derby and the Community of Mowanjum in the western Kimberley, and further to the northeast in Imintji, Kupungarri

Text	*Wanalirri*	*wa*	*yamowul yamowul yamowul*
Gloss	Wanalirri [name of Wanjina spirit]	Ø [dummy syllable]	boggy ground Spoken form: yawul yawul [Ungarinyin language]

Figure 8.1 Wanalirri song from the Wanalirri Junba composed by Wati Ngerdu, circa 1960. Text transcription by Sally Treloyn with Pansy Nulgit. Analysis by Thomas Saunders.

and Dodnun Communities between 2000–02 and 2010–12 indicate a rich and prolific history of at least 35 Ngarinyin, Wunambal and Worrorra Junba composers through the 20th century, responsible for the composition of over 50 repertories of song. Of the 1500–2000 songs that would have made up these repertories at their peaks, over 500 unique songs have been recalled, performed and documented since 1997. Of these, fewer than 20 songs are regularly performed with dance today, attributed to the following composers:

- Sam Woolagoodya, whose Baler Shell corroboree is continued by his son Donny Woolagoodya;
- Wati Ngerdu, whose Wanalirri Junba repertory (see Figure 8.1) is performed at almost all major Ngarinyin cultural events; and
- Scotty Martin, whose Jadmi-type Junba repertory has recently been revived after a hiatus of several years following the passing of two of its prominent dancers.

While many factors guide which of the songs and distinct repertories come to be performed at a public event, it is evident from available recordings of unelicited public performances recorded between circa 1960 and 2012 that the number of repertories and songs performed at these events has decreased substantially. Figure 8.2 presents data from nine recordings of unelicited danced performances made by:

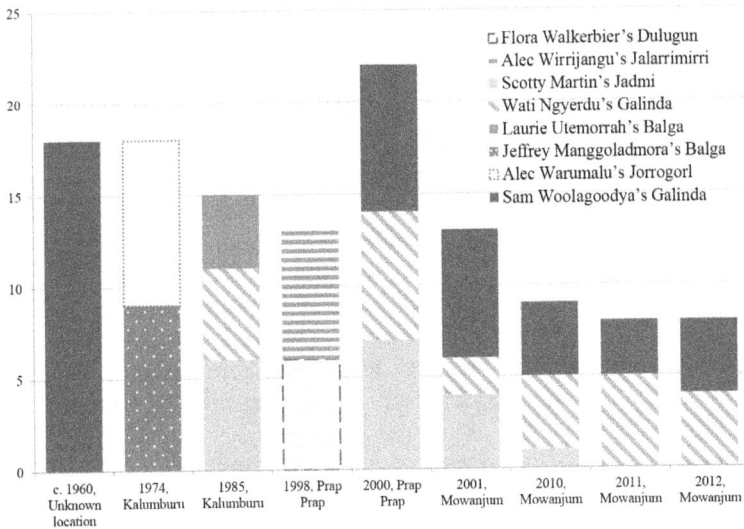

Figure 8.2 Number of unique songs by repertory performed at selected, unelicited, danced public events.

- An unknown recordist in Mowanjum or Bangarun circa 1960 (tape held by elder Mabel King (dec.) in 2001);
- Lesley Reilly (recorded in Kalumburu 1974);
- Ray Keogh (recorded in Kalumburu 1985);
- Linda Barwick (recorded in Prap Prap 1998); and
- Sally Treloyn (recorded in Prap Prap 2000, and Mowanjum in 2001, 2010, 2011, 2012).

Figure 8.2 indicates some attrition of the number of songs in common usage for such events, from 13 to 22 in the period circa 1960–2001, to eight or nine in the period 2010–12. It also indicates a reduction in the variety of repertories that are being performed, with some eight composers represented in the period between 1960 and 2001, and only three in the period 2010–12 (although this is partly due to the single location of data in later years). While Junba remains strong, this indicates some degree of endangerment.[2]

Communities and leading elder songmen and women, including Scotty Martin, his son Matthew Martin and Pansy Nulgit, along with emerging elders such as one of the co-authors of this paper, Rona Googninda Charles, have sought to address this endangerment through their engagement with researchers such as Treloyn and the Mowanjum Art and Culture Centre. Underpinning the urgency and importance of this task is the role that Junba practices play, as noted, in maintaining and achieving the wellbeing of Country, spirits and living ancestors: the wellbeing of individuals and communities is tied to the wellbeing of song traditions (see Treloyn and Martin 2014). In this chapter, we will discuss the core activities of a project centred on fostering community-led discovery and repatriation of recordings from legacy collections, hand in hand with traditional teaching and learning on Country. We present the perspectives of cultural heritage stakeholders on these ac-tivities, and on associated research methods, through transcribed dia-logues and conversations. First, we briefly outline legacies of research on Junba.

Legacies of Junba research, 1938–2002

Junba has been the focus of several research projects, dating back to the ethnographic expedition of the German Kulturmorphologisches Insti-tut to the northwest Kimberley in 1938–39.[3] While no recordings from the expedition are currently known to the authors, the leader, Andreas Lommel, transcribed lyrics and prepared glosses of some 43 Junba song texts with their Worrorra composer, Alan Balbangu, along with de-

---

2   Catherine Grant identifies 12 factors to assess the health of a musical tradition in a 'Music Vitality and Endangerment Framework' (MFEV) (Grant 2014, 163). While a detailed investigation of the Junba traditions within the Kimberley is yet to be done in relation to the MVEF, the suggested attrition of Junba since the 1980s may correspond to MVEF Factor 4, 'change in the music and music practices'. Further research is needed, however, to take into account cultural factors and local perspectives on change and innovation within Junba.
3   It is possible that earlier recordings made by Yvnge Laurell in 1910 on Sunday Island in the southwest Kimberley contain some Junba; however, detailed listening with Ngarinyin, Worrorra and Wunambal Junba singers has yet to be done.

scriptive accounts of song conception experiences and dances. These were later published in the text *Die unambal* (Lommel 1952, trans. to English 1997), and further discussed by Lommel with Ngarinyin lawman David Mowaljarlai (Lommel and Mowaljarlai 1994) and then in 2001–02 by Treloyn with Ngarinyin elders who recalled Lommel's 1938–39 visit (Treloyn 2006a). From the 1960s through the 1980s substantial collections of Junba were recorded in Derby, Mowanjum, Kalumburu, Kununurra and Wyndham by numerous people, including Alice Moyle, Peter Lucich, Wayne Masters, Ian Crawford, Lesley Reilly, Ray Keogh and Ambrose Cummins.

While Alice Moyle undertook a number of transcriptions of Junba songs, elicited song texts with performers and described the instrumentation and aspects of performance practice (1974, 1978, 1981), work to investigate the entire sample of Junba that Moyle recorded is only now being undertaken. Although substantial recordings of Junba were made in the 1960s–1980s, it was not until the mid to late 1990s that ethnomusicologists returned to Junba. Between 1997 and 1999, Allan Marett and Linda Barwick collaborated with anthropologist Anthony Redmond, the Ngarinyin Aboriginal Corporation based in Derby, community leaders and singers to record several repertories of Junba: the Jalarrimirri Junba composed by Alec Wirrijangu, the Dulugun Junba composed by Flora Walkerbier (dreamt by Bruce Nelji), Wati Ngerdu's Wanalirri Junba, and Scotty Martin's Jadmi and Jorrogorl Junba repertories. These recordings subsequently formed the starting point for Treloyn's doctoral study of Junba. In 2000–2002, Treloyn worked with a group of elder men and women identifying as Ngarinyin, Worrorra and/or Wunambal to record and transcribe known Junba songs and research their histories and cultural significance (see Treloyn and Charles 2014). Treloyn (2006a) focused on analysis and ethnography of the Junba performance practice and composition, centred on the Jadmi-type Junba repertory composed by Scotty Martin.

Throughout Treloyn's postgraduate fieldwork between 2000 and 2002, it was evident that elders of the community valued the legacy recordings produced by earlier research. As well as seeking to document their own knowledge of Junba, two elders brought to her cassette tapes copied from recordings made in the 1960s to discuss and, in one case, repair. The repaired tape included a substantial collection of songs composed by Laurie Utemorrah and Paddy Lalbanda, known as the Bayerra repertory. The renewed interest in the songs, promoted by dissemination of copies on cassette and CD, led elder Ngarinyin siblings Mabel King (dec.) and Jimmy Maline (dec.) to 'wake up' the Junba (i.e., to stage the Junba after a hiatus of some years). This tape, and several cassette copies of recordings made by Barwick and Marett, became like a soundtrack for fieldwork, almost constantly playing on the cassette player in Treloyn's Toyota at the request of elder ladies with whom she travelled. This became a way for Treloyn to learn the songs and singing, at the encouragement of leaders such as Pansy Nulgit, and also stimulated sessions of documentation. In the course of Treloyn's fieldwork, the texts and histories of the repertories contained in Barwick and Marett's collection, as well as Ray Keogh's collection, with the addition of the aforementioned tapes held by the elders, were documented by groups of elders led by Jack Dann (dec.), Paddy Neowarra, Scotty Martin, and Pansy Nulgit. After Treloyn's return to Sydney, requests for access to additional copies of cassettes and CDs continued. Additionally, Scotty Martin – an important proponent of the continuation of the Junba tradition through his composition of two repertories, and his leading of Worrorra and Wunambal repertories at annual Mowanjum Festivals and other cultural events – requested that Treloyn return to the Kimberley to undertake activities to support increased youth engagement with Junba.

While Barwick and Marett returned copies of their research to the communities of origin as did Redmond and Treloyn, and elders held earlier selected copies of recordings made during 2000–02, longer-term, local access to the results of research remained inadequate. Moreover, it seemed that to support intergenerational engagement around Junba, research needed to move beyond the traditional model of recording, documenting, analysis and archiving, to include communities in these discovery, collection and preservation processes. Following consultations through 2008–09 a project – which became known locally as the Junba Project – was developed, supported initially by the Australian Institute of Aboriginal and Torres Strait Islander Studies (AIATSIS) and later by the ARC, in partnership with the Mowanjum Art and Culture Centre (located in the Mowanjum Community close to Derby) and the Kimberley Aboriginal Law and Culture Centre (KALACC).[4]

The Junba Project

The primary aim of the Junba Project was to determine effective methods for repatriating, recording and documenting recordings of song and dance to support intergenerational knowledge transmission and production around Junba. The project was based on assumptions about the positive impact that recordings and other products of ethnomusicological research can have on endangered traditions and cultural heritage communities. There were numerous anecdotal accounts of the role that recordings could play in supporting creative innovation and the memory and recovery of songs (see, for example, Marett and Barwick 2003). Deakin's observation of an audiocassette in a Wurnan package (Deakin 1978) suggested that new technologies may be readily incorporated alongside more traditional modes of teaching and learning Junba over the vast distances of the Wurnan system. And, as noted, Treloyn had observed and played a role in elders' efforts to wake up a repertory, initially stimulated by the repair of a cassette tape in 2001. In doing so, however, Treloyn was also mindful of the potential harm that the recordings might have done due to the reifying and distorting potential of recording media (Kirshenblatt-Gimblett 2006) on creative, fluid forms (Knopoff 2004, 181), as well as on the diverse knowledges that circulate around particular songs (Wild 1992, 13) (see Treloyn and Emberly 2013). As the project proceeded, we were interested to note how community leadership and use of repatriation and dissemination as strategies to sustain the Junba tradition mitigated against this potential adverse effect of repatriated recordings.

---

4 'Sustaining junba: Recording and documenting endangered songs and dances in the northern Kimberley' (AIATSIS G2009/7458, researchers Sally Treloyn, Scotty Martin and Matthew Martin); 'Strategies for preserving and sustaining endangered Aboriginal song and dance in the modern world' (Australian Research Council, LP0990650, researchers Sally Treloyn and Allan Marett).

The primary materials that were repatriated to the community were selections of collections recorded by Treloyn between 2000 and 2002, by Barwick and Marett between 1997 and 1999, by Ray Keogh in 1985, and by Lesley Reilly in 1974. A core group of stakeholders also attended the AIATSIS Access Unit in November 2012 with Treloyn and Marett to discover, review and order copies of subsequent recordings and photographs by Alice Moyle, Peter Lucich and Ian Crawford, among others. These were received in 2014. Recordings and documentation repatriated or produced by the community and researchers in the course of the project were subsequently used by multiple generations to produce knowledge about Junba and contribute to intergenerational engagement with the tradition. We present here excerpts of dialogues and stories of repatriation, dissemination and use by cultural heritage stakeholders. The dialogues and stories are from two generations of stakeholders: Matthew Dembal Martin, a senior *manambarra* (lawman) and leader of Junba singing and dancing, and Rona Googninda Charles, co-author of this chapter and an emerging leader for Ngarinyin peoples and researcher of Junba. These stakeholders describe and critically assess the research process, consider benefits, and make recommendations for future research. We do not intend for these accounts to be exhaustive, but rather to set out a range of uses and reflections on the experience and use of repatriation, dissemination of recordings, as well as documentation activities, within the diverse community.

Recordings as a conduit to ancestors and place

In our presentation to the Research, Records and Responsibility (RRR) conference, Charles emphasised the personal significance of recovering records of her family in the collections. In doing so she also stressed the importance of there being a new repository – or 'home' – for digital records of these collections in a local archive located within her community (in this case the Wurnan Storylines community archive developed by Katie Breckon at the Mowanjum Art and Culture Centre):

> We went to the archive, Canberra. And I was so amazed. I found lot of the old stuff: a lot of photographs of Junba, and also my old people

that I grew up with and I knew. We were able to go and get copies and bring him back because our Art Centre [Mowanjum Art and Culture Centre] is establishing an archive. [Because of this] we [are] getting all the archive material from Canberra and maybe Western Australia to put them in our own system in the community. (Rona Googninda Charles, 2 December 2013, Research, Records and Responsibility, University of Melbourne)[5]

Elsewhere elder Matthew Martin has reflected on the presence of ancestors in recordings held in the AIATSIS archive. He stresses the importance of bringing copies of these recordings that provide a conduit to these ancestors back to the hereditary Country to which they belong:

[I]t was good [to] see those old, old things from old people, and the song. [We] pick the song from old, old people. They [the old people] are still there [in the recordings]: like the old people are gone but their spirit is still there. What you call that place? They still there, they still remain. Can't forget them ... [We need to] bring the whole lot back ... bring them back to Country. (Matthew Dembal Martin, 16 January 2014, Mowanjum Community)[6]

Martin's explanation of the need to bring records of ancestors' songs and voices back to Country corresponds to the need to repatriate the physical remains of ancestors' bodies back to Country. Historian Martin Thomas explains the subject status of human remains for elders from Arnhem Land who journeyed to the Smithsonian Institute to accompany the remains of deceased family back to Country: '[f]or Gumbula ... death has not altered their subject status. And as was the case when they were living and breathing, they can still expect to connect with, and reside within, their ancestral country' (Thomas 2014, 134). Like bones, recordings are not the objective relics of past research, but rather are subjective remains of ancestors with which living people have active responsibilities and relationships.

---

5   Audio recorded by Nick Thieberger, 2 December 2013, http://hdl.handle.net/2123/12254.
6   Audio recorded by Sally Treloyn, 16 January 2014.

Recordings and teaching/learning

For Martin, the need to bring back recordings relates to his own responsibilities as a teacher of Junba to pass on Junba knowledge to the generations that follow him. The following dialogue between Treloyn and Martin illustrates the role played in teaching and learning by the recordings, and by the ancestors to whom the recordings provide a conduit:

> Treloyn: So, [is there] anything you want to say about why it's important to bring those old recordings back from Canberra, and how you have been using those old recordings for yourself, to teach kids?
>
> Martin: Yeah, well the main thing is learning [teaching] kids – our next generation coming up – before they [the songs and dances] die away, you know ...
>
> Treloyn: How do you teach the kids to dance with the old recordings?
>
> Martin: Well, that's the recording, you go by the words: the meaning, you know. The meaning of the songs and what it's about: Country or ... the spirit, [or] birds. Just follow that ... Follow the spirit. [The] spirit [will] always be there.
>
> Treloyn: And what does it mean ... if you have an old recording with old, old people singing in it and you can hear their voices?
>
> Martin: It's sort of bringing in to it, you know. Old old songs, old old people what been passed away, like you bringing the spirit back to you. So you, you can carry on ... [as] the teacher for them, for the next generation.
>
> Treloyn: It's like the spirits are helping you do the teaching.
>
> Martin: Yeah, it's like the old spirit comes back. You can't see it but you can feel it ... Singing ... Dancing it brings memories back to, from the old time ... When young people dance, it brings back the memories of old people. They [the old people that have passed] are teaching them. Its just like they're, they're happy to dance and you see the young kids running around. They are willing to dance. The spirit comes back to them ... [unclear] spirit to their spirit you know ... It sort of draws them in. (Matthew Dembal Martin, 16 January 2014, Mowanjum Community)

Charles has similarly used recordings to support her own endeavours to teach and learn Junba (see Treloyn and Charles 2014).

Recordings as a conduit to wellbeing

Given that reference to and memories of deceased family members may induce feelings of sorrow for Indigenous peoples in the Kimberley, as elsewhere in Australia (to the extent that there is avoidance and often a prohibition on saying the name of the deceased), it is logical that we consider what impact playing and listening to recordings of the voices of ancestors in legacy recordings has on living, listening family members. In the following dialogue, Martin explains that while listening may bring feelings of sadness, the experience of receiving songs from the spirits of ancestors, via recordings, and then carrying these songs on into the future, brings good *liyan* or 'gut feeling' (Redmond 2001a), that encompasses personal wellbeing as well as that of the speaker's community and broader world (Dodson, cited in Yu 2013).

> Treloyn: When you hear an old old recording of old people, how does that make you feel?
>
> Martin: Ah, it makes you a bit sad. But you know you [are] getting those old songs back, so ... you can have it here from the old people singing to your time [that is, singing from the past into the present] ... [You] feel sad for listening to their voice; the old people's voice sort of makes you feel off. But when you start singing it [the song that they teach you] you feel the power coming into you. [It is] just like the old spirit [of your ancestor] comes into you. So you start singing, and you don't miss a word. You pick songs up. You listen to it a couple of times maybe, and you pick it up ... You feel it in your body. Sad, next one you feel happy now. [You] start [to] sing that old old songs ... The spirit comes out and you [are] the boss man now. Just like the spirit been leave it up to you now. That *anguma* [spirit of deceased person], you know, *anguma* ...
>
> Treloyn: When you [are] happy for singing a song that you have picked up and that spirit's come and handed it over, do you feel that feeling of *liyan*?

Martin: ... That *liyan* make you feel happiness come to you more. [When you] start singing the song after the old people come to you, [it] make you feel proud. Proud. Make you carry on [from] the old people. (Matthew Dembal Martin, 16 January 2014, Mowanjum Community)

Liyan is dependent on relationships between individuals, their families and their Country (Dodson, cited in Yu 2013). Insofar as recordings are used as a conduit to past family and place, and Junba singing and dancing serve to reinforce connections to place (see Redmond 2001b), the importance of repatriation of recordings for stakeholders such as Martin is perhaps predicated on the contribution that recordings can make to a person's and a community's wellbeing.

The extent to which recordings may serve as a therapeutic tool is yet to be the subject of research. However, Charles recounts a compelling story of the beneficial effects of playing Junba recordings, arranged into an iTunes playlist prepared in the course of the Junba Project, to an elderly singer who had been recently admitted to residential aged care in the town of Derby, several hundred kilometres from her Community and immediate family.

Charles: There's an old lady that was one of our main singers and she's also a composer. She was put in an old nursing home and ... she had [been told she had] dementia. I went there one day, and I took her sister along. She [the old singer] was in bed. It was ten o'clock [in the morning] and one of the staff was saying to us, 'Oh, we can't get [her] out of bed, she refuse[s] to get out of the bed. She's so depressed and we don't know what to do with her. She's just going to lay there.' I took the laptop with me and I went in there and I sat down. She was just staying there covered up with the blanket. I put on the music; I put on one of the Junba songs for her. She was laying down listening, and I could see her lips moving. She got out of bed, sat down and started singing! I thought to myself, if she had dementia [as her carers had said], she wouldn't remember any of these songs, but she was singing! And she started singing! And I put on the next one and she sang it. I got her to get up, to have a shower [and] make her bed up. And she ... came alive. The music made her come alive, you know ...

(Rona Googninda Charles, 2 December 2013, Research, Records and Responsibility, University of Melbourne)

Noting that this elderly singer's experience is not unique, Charles suggests that recordings of Junba might be used on a regular basis as a tool to improve the lives of the broader community of elderly people who move from their Communities throughout the Kimberley into towns for care.

> Thinking about some of our old people at the nursing home in the town, when we [their families] live in the Communities, we thought, 'We'll take CDs there for them, and put them on while they are there, [and they can be] listening to the CDs all day, [or at] morning tea or lunch break. We found that it was very useful for us to take these CDs for the old people['s] home [i.e., the residential aged care facility]. It amazes me because they [the staff] say they [the old people] can't remember anything, but when you put on the Junba they start singing. (Rona Googninda Charles, 2 December 2013, Research, Records and Responsibility, University of Melbourne)

Waking up dance-songs and strengthening the tradition

Over the three years of the Junba Project, members of the cultural heritage community have had greater access to legacy records of Junba, including audio recordings, video and photographs. The Mowanjum Art and Culture Centre archive, managed by Katie Breckon, has been instrumental in this. Martin has used audio and video recordings, now held in the archive, to recall songs to assist in his own role as song-leader. He has also used video of his own performances as a dancer in the 1990s and early 2000s to teach young emerging dancers. Charles continues this practice and has instructed her sons on dances from Scotty Martin's Jadmi-type Junba repertory, recorded by Barwick and Marett in 1997 at Bijili in the Northern Kimberley.

In Figure 8.2 we saw evidence of a decline in the number and diversity of repertories and songs being performed at public unelicited performance events between the 1960s and 2012. Figure 8.3 sets out the repertories and songs performed at the 2013 and 2014 Mowanjum

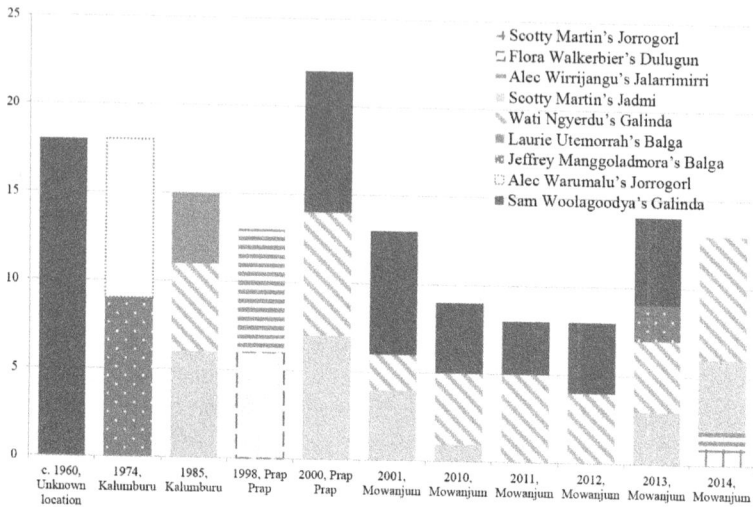

Figure 8.3 Number of unique songs by repertory performed at selected unelicited, danced public events to 2014.

Festivals, recorded by Treloyn and Maitland Ngerdu respectively. Whereas between 1985 and 2012 we saw a decrease in the number of repertories and songs performed, in 2013 and 2014 there was an increase back to the numbers of the 1980s and 1990s. Many factors may influence the rise and fall of particular repertories, including the format and time constraints of festival programs, funding availability, the entry and departure and re-entry of songs from repertories with the passing of songmen and dancers, as well as a decline in the number of performers. However, given the coincidence of the increase in unique songs and in the diversity of repertories at the 2013 and 2014 Festivals with the mid to final stages of the Junba Project, it appears that increased access and use of legacy materials in the community, and the revision of research design to include cultural heritage stakeholders across generations in the repatriation, recording, dissemination and documentation processes, may play a role in strengthening and sustaining endangered practices.

Conclusion

In this chapter we have discussed community-led engagement activities around the discovery, return and use of records of Junba, and viewed data indicating the relative health of the Junba tradition from the 1960s to 2014. We have noted a coincidence between the maturation of the Junba Project and a revival in the number and diversity of songs and repertories performed at the annual Mowanjum Festival. The project falls within a history of intercultural research engagements around Junba dating back to at least 1938. Predominantly focused on collection, documentation and preservation, the large majority of these records are held in archives. However, there is a long history of recordings circulating in the Kimberley, incorporated into traditional systems of knowledge transmission embedded in and delineating the Wurnan. Through contextual details, data on the health of the Junba tradition, and dialogue with cultural heritage stakeholders, we have provided evidence of the benefits of multi-level community engagement in song research and repatriation, including the use of recordings as a conduit to ancestors and place, and thereby as a conduit to wellbeing. Through dialogues and stories told by multiple generations of singers, dancers, teachers and learners, we see how cultural heritage stakeholders can discover, use and create records of their songs to strengthen practices and research collaborations into the future.

Acknowledgements

Research presented in this paper was supported by AIATSIS (G2009/7458) and the ARC (LP0990650) with industry partners the Mowanjum Art and Culture Centre and the Kimberley Aboriginal Law and Culture Centre. The authors would like to thank the Ngarinyin, Worrorra and Wunambal cultural heritage communities whose traditions and knowledges inform this research, and particularly recognise Matthew Dembal Martin for his contribution to this paper.

Works cited

Deakin, Hilton (1978). 'The Unan cycle: A study of social change in an Aboriginal community.' PhD thesis, Monash University, Melbourne.

Grant, Catherine (2014). *Music Endangerment: How Language Maintenance Can Help.* New York: Oxford University Press.

Kirshenblatt-Gimblett, Barbara (2006). 'World heritage and cultural economics.' In *Museum Frictions: Public Cultures/Global Transformations*, edited by Ivan Karp, Corinne A. Kratz, Lynn Szwaja and Tomas Ybarra-Frausto, 161–203. Durham: Duke University Press.

Knopoff, Steven (2004). 'Intrusions and delusions: Considering the impact of recording technology on the subject matter of ethnomusicological research.' In *Music Research: New Directions for a New Century*, edited by Michael Ewans, Rosalind Halton and John A. Phillips, 177–86. London: Cambridge Scholars Press.

Lommel, Andreas (1952). *The Unambal: A Tribe in Northwestern Australia.* Primary translation by Ian Campbell. Carnarvon: Takarakka Nowan Kas Publications, 1997.

Lommel, Andreas and David Mowaljarlai (1994). 'Shamanism in northwest Australia.' *Oceania* 64(4): 277–87.

Marett, Allan and Linda Barwick (2003). 'Endangered songs and endangered languages.' In *Maintaining the Links: Language Identity and the Land. Seventh conference of the Foundation for Endangered Languages*, edited by Joe Blythe and Robert McKenna Brown, 144–51. Bath: Foundation for Endangered Languages.

Moyle, Alice (1974). 'North Australian music. A taxonomic approach to the study of Aboriginal song performances.' PhD thesis, Monash University, Melbourne.

Moyle, Alice (1978). *Aboriginal Sound Instruments.* Canberra: Australian Institute of Aboriginal Studies.

Moyle, Alice (1981). *Songs from the Kimberleys.* Canberra: Australian Institute of Aboriginal Studies.

Redmond, Anthony (2001a). 'Rulug Wayirri: Moving kin and country in the northern Kimberley.' PhD thesis, University of Sydney.

Redmond, Anthony (2001b). 'Places that move.' In *Emplaced Myth: Space, Narrative, and Knowledge in Aboriginal Australia and Papua New Guinea*, edited by Alan Rumsey and James F. Weiner, 120–38. Honolulu: University of Hawai'i Press.

Redmond, Anthony (2008). 'Captain Cook meets General Macarthur in the northern Kimberley: Humour and ritual in an Indigenous Australian life-world.' *Anthropological Forum* 18(3): 255–70.

Thomas, Martin (2014). 'Turning subjects into objects and objects into subjects: Bones as a bridge between worlds.' In *Circulating Cultures: Exchanges of Australian Indigenous Music, Dance and Media*, edited by Amanda Harris, 129–66. Canberra: ANU Press.

Treloyn, Sally (2003). 'Scotty Martin's jadmi junba: A song series from the Kimberley region of northwest Australia.' *Oceania* 73: 208–20.

Treloyn, Sally (2006). 'Songs that pull: Jadmi junba from the Kimberley region of northwest Australia.' PhD thesis, University of Sydney.

Treloyn, Sally and Andrea Emberly (2013). 'Sustaining traditions: Ethnomusicological collections, access and sustainability in Australia.' *Musicology Australia* 35(2): 159–77.

Treloyn, Sally, Rona Googninda Charles and Sherika Nulgit (2013). 'Repatriation of song materials to support intergenerational transmission of knowledge about language in the Kimberley region of northwest Australia.' In *Endangered Languages Beyond Boundaries: Proceedings of the 17th Foundation for Endangered Languages*, edited by Mary Jane Norris, Erik Anonby, Marie-Odile Junker, Nicholas Oster and Donna Patrick, 18–24. Bath: Foundation for Endangered Languages.

Treloyn, Sally and Matthew Dembal Martin (2014). 'Perspectives on dancing, singing and wellbeing from the Kimberley region of northwest Australia.' *Journal for the Anthropological Study of Human Movement* 21(1).

Treloyn, Sally amd Rona Googninda Charles (2014). 'How do you feel about squeezing oranges?: Reflections and lessons on collaboration in ethnomusicological research in an Aboriginal Australian community.' In *Collaborative Ethnomusicology: New Approaches to Music Research Between Indigenous and Non-Indigenous Australians*, edited by Katelyn Barney, 169–86. Melbourne: Lyrebird Press.

Wild, Steven (1992). 'Issues in the collection, preservation and dissemination of traditional music: The case of Aboriginal Australia.' In *Music and Dance of Aboriginal Australia and the South Pacific: The Effects of Documentation on the Living Tradition*, edited by Alice M. Moyle, 7–15. Sydney: Oceania Publications, University of Sydney.

Yu, Peter (2013). 'Process from the other side: Liyan in the cultural and natural estate.' *Landscape Architecture Australia* 139: 26–27. http://architectureau.com/articles/ process-from-the-other-side-liyan-in-the-cultural-and-natural-estate.

Postscript

Report on the establishment of a new archive

9

The Western Australian New Music Archive: performing as remembering

Cat Hope, Lisa MacKinney, Lelia Green, Meghan Travers and Tos Mahoney

'New music' refers to experimental, exploratory music. The definition adopted for the Western Australian New Music Archive (WANMA) is that used by the Australian Music Centre to define 'composition in sound'. It includes notated composition, electroacoustic music, improvised music (including contemporary jazz), electronica, sound art, installation sound, multimedia, web and film sound, and related genres and techniques.[1] The curation of WANMA is guided by, and confronts the challenges presented by, such a broad definition, with a focus on constructing a representative canon of Western Australian new music history from 1970 to the present day. A drawback of the Western Australian music collection at the State Library of Western Australia (SLWA), and indeed of many other Australian music collections (such as that at the Australian Music Centre and UWA's Callaway Collection)

---

1   Australian Music Centre. Artist Representation.
http://www.australianmusiccentre.com.au/about/representation.

is the limited nature of the music genres and artefacts included. In the past, archives and libraries have cultivated paper scores and, in some cases, analogue recordings of performances of these scores. Music has moved beyond these paradigms and into areas of improvisation (non-notated music), electronic music, installation (which has physical and visual elements as well as sonic aspects) and applied music (for dance, film and on the internet). WANMA includes materials that reflect contemporary recognition of improvisation and sound art as composition, and therefore the role of recordings as an alternative score, and video as an important documentation device for sound art. As with other contemporary information, WANMA reflects the increasing movement of information into the digital realm, either as digitised or born-digital materials, and seeks to provide both digitisation and digital preservation of materials, allowing for both ongoing availability and access.

Western Australia has had a vibrant new music scene for many years, having long contributed to the wider Australian musical context by producing some of Australia's most important musical figures. These include internationally renowned sound artist Alan Lamb, composer and declared National Treasure Roger Smalley, and composers Ross Bolleter, Jonathan Mustard, Cathie Travers (see Figure 9.1) and Lindsay Vickery, to name a few. And, since its establishment in the mid-1980s, Perth organisation Tura has played a central role in supporting new and exploratory musical endeavours in Western Australia. This takes the form of organising performances by local and international artists, securing funding, assisting with promotion, and supporting the creation, development, presentation and distribution of new music for its artists, organisations and audiences. However, despite the intense level of activity in Western Australia, the wealth of national archival information on new music and its creators is currently based around artists from other states. There is a general lack of awareness of the range of activity in Western Australia, and the future launch of the WANMA will make this activity far more visible and accessible.

210

Figure 9.1 Western Australian composer and performer Cathie Travers, circa 1992. Photo by Chris Ha.

A curated collection

There are issues of artistic as well as historical judgement in the determination of the authenticity and reliability of materials archived that make WANMA a curated collection. Chief Investigator Dr Cat Hope (Western Australian Academy of Performing Arts) and Partner Investigator Tos Mahoney (Tura) act as curators, having a detailed knowledge of Western Australian new music practice, and have led the

WANMA research since a pilot project was established in 2009. This was when Tura made its entire collection of materials available for an archival analysis and digitisation project, along with its extensive database of Western Australian composers and sound artists. The WANMA will initially incorporate this body of material, which includes audio, video, scans of documents, album covers, newspaper clippings and other ephemera. Once this is completed, the project staff will scope possibilities for other materials to be included as the project progresses. Mahoney's interest in and ongoing support for regional agendas for new music has also been vital for maintaining WANMA as a truly state-based collection, as opposed to a collection from the city of Perth and its surrounds.

One of the many challenges for the WANMA project has been the definition of 'Western Australian'. Although it applies largely to printed matter, the policy governing the collection of heritage materials by the SLWA has applications for our decision-making process. Those criteria are:

- A significant proportion of the content is about Western Australia.
- The work was:
  - Written or created by a person born in Western Australia and/or who has spent a significant amount of time living in Western Australia;
  - Published or created in Western Australia;
  - Written or created by a corporate body identified as primarily Western Australian;
  - Produced in or about the Indian Ocean Territories.

It is immediately apparent that there is a degree of discretion inherent in these criteria – 'significant proportion', 'significant amount of time', 'primarily Western Australian' – and that those curating the archive must make decisions about what constitutes 'significant' to Western Australia, Western Australians and music practice in general.

There are arguments for including material for which there is a less obvious Western Australian component – for instance, recordings or ephemera relating to Western Australian premieres of international works, and significant performances by international and interstate composers and performers, particularly if local artists were on the bill or collaborating in some way. A good example of this is provided by Jon Rose, an extremely prolific experimental violinist from Sydney whose work is included in the body of material digitised by Tura. Jon Rose was (perhaps inadvertently) instrumental in the formation of Tura, a process which began when Perth flautist and improviser Tos Mahoney attended and performed at Jon Rose's Relative Band Festival (a festival of experimental music) in Sydney in 1984 (White 1991, 8). Using this event as a model, Mahoney organised the inaugural Perth Festival of Improvised Music at the Praxis Gallery, Fremantle, in April, 1985. This festival brought together local, interstate and international experimental musicians for a series of public performances and workshops – many captured on an LP released shortly afterward (see Figure 9.2). After a successful second festival in 1986, Mahoney founded Evos Music, an organisation named to reflect and support the idea of music as a constantly evolving art form (Mitchell 1998, 9). In 1997, in conjunction with the inaugural Totally Huge New Music Festival, Evos Music evolved into Tura, which remains the peak body for experimental music in Western Australia. Jon Rose has performed in Perth for Tura on many occasions, most recently in 2010 for the Sounds Outback Festival at Wogarno in regional Western Australia. So, although Rose has never lived in WA, and his recordings are not, for want of a better way to put it, 'Western Australian themed', his work, performances, and involvement in experimental music networks have certainly had an impact on the development of new music in Western Australia.

Initial work on curating the archive began with meetings of Hope, Mahoney and the SLWA WANMA project officer. Together, they will sort through the materials in the Tura pilot archive and select items of significance for inclusion in WANMA based on their local knowledge and experience. It is hoped that this process will provide training for the library project officer that will go on to benefit WANMA after the conclusion of the Australian Research Council funding supporting the project at the end of 2015. This is a pivotal factor for the preservation of WANMA, as the project is funded only for a fixed three years (2013–15). However, there is also the danger that the collection will not be curated beyond the period of the project. In an attempt to reduce this danger, the current project officer is working with SLWA's Liaison, Acquisition and Development section to formulate a collection

Figure 9.2 The cover of the LP *Live at Praxis*, a recording of highlights from the inaugural Perth Festival of Improvised Music, released by Impro Records, Perth, 1985.

development policy. This will ensure that, at the end of three years, systems are securely locked in place to guarantee the continued development and progress of the archive. We hope that these policies may also be of use to other institutional projects funded by competitive grants for finite periods.

A community of practice

The community of practice which frames the composition, performance and consumption of Western Australian new music is of critical importance to the delivery and design of WANMA. Discussing communities of practice in the creative industries in Italy, Marco Bettiol and Silvia Sedita argue that communities of practice develop:

> ... a pool of skilled people within which it is feasible to develop projects. Communities of practice improve knowledge sharing and help the development of a common identity and social relationships. It is not just a matter of knowhow but also of who knows what that is at the heart of a community of practice. In our perspective, this role [of knowing about others' work] is necessary to select and further involve qualified people in the project. Projects do not develop in [a] vacuum but within a social structure. (Bettiol and Sedita 2011, 468)

Our archive is designed to be sufficiently nuanced to allow for investigation of the influence of key events and performances upon the genesis of artworks that follow. It is hoped that this will enable explorations of the rich inter-relationships and communication channels between creators, performers, events, genres, venues and organisations in Western Australia's musical heritage. For example, the wide range of materials in the Tura archive includes more than music and scores; there are also planning documents, contracts, invoices and curricula vitae. The importance of such supporting materials has been highlighted by the National Archives of the UK in their Archiving the Arts project (The National Archives [UK] 2014). In some cases, these items will enable the curators to find contributors of specific materials. For example, the recording engineer who was paid to record a concert is likely to be identified by way of invoices, rather than by any information on the recorded materials in Tura's collection. This is important as there is often copyright held in the recording of a musical work by the recording engineer and/or publisher, in addition to the rights of composers and performers (Australian Copyright Council 2012).

A performing archive

An important element of WANMA has been the close link of archival materials to actual performances that have taken place in Perth, a characteristic reflected in the nature of Tura's collection used in the pilot study. This element will continue to mark part of the WANMA project into the future, by actually fuelling future growth. With the involvement of the ABC Classic FM team of producers, audio engineers and presenters in the forthcoming phase of the archive's implementation, an ongoing commitment to recording and broadcasting new concerts of Western Australian works – new or newly rediscovered – feeding them back into the archive and incorporating linkages to related performers, composers, venues and other associated data is innovative in conception and serves as a model for future 'living' archives. In addition, Tura's ongoing involvement will ensure public awareness of the project, through the organisation's marketing and production support. In the past, ABC Classic FM's Australian Music Unit has had something of an ad hoc approach to choosing Western Australian content to record for its broadcasts. Their partnership in this project will also provide curatorial advice as to the most valuable and relevant Western Australian materials to record, both as part of WANMA, and in their programming generally. As public awareness increases, and there are more communications around WANMA and its mission, so there are increased opportunities for holders of collections to learn about the project, and to use the archive and come forward, thus expanding the content in WANMA (Marres 2011).

Another aspect of community involvement WANMA plans to explore is crowdsourcing. Unlike the National Library of Australia's (NLA) spectacularly successful newspaper correction program (the Australian Newspapers Digitisation Program), for WANMA this would likely focus more on the inclusion, rather than correction, of materials. This could include the addition of links to photographs, posters, flyers, newspaper and magazine reviews, 'bootleg' recordings and other ephemera relating to a performance of a particular work in the archive. It could also be an extremely valuable aid to identification of personnel in materials where this is unknown, through the use of techniques like the 'tagging' technology available to social media. The SLWA has successfully implemented a pilot project of a similar nature with 'Storylines', a central access point for digitised heritage collections relating to Aboriginal history in WA.[2] The project uses the Ara Irititja software, a purpose-built platform developed in South Australia for the project of the same name, which allows the tagging and linking of a variety of materials including video and audio, as well as public uploading. 'Storylines' will be consulted as a model for future crowdsourcing of materials once the curation of Tura's pilot collection has been finalised and entered into the catalogue.

Digitisation and digital preservation

Digitisation for preservation and digital preservation are closely related, 'but the underlying standards, processes, technologies, costs, and organisational challenges are quite distinct' (Conway 2010). Digitisation (whether for preservation or access purposes) implies that the original material is in a non-digital form, while digital preservation is the act of preserving materials that were created digitally – these may ultimately include digitised materials, but it is the born-digital content that presents the greater challenges, including interactive and multimedia works.

This project will initially produce digitised content from analogue source materials, with outputs of digital content in formats suitable for both online access and for preservation. Looking ahead, WANMA seeks to work with the community of Western Australian composers and performers to develop ways for their digital works to be taken into the collection and for preservation activities to commence early in the lifecycle of the material. This reflects recent changes to the legal transfer times (that is, the time after which material deemed to have archival value must be transferred to an archive) for archival material in government, including in Australia in 2011 (Commonwealth of Australia 1983), and brings the archival material closer to the concept of the

---

2   State Library of Western Australia. Storylines. http://www.slwa.wa.gov.au/for/indigenous_australians/storylines.

'living archive'. It acknowledges the Australian concept of Records Continuum Theory (McKemmish 2001) in information management. Records Continuum Theory suggests that records are simultaneously contemporary and historical from the moment they are created: 'By definition they are frozen in time, fixed in a documentary form and linked to their context of creation. They are thus time and space bound, perpetually connected to events in the past. Yet they are also disembedded, carried forward into new circumstances where they [are] re-presented and used' (John Curtin Prime Ministerial Library, 2004). This will also bring otherwise fragile digital materials into a managed environment that provides for their long-term sustainability and access, without blocking but in fact further encouraging their re-use in the current time, and linking materials to a wide cultural heritage while they are still contemporary. This future work will develop a unique collection and portal to a history as it is created.

Early communications of the archive

One of the earliest WANMA 'communications' was the staging of a small exhibition at the SLWA to coincide with the Totally Huge New Music Festival, which also incorporated the International Computer Music Conference, in August 2013 (see Figure 9.3). Lisa MacKinney had recently commenced a temporary role as project officer for WANMA, and one of the early tasks required was determining what materials in the State Library's collection might qualify for inclusion in digital form as part of WANMA. Posters of historical interest, some of which were uncatalogued, were located in the library. We asked a number of local composers to lend us material and they were positive about their possible participation and thought it a worthwhile contribution. As word spread, other offers were forthcoming, including a mid-1990s computer with music-composing software that we were able to have running as part of the exhibition. The variety of materials presented – such as computer software programs on floppy disc, diaries, posters, cassettes and a range of audio and video formats – point to the upcoming challenges of digitising new music practices and the ephemera surrounding them. This is not a new phenomenon, as evidenced by

Figure 9.3 Some items from the Western Australian New Music Archive on display at the State Library of Western Australia during the International Computer Music Conference in August 2013. Photograph by Dana Tonello-Scott.

Rothenberg's observation in 1995 that 'digital information lasts forever – or five years, whichever comes first' (Rothenberg 1995); however, the project acknowledges this, and seeks not only to digitise materials in analogue format, but also to develop early-intervention digital preservation practices, such as the movement of digital materials from their creation format into a format likely to survive more than one generation of computing technology, for born-digital, interactive materials. These may be in formats such as Adobe Flash or MaxMSP code, which form a large part of the contemporary music landscape today, but, based on the experience of previous popular software formats such as Macromedia Director, are unlikely to be able to still be read in as little as 20 years' time.

In acknowledging the differences between digitisation and digital preservation, we are hopeful that the composers who lent us material might agree in the future to allow it to be preserved for inclusion in the digital archive. In this manner, the WANMA exhibition was an important investment in the future of the archive, as well as valuable promotion for it. It is also hoped, in later stages of the project, that composers and performers will contribute their interactive works as they are being developed, potentially allowing a better preservation outcome for these materials. Before we can approach composers and performers to contribute, we will need to be confident that we have a full collection policy as well as copyright and contractual clearances in place.

The Australian Broadcasting Corporation is an important partner for WANMA as the national flagship for the kind of music WANMA represents. As the area of the ABC most closely aligned with the project, ABC Classic FM's Australian Music Unit will also be making its own archive of Western Australian recordings (which are currently not publically accessible) available to WANMA for digitisation and inclusion in the archive though a connection with their Classic Amp/Rewind project – an example of some of their work is seen in Figure 9.4. In this way, WANMA will access ABC material while supporting the ABC's goal of getting more archival content recorded and available online, as well as increasing Western Australian performance content for their broadcasts.

Intellectual property and ownership

The collection and long-term preservation of digital content poses challenges to formal intellectual property agreements. Original hardcopy materials will not be gathered by the project; rather, the database will point to their location and availability. The integration of an intellectual property framework within the archive to manage the complex rights inherent in musical works and related materials is a vital part of the research, as it is crucial to achieve an appropriate balance between copyright owners, the music community and WANMA users. This is a topic of ongoing debate in legal and policy circles, and our research also contributes to debates around copyright, copyleft (Free Software Foundation 2014), and Creative Commons approaches to artworks.[3] The purpose of an archive, its subject matter, the manner in which it will acquire copies, as well as who will have access to the archive, from where, and under what conditions, all come with copyright implications that are critical to determine. We are currently in the process of engag-

---

3   Creative Commons. 'About the Licenses'. http://creativecommons.org/licenses.

Figure 9.4 A screenshot from the ABC Classic FM 'Rewind' webage for a work by Western Australian composer David Pye, performed by Western Australian artists, created by the Australian Music Unit at ABC Classic FM.

ing a digital copyright consultant to guide us through these complex processes, particularly in light of changes to Australia's copyright laws (Commonwealth of Australia 2006) that make some special provisions for libraries and collecting institutions, and the recent inquiry into further proposed changes to the Act (Senator the Hon. George Brandis QC 2014).

One response to these challenges will be the use of high-speed scalable storage and network infrastructure that can support streaming video and sound so that materials are experienced direct from the archive, rather than requiring downloading; they will thus meet exemptions made to the *Australian Copyright Act* in 2006 for the storage of temporary copies in computer memory. But these issues are further complicated for WANMA by the fact that, although the archive will be accessible through the SLWA's catalogue and website, only copies of hard-copy materials will be in the library collection. The copyright clearance for and ownership of such materials has been an ongoing and delicate process of negotiation with the library that has required an understanding of other collections of digital materials, such as photographs and the oral history recordings made for the Oral History Record Rescue project. The digital copies that make up WANMA will belong to the library and reside digitally in its Heritage Collection even if the original 'hard copy' resides elsewhere. This is enabled through a process known as the 'deed of gift', an agreement entered into by both the SLWA and the donor. The 'deed of gift' arrangement enables WANMA and the SLWA to provide digital access copies for research purposes. In this way, the WANMA materials reside in the SLWA, enabling the preservation processes already in place in the library to be extended to WANMA materials.

As the WANMA materials will appear in the SLWA catalogue, they will in turn feed into the NLA's TROVE catalogue. They are also searchable in a unique web portal for WANMA, through the use of a specially constructed application programming interface (API). In addition, the WANMA portal will connect directly to other partners, such as Tura, the ABC, as well as to the public through the development of other APIs. The benefit of a standalone interface in addition to the SLWA catalogue is that it enables WANMA to have its own unique presence and identification, and to operate as a place where all WANMA activities, such as new additions, recordings and performances, can be promoted and shared.

The pilot study discovered that the primary users of WANMA would be artists and musicology and intermedia researchers, and that there would be accessibility benefits flowing on to a global and general audience. We plan to make WANMA an open access archive, as is the current full SLWA catalogue, implementing similar deeds and contracts to facilitate this. More user-experience research will be undertaken in order to determine more precisely the manner in which access to the archive will operate, and what capabilities the software should include. But it was also determined that this flow-on would only be possible with knowledge of international bibliographic standards and a requirement that WANMA be interoperable with Australia's national bibliographic infrastructure. We have begun discussions with the NLA, ABC Classic FM and, in an advisory capacity, the Australian Music Centre, who recently digitised their extensive collection of scores and recordings, to discuss ways to enable this.

Conclusion

WANMA addresses manifest gaps in national and international collections of new music. As these have been developed over the years they have failed to include Western Australian new music at the depth and breadth required to understand and investigate the many interconnections between people, place, artworks and shared experiences.

The archive is more than a historical repository of new music and its supportive and peripheral elements, however. It is a curated collection with the capacity to influence the present and the future through a commitment to performative research. As a result of this aspect of the project, new compositions and recovered artworks will be produced by research partner ABC Classic FM, informing the future direction of new music while at the same time building WANMA's collection.

Communication is at the heart of this project, which we hope will form a core for the existence of a community of practice, and for the continuation and development of such a community over time. Relevant communication extends beyond the spoken and the written to the experiential – shared non-verbal communication arising out of artistic engagement between new music audience members and participants, composers and musicians. This project has the further benefit of making Western Australian new music visible and according it appropriate importance, creating a dynamic which will attract the interest of people as yet unknown who will be moved to engage with the archive and, possibly, donate materials as yet unidentified. Although WANMA is in its early days and is not yet publicly accessible, it has already raised a range of issues around copyright and definitions of relevance. New music is a complex and evolving artform and WANMA recognises and celebrates this in its conception and ongoing construction.

Works cited

Archives Act 1983 (Cth).

Australian Copyright Council (2014). Music and Copyright Information Sheet G012v14. http://tiny.cc/acc-g012v14.

Australian Law Reform Commission (2014). *Copyright and the Digital Economy* (Final Report). Sydney: Commonwealth of Australia. http://alrc.gov.au/ publications/copyright-report-122.

Australian Music Centre (2015). 'Artist representation.' http://www.australianmusiccentre.com.au/about/representation.

Bettiol, Marco and Silvia Rita Sedita (2011). 'The role of community of practice in developing creative industry projects.' *International Journal of Project Management*, 29(4): 468–79.

Conway, Paul (2010). 'Preservation in the age of Google: Digitization, digital preservation and the dilemmas.' *Library Quarterly* 80(1): 61–79.

Copyright Amendment Act 2006 (Cth).

Creative Commons (2015). 'About the licenses.' http://creativecommons.org/ licenses/.

Free Software Foundation (2015). 'What is Copyleft?' http://www.gnu.org/copyleft.

Haunton, Melinda (2014). 'Talking "Archiving the Arts"'. Blog. The National Archives. http://blog.nationalarchives.gov.uk/blog/talking-archiving-arts.

John Curtin Prime Ministerial Library (2004). 'Australian contributions to recordkeeping.' *Understanding Society Through Its Records.* http://john.curtin.edu.au/society/australia.

McKemmish, Sue (2001). 'Placing records continuum theory and practice.' *Archival Science* 1(4): 333–59.

Marres, Noortje (2011). 'The costs of public involvement: Everyday devices of carbon accounting and the materialization of participation.' *Economy and Society* 40(4): 510–33.

Mitchell, Lynne (1998). 'ABC attitude to Australian and contemporary music is absolutely pathetic.' *Music Maker* 6(5): 9.

National Library of Australia (2015). 'Australian Newspaper Digitisation Program.' http://www.nla.gov.au/content/newspaper-digitisation-program.

Pye, David, composer and creative director (2004). *Karakamia*. Audio. Perth: Australian Broadcasting Commission. http://tiny.cc/2004-pye-karakamia.

Rothenberg, Jeff (1995). 'Ensuring the longevity of digital documents.' *Scientific American* 272(1): 42–47.

State Library of Western Australia (2013a). 'Collection profile for music.' http://tiny.cc/2013-slwa-music.

State Library of Western Australia (2013b). 'Oral histories.' http://www.slwa.wa.gov.au/find/wa_collections/oral_history.

State Library of Western Australia (2014). 'Collecting profile – J. S. Battye Library of West Australian History.' http://tiny.cc/2014-slwa-battye.

State Library of Western Australia (2015). 'Storylines.' http://www.slwa.wa.gov.au/for/indigenous_australians/storylines.

White, Terry-Ann (1991). 'Testing the tensions.' *Fremantle Arts Review* 6(4): 8–9.

About the contributors

Linda Barwick is a musicologist, specialising in the study of Australian Indigenous and immigrant musics and in the digital humanities (particularly archiving and repatriation of ethnographic field recordings as a site of interaction between researchers and cultural heritage communities). Linda has studied community music practices through fieldwork in Australia, Italy and the Philippines. Themes of her research include analysis of musical action in place, the language of song, and the aesthetics of cross-cultural musical practice. She also publishes on theoretical issues, including analysis of non-Western music, and research implications of digital technologies.

Andrea L. Berez is an assistant professor in the department of linguistics at the University of Hawaiʻi at Mānoa, where she teaches in the language documentation and conservation track. She is also the director of Kaipuleohone, the University of Hawaiʻi digital language archive, and the current president of DELAMAN, the Digital Endangered Languages and Music Archiving Network. Her current linguistic fieldwork is in the highlands of Papua New Guinea.

Catherine Bow is a linguist with experience in both descriptive and applied linguistics, currently working as project manager for the Living Archive of Aboriginal Languages at Charles Darwin University.

Rona (Googninda) Charles (Ngarinyin/Nyigina) is a cultural, natural-resource and research consultant and advisor based in the Kimberley region of northwest Australia. Rona has worked extensively on the Junba Project as a facilitator and researcher, and has presented the results of the project in arts, health, and language forums in Australia and Canada.

Michael Christie worked between 1972 and 1982 at Milingimbi School in East Arnhem Land, where he was the first teacher linguist in the bilingual program. He was teacher linguist at Yirrkala School from 1986 until 1994, when he moved to Darwin to set up and coordinate the Yolngu Studies program at Northern Territory University (now Charles Darwin University). He is currently professor of education, heading up the Contemporary Indigenous Knowledge and Governance Research Group at the Northern Institute, Charles Darwin University, and is a chief investigator in the development of the Living Archive of Aboriginal Languages.

Brian Devlin has worked in two bilingual schools in East Arnhem Land: as teacher linguist at Yirrkala and as principal at Shepherson College on Elcho Island. He has been guest professor of Australian and Indigenous studies at the University of Köln, Germany, and visiting foreign expert at Xinghua University in Beijing. Designated an 'expert of international standing' by the Australian Research Council College of Experts in 2007, he is currently associate professor of bilingual education and applied linguistics at Charles Darwin University.

Andrea Emberly is an ethnomusicologist whose work focuses on the study of children's musical cultures. She is currently assistant professor of children's studies at York University in Toronto, Canada and honorary research fellow at the University of Western Australia. At present she is focused on two major research projects, one on initiation schools in Vhavenda communities in South Africa (SSHRC Insight Development) and another on language, music and education in remote communities in the Kimberley region of Western Australia (ARC Linkage).

Lelia Green is professor of communications in the School of Communications and Arts at Edith Cowan University, and director of the Centre for Research in Entertainment, Arts, Technology, Education and Communications (CREATEC). She is an active ethnographer with a range of nationally funded research projects. Lelia is a co-chief investigator on the Australian Research Council Linkage Grant that established the Western Australian New Music Archive.

Amanda Harris is research associate on the Australian Research Council Discovery Project 'Intercultural Inquiry in a Trans-National Context' at the University of Sydney and has worked with PARADISEC since 2003. Her current work focuses on intercultural Australian history, with a focus on cultural and gender histories. Her edited book *Circulating Cultures: Exchanges of Australian Indigenous Music, Dance and Media* was published by ANU Press in 2014, and other publications have appeared in *Women and Music, Life Writing, Women's History Review, History and Anthropology*, and *Lilith: A Feminist History Journal*.

Cat Hope is an academic with an active profile as a composer, sound artist, soloist and in music groups based in Western Australia. She is the director of the award winning new music ensemble Decibel and has toured internationally. Her's composition and performance practices focus on low-frequency sound, drone, graphic notation, noise and improvisation. Her works have been performed at festivals internationally and broadcast on Australian, German and Austrian radio. In 2013 she was awarded a Churchill Fellowship to study digital music notations internationally. She is an associate professor at the Western Australian Academy of Performing Arts at Edith Cowan University.

Daniela Kaleva is a lecturer in music at the University of South Australia. Her research focuses on interdisciplinary approaches to music research, including research within the performative paradigm. Her main interests are plurimediality in opera and theatre, and the performance and production of baroque opera. She has co-edited a special issue of *Musicology Australia* on music performance and performativity (Vol. 36/2). Kaleva has qualifications in information management and systems and has worked in information roles at the ABC Sound Library and the State Library of Victoria, and research support roles at the University of Sydney and Deakin University.

Lisa MacKinney is a musician and historian who lived in Perth for eight years. During this time she was actively involved in the Western Australian experimental music community and worked as a project officer with ARC Linkage Partner the State Library of Western Australia. Lisa also liaised and collaborated with the other Western Australian New Music Archive industry partners (the National Library of Australia, ABC Radio Classic FM and Tura New Music) and laid the foundations for turning the Tura collection into an accessible new music archive.

Tos Mahoney is the founder and artistic director of Tura New Music and principal convenor of the Totally Huge New Music Festival, both based in Western Australia with a statewide reach. Tura's music recordings and ancillary collections, stretching back over a quarter century, form the basis of the Western Australian New Music Archive. A musician himself of many years' standing and a long-time colleague and collaborator with Cat Hope, Tos is a central figure in new music in Western Australia.

David Nathan is the language co-ordinator at the Centre for Australian Languages and Linguistics at Batchelor Institute. Formerly the director of the Endangered Languages Archive at SOAS University of London, he has 20 years' experience in educational and computing support for Indigenous and endangered languages. He developed digital platforms and applications for language research, education and publication and has taught computing, linguistics, cognitive science, multimedia, language documentation and archiving. His publications include the textbook *Australia's Indigenous Languages*, and papers on archiving, language documentation, audio, multimedia, lexicography and the internet. He has co-produced multimedia apps for several languages, and was co-author (with Peter Austin) of the web's very first dictionary, for Gamilaraay in New South Wales.

Jennifer C. Post is an ethnomusicologist whose current work focuses on the production and use of musical instruments and on traditional ecological knowledge and music in Inner Asia. Her archival training has also enabled her to complete in-depth projects on the conservation, organisation, and representation of music and musical instruments in the United States, the Pacific and Africa. Currently teaching at the School of Music, University of Arizona, she is also honorary senior research fellow at the University of Western Australia.

Nicholas Thieberger wrote a grammar of South Efate, a language from central Vanuatu. In 2003 he helped establish the Pacific and Regional Archive for Digital Sources in Endangered Cultures and is now its director. He is interested in developments in digital humanities methods and their potential to improve research practice for creation of reusable data sets from fieldwork on previously unrecorded languages. He is the editor of the journal *Language Documentation and Conservation*. He is an Australian Research Council Future Fellow at the University of Melbourne.

Meg Travers works as a digital archivist and is also a PhD candidate at the Western Australian Academy of Performing Arts, researching the preservation of early electronic musical instruments and the role of archives and museums in this area. She is an active composer and performer of electronic music with her ensemble MotET.

Sally Treloyn is a research fellow in ethnomusicology at the University of Melbourne with expertise in the song traditions of the Kimberley and Pilbara, applied ethnomusicologies, musical analysis, and an interest in collaborative intercultural research methodologies. Sally currently leads three ARC-funded projects discovering ways to sustain the vitality of song traditions in northwestern Australia.

Peter Withers is a scientific software developer at the Max Planck Institute for Psycholinguistics, where he developed the software applications Arbil and KinOath. He has also worked at the Radboud University Nijmegen, developing scientific mobile apps and experiment software within the artificial intelligence department and the, Centre for Cognition, Donders Institute for Brain, Cognition and Behaviour.

Index

Index

www.ingramcontent.com/pod-product-compliance
Lightning Source LLC
Chambersburg PA
CBHW071018280326
41935CB00011B/1405